Countertrade

WILEY PROFESSIONAL BANKING AND FINANCE SERIES
EDWARD I. ALTMAN, Editor

Countertrade
Practices, Strategies, and Tactics

COSTAS G. ALEXANDRIDES
Professor of Management, Georgia State University
Director, International Market Information System
Atlanta, Georgia

BARBARA L. BOWERS
Associate Director, International Market Information System
Atlanta, Georgia

JOHN WILEY & SONS

New York · Chichester · Brisbane · Toronto · Singapore

Library of Congress Cataloging in Publication Data:

Alexandrides, Costas G.
    Countertrade : practices, strategies, and tactics.

    (Wiley professional banking and finance series,
0733-8945)
    Bibliography: p.
    Includes index.
    1. Countertrade. I. Bowers, Barbara L. (Barbara
Lynn), 1948–   . II. Title. III. Series.

HF1414.3.A44 1987   382   87-12966
ISBN 0-471-84711-9

Printed in the United States of America

10 9 8 7 6 5 4 3 2 1

For Sophia Alexandrides
and Helen Acree Kramer

Foreword

With this volume, Dr. Alexandrides and Ms. Bowers have set the standard for serious discussion of countertrade. Meticulously researched, thoughtfully organized, and highly readable, *Countertrade* will open many eyes to new ways of conceptualizing international business. Far from being a peculiar and seldom-used trading practice, countertrade—accepting goods as partial or complete payment for sales instead of foreign exchange—now comprises approximately 20% of all global trade. An increasing number of governments treat it today as the preferred method of compensation. The alarming level of the current U.S. trade deficit, unless arrested and reversed, will adversely affect the American economy at home and the strategies of the United States in the world market. Countertrade can be an important part of the solution to the deficit problem.

In many cases foreign firms have mastered the techniques of countertrade to a much greater extent than the American business community. Perhaps this can be explained by the commonly held view of countertrade as being too risky. In fact, American companies can use countertrade to set up long-term and mutually beneficial trading relations in a host of countries, creating entirely new markets in the process.

To be sure, the risks associated with countertrade are real, but precautions can be taken. Clear thinking must dominate at the policy-making level in business as well as in government before an appropriate strategy and organizational structure for countertrade operations are adopted. The authors' coverage of these areas is original and thought-provoking, and cannot help but increase the quality and effectiveness of corporate consideration of countertrade.

This book will hopefully reach a broad audience, from academia to the corporate boardroom. The trade competition we face as a nation is increasingly intense and sophisticated, encompassing a greater number of goods and services than ever before. The work of Dr. Alexandrides and Ms. Bowers should help American business meet that competition head-on.

CHARLES H. PERCY
President
Charles Percy & Associates

Washington, DC
August 1987

vii

Series Preface

The worlds of banking and finance have changed dramatically during the past few years, and no doubt this turbulence will continue through the 1980s. We have established the Wiley Professional Banking and Finance Series to aid in characterizing this dynamic environment and to further the understanding of the emerging structures, issues, and content for the professional financial community.

We envision three types of book in this series. First, we are commissioning distinguished experts in a broad range of fields to assemble a number of authorities to write specific primers on related topics. For example, some of the early handbook-type volumes in the series concentrate on the Stock Market, Investment Banking, and Financial Depository Institutions. A second type of book attempts to combine text material with appropriate empirical and case studies written by practitioners in relevant fields. Finally, we are encouraging definitive, authoritative works on specialized subjects for practitioners and theorists.

It is a distinct pleasure and honor for me to assist John Wiley & Sons, Inc. in this important endeavor. In addition to banking and financial practitioners, we think business students and faculty will benefit from this series. Most of all, though, we hope this series will become a primary source in the 1980s for the members of the professional financial community to refer to theories and data and to integrate important aspects of the central changes in our financial world.

EDWARD I. ALTMAN

Professor of Finance
New York University,
Schools of Business

Preface

This book is intended to help corporations understand countertrade and practice it successfully. Countertrade has become an established feature of international trade, now accounting for about 20% of world trade; it is too big a trend to ignore. It is also too good an opportunity to pass up. Selling through countertrade can enable corporations to enter otherwise inaccessible markets, increase market share, and create new business through trading.

Despite these opportunities, many American corporations participate in countertrade only when forced to, and resent having to take products instead of cash as partial payment for their sales. We believe that these negative attitudes are due not so much to the inconvenience and complexity of countertrade transactions as to the traditional resistance of the American business community to exporting. When we developed our trade data base several years ago, we frequently got calls from anxious export managers who wanted trade data for their products. "I'm trying to prove to the company that we can increase our exports, but I can't get top management to support me," they would say. In the conversations we had with countertrade managers while this book was in progress, we kept hearing eerie echoes of that statement: "I could do much more business through countertrade if only I had the support of top management." This is a case of history repeating itself. During the 1970s, American companies were so hurt by foreign competition in the U.S. market that they were forced to export and go multinational in order to compete. In the 1980s, foreign companies began to cut into American multinationals' world markets by countertrading. Now the Americans must learn to compete through countertrade.

We believe that this book is different from other books on countertrade because it integrates countertrade with international trade and international business. Furthermore, it includes a substantial amount of new material and original research. The book is divided into three sections: Part 1, Development of the Countertrade Environment; Part 2, Corporate Countertrade Practices; and Part 3, Countertrade Practices in Selected Countries. Each section builds upon the information presented in the previous section.

In Part 1, we have traced the postwar economic and trade developments that led to trade management and countertrade in developing, socialist, and industrial countries. Seen as a part of larger trends in international industrial development, trade, and finance, countertrade emerges as an inevitable result of unbalanced world economic development rather than as a sudden and desperate reaction to the 1982 cutoff in bank lending. The banking crisis, which was itself the result of a buildup of international economic and trade problems, served as a catalyst to countertrade, not as its cause. This information may strike some people as academic, but we contend that it is vital for the formulation of successful countertrade strategy. Learning to countertrade is like learning a foreign language. When you study a foreign language, you must learn something about the country's history and culture; when you become involved in countertrade, you must learn something about the buyer country's trade and economic development as well as trends in world trade. Furthermore, the exporter must remember that in countertrade he will usually be dealing with a government entity rather than a private buyer. Private buyers do not care whether their vendors are well-informed about the country's trade needs, but governments care very much. Buyer country governments expect vendors proposing countertrade to show an understanding of the country's trade and industrial development goals, and to design a proposal that addresses these needs.

In Part 2, we have covered corporate countertrade practices: countertrade policies and strategies, organization of in-house countertrade units, countertrade service organizations, market research for countertrade products, countertrade insurance, countertrade financing, and a case study on the Saudi Arabian Peace Shield offset.

Chapter 5 (Countertrade Policies and Strategies) represents the first attempt that we know of to define and classify corporate countertrade policies and strategies. We arrived at these classifications through observation of American countertrade practices and extensive interviews with countertrade managers. The two policy definitions we developed through this research are *company advantage,* in which countertrade is done primarily for the company's benefit, with the trade and economic needs of the buyer country being a secondary consideration; and *mutual advantage,* in which the company considers the buyer country's needs to be of equal importance to its own and designs mutually beneficial countertrade projects. The four strategy definitions we arrived at are *defensive, passive, reactive,* and *proactive.* We believe that companies can achieve the greatest success in countertrade with a mutual advantage policy and a proactive strategy. Chapter 5 also includes a countertrade synergy matrix illustrating how the choice of strategy affects the level of synergy and the financial position of the company's countertrade unit. Additionally, we devised a strategic process chart for countertrade transactions. This chart shows a step-by-step process of a transaction, from analysis of countertrade needs and cost–benefits up to fulfillment of the countertrade obligation; it includes many elements discussed in Part 1 of the book, such as the buyer country's needs in areas such as export development. The matrix and the strategic process chart are also original contributions.

In Part 3, we have given a representative sample of world countertrade practices by describing countertrade regulations, countertrade transactions, and international trade patterns in 11 countries. We chose a mix of countries that are in different stages of economic development: five developing countries (Argentina, Brazil, Colombia, Egypt, Malaysia), three industrial countries (Australia, Canada, Greece), two socialist countries (China, Soviet Union), and one OPEC country (Algeria). Our descriptions of country countertrade practices differ from those provided in other books in two ways: first, the information is provided in a standard format; second, we include analyses of imports and exports which we then relate to the countries' countertrade needs. These analyses are related to the trade trends discussed in Part 1. We have listed a total of 86 countertrade transactions for the 11 countries, which are intended to be examples rather than comprehensive records of each country's countertrade. All types of transactions are represented, from simple counterpurchases up to complex offsets.

The Appendix contains a directory of selected countertrade service organizations, with addresses and telephone and telex numbers.

We would like to thank the following persons for their input and advice: James I. Walsh, Senior International Economist, U.S. Department of Commerce; Michael Morrison, Editor, *Countertrade Outlook;* Peter W. Harben, Editor, *Countertrade and Barter Quarterly;* Dan West, Director of Countertrade, Monsanto International; Patrick M. Hall, Vice President, Rockwell International Trading Company; Patricia Ballard, President, International Countertrade; H. Charles Langford, President, China/Tech; John Ong, United Nations Statistical Office; and Frederick N. Schnurr, formerly Countertrade and Trade Finance Manager, American Standard and Sumitomo Bank. We are indebted to John P. Angelidis, Research Associate of IMIS, for his research contributions. Our special thanks to Sylvia A. Wyatt, Rosalind Perry, Cynthia A. Barnes and Aprile F. Kelly for their help in production of the book.

Costas G. Alexandrides
Barbara L. Bowers

Atlanta, Georgia
August 1987

Contents

List of Abbreviations

ACA	American Countertrade Association (private U.S. organization)
ALADI	See LAIA, Latin American Integration Association. ALADI is the French translation: Association Latino-Américaine d'Integration
ALESA	American League for Exports and Security Assistance (private U.S. organization)
ASEAN	Association of Southeast Asian Nations
AWACS	Airborne Warning and Control System
bbl	Barrels of petroleum
bpd	Barrels of petroleum per day
BEFIX	Brazilian tax benefit program for exporters
BTN	Brussels Tariff Nomenclature
CACEX	Carteira do Comercio Exterior (government of Brazil)
CACM	Central American Common Market
CAST	Chinese Association of Science and Technology (government of China)
CCC	Commodity Credit Corporation of the U.S. Department of Agriculture (government of United States)
CEPEX	Countertrade division of the export division of the Department of Promotion and Markets (government of Brazil)
CERT	Tax reimbursement certificates issued by the government of Colombia
CIBA	Canadian Industrial Benefits Association (government of Canada)
CMEA	Council for Mutual Economic Assistance (formerly known as COMECON)
CNCE	Conseil Nationale du Commerce (government of Algeria)
COMECON	See CMEA. COMECON is the old acronym for Council for Mutual Economic Assistance.

COMEX	Institut Nationale Algerien du Commerce Exterieur (government of Algeria)
CONCEX	National Council of Foreign Trade (government of Brazil)
CPE	Centrally planned economy
CPU	Central processing unit
C31	Command, Control, Communications and Intelligence (part of AWACS system)
DEPM	Department of Promotion and Markets (government of Brazil)
DIOA	Defense Industry Offset Association (private U.S. organization)
DPEPS	Department for Promotion of Exports of Products and Services (government of Greece)
EC	European Community
ECGD	Export Credit Guarantee Department (government of United Kingdom)
EDIMEL	Algerian state enterprise responsible for the export of electric appliances
EEC	European Economic Community
EFTA	European Free Trade Association
EMBRAER	Brazilian state enterprise; aircraft manufacturer
ENADQ	Algerian state enterprise responsible for the export of wheelbarrows and similar products
En.B.C.R.	Algerian state enterprise responsible for the export of bolts, pipe traps, etc.
ENL	Algerian state enterprise responsible for the export of cork products
ENOF	Enterprise Nationale des Produits Miniers Non Ferreux (Algerian state enterprise responsible for the export of nonferrous minerals)
ENPMH	Algerian state enterprise responsible for the export of water valves
EPG	European Participating Governments
ETC	Export trading company
FCIA	Foreign Credit Insurance Association (government of United States)
FELDA	Federal Land Development Authority (government of Malaysia)
FERPHOS	Enterprise Nationale du Fer et Phosphates; Algerian state enterprise responsible for the export of iron and phosphates

FIRA	Foreign Investment Review Board (government of Canada)
FMS	Foreign Military Sales (U.S. law)
FTO	Foreign trade organization (state trading enterprises of various governments); same as STO, state trading organization
GATT	General Agreement on Tariffs and Trade
GOFI	General Organization for Industrialization (government of Egypt)
GNP	Gross national product
GSP	Generalized System of Preferences of the General Agreement on Tariffs and Trade
IBC	Brazilian Coffee Institute (government of Brazil)
ICP	Integrated Commodity Program of the New International Economic Order
IMF	International Monetary Fund
INCOMEX	Instituto Colombiano de Comercio Exterior; Colombian Institute of Foreign Trade (government of Colombia)
ITCO	International Trading Company (government of Greece)
LAIA	Latin American Integration Association; same as ALADI, Association Latino-Américaine d'Integration
LDC	Least developed country
LOA	Letter of Agreement
MBO	Management by objectives
MFA	Multifiber Arrangement
MITCO	Malaysian International Trading Corporation (government of Malaysia)
MMC	Malaysian Mining Corporation (government of Malaysia)
MMTC	Minerals and Metals Trading Corporation (government of India)
MNC	Multinational (transnational) corporation
MOFERT	Ministry of Foreign Economic Relations and Trade (government of China)
MOIC	Malaysian Overseas Investment Corporation (quasi-government)
MTN	Multilateral trade negotiations
mw	Megawatt
NASCO	Nasr Automotive Manufacturing Company (government of Egypt)
NATO	North Atlantic Treaty Organization
NIC	Newly industrialized country

NIEO	New International Economic Order
NIMEXE	Nomenclature of goods for the external and trade statistics of the European Community and trade between the member countries
NTB	Nontariff barrier
ODA	Official Development Assistance (foreign aid)
OECD	Organization for Economic Cooperation and Development
ONCV	Algerian state enterprise responsible for the export of wine
OPEC	Organization of Petroleum Exporting Countries
PC	Personal computer
PNA	Algerian state enterprise responsible for the export of garden rakes and similar products
PROMETAL	Algerian state enterprise responsible for the export of sanitary wares
PSP	Peace Shield Program
PTBA	Parallel Technical Banking Agreement
R&D	Research and development
RFP	Request for proposal
SBU	Strategic business unit
SEC	State Economic Committee (government of China)
SEIC	Systemas Especiales de Intercambio Commercial (export promotion mechanism, government of Colombia)
SIC	Standard Industrial Classification
SITC	Standard International Trade Classification
SONAREM	Algerian state enterprise responsible for the export of minerals
SONATRACH	Société Nationale pour la Recherche, la Production, le Transport, la Transformation et la Commercialization des Hydrocarbures (Algerian state enterprise responsible for the export of petroleum and petroleum products)
STO	State trading organization (state trading enterprises of various governments); same as FTO, foreign trade organization
UNCTAD	United Nations Conference on Trade and Development
UNIDO	United Nations Industrial Development Organization
USAF	U.S. Air Force (government of United States)
USDOC	U.S. Department of Commerce (government of United States)
WTC	World trading company

PART 1 The Countertrade Environment

It is a myth that countertrade was caused by the 1982 global banking crisis. Countertrade was certainly accelerated by the banking crisis, but countertrade is a trade management mechanism, and pressures for trade management have been building up since World War II. All countries practice trade management, no matter how strongly their governments may advocate free trade. The United Nations estimates that 50% of world trade today is managed trade. Managed trade, defined as trade that is not subject to free market forces, includes all mechanisms coming under the heading of protectionism (nontariff barriers, import quotas, voluntary export restraints, etc.), as well as countertrade and offsets.

The purpose of Part 1 is to familiarize exporters with postwar trade management trends in developing, socialist, and industrial countries, with the objective of helping exporters understand the forces behind countertrade/offset and prepare successful compensation trade proposals. An exporter who thinks that a developing country wants countertrade only because it cannot get new loans to pay for imports, for example, is not seeing the big picture and thus cannot formulate a successful strategy for sales growth in the market. Likewise, loans and repayment difficulties have little to do with countertrade in socialist countries, and nothing at all to do with offsets in industrial countries. The exporter who understands the trade situation in prospective markets is the one most likely to succeed.

Chapter 1, "Forms of Countertrade," lists the different forms of countertrade with brief descriptions of each type. Most exporters are familiar with these categories, although there is considerable difference of opinion on some definitions of countertrade types. Many people do not consider joint venture/buyback to be countertrade, for example. The types of countertrade discussed are barter, counterpurchase, reverse countertrade, compensation/buyback, bilateral clearing and switch, evidence accounts, offsets, countertrade linkage and joint ventures. Although *offset* is given a specific definition in Chapters 1 and 4, elsewhere in the book the terms *offset* and *countertrade* are used interchangeably.

Chapter 2, "The Developing World," traces the postwar economic and trade developments that have pressured developing countries to practice trade management. This chapter goes into much greater detail than Chapters 3 and 4 because trade management in developing countries is poorly understood by the Western business community. Areas covered regarding industrial country obstacles to Third World export development include North–South friction; the problems arising from low and/or volatile commodity prices; the proposed New International Economic Order and the associated Integrated Commodity Program; export diversification from primary commodities to manufactures; tariff and nontariff barriers to developing country exports of manufactures; and the Multifiber Arrangement, the classic example of protectionism. Following this is a section on tariff and nontariff barriers within the developing countries, which shows that developing countries are in fact more protectionist than industrial countries, and tells how exporters can overcome some of this protectionism through countertrade. There is also a discussion of problems with the export of manufactures which are not due to protectionism, such as low product quality and lack of demand for products in desired markets. This portion of the chapter is written with countertrade strategy in mind, and includes many references to strategic solutions to trade problems.

Chapter 2 concludes with an extensive discussion of OPEC's role in the development of the current countertrade environment, in regard to the effect of oil price increases on the accumulation of debt from commercial banks (excess liquidity from oil surplus money), the intensification of North–South friction, strengthening of the trade management trend worldwide and oil barter. There is a high level of detail included because few people realize how powerfully OPEC has affected countertrade; in some ways, OPEC can actually be said to have caused countertrade. The information in this section is not of merely historical value. Oil prices have already skyrocketed twice, and it is entirely possible that they could do so again. By understanding the effect OPEC has had on countertrade, exporters can be better prepared if there is another oil price shock.

Chapter 3, "The Socialist Countries," points out the difference in countertrade motivations between developing and socialist countries, as well as the difference in motivations between Eastern Europe and socialist China. It also addresses the great influence Eastern Europe has had on the countertrade strategies of both Western exporters and developing country governments; Eastern Europe has long been the countertrade center of the world, and exporters who accordingly associate countertrade with socialist countries are probably using the wrong strategy in other countries. This chapter traces the development of countertrade in Eastern Europe and provides a few statistics on East–West trade. These statistics demonstrate that export/countertrade opportunities are greater in China than in Eastern Europe, and show that Western exporters have not shown much interest in either market area, despite a reasonably good demand for Western products and technology.

The emphasis in Chapter 4, "The Industrialized Nations," is on military and civilian offsets in trade between developed countries. The first part of the chapter is a discussion of the postwar development of military offsets and the gradual progression from direct offsets to increasingly large indirect offsets. The second part discusses civilian offsets in industrial countries, primarily Canada, Australia, New Zealand, and Greece. The motivation for civilian offsets in these countries is export diversification; statistics are provided to show that these four countries have export structures similar to those of developing countries.

1 Forms of Countertrade

There is a great deal of confusion over the definition of countertrade and its various forms in the government and business communities. Governments of developed countries that have practiced countertrade for many years call it by some euphemism such as "industrial benefits programs" and reserve the term "countertrade" for the practices of developing countries and centrally planned economies. The segment of the business community that is new to countertrade does not know what to think. The business press persists in describing countertrade as "trade without money," which understandably frightens many companies; however, in most forms of countertrade, there is at least a partial payment of hard currency. Moreover, in countertrade between developed countries, full payment is usually made in cash, with the countertrade or offset obligations satisfied under a separate contract.

There are several well-defined forms of countertrade, which are described in the following sections: barter, counterpurchase, reverse countertrade, compensation/buyback, bilateral clearing and switch, evidence accounts, offset trade, countertrade linkage, and joint ventures. It should be noted that many transactions do not fit neatly into these categories, however. Offset trade in particular usually combines several techniques of countertrade, and can involve a network of very complex transactions.

BARTER

Simple barter consists of a direct exchange of goods or services of equivalent value without the use of currency. It is handled through a single contract between the trading parties; there is usually no third party involved. There are no documentary letters of credit; financial arrangements for security may consist of standby letters of credit, performance bonds, or escrow accounts. Simple barter occurs most often in one-time, spot transactions, and is used primarily by countries that have no foreign exchange and no outside sources of credit. Many transactions between Western exporters and Latin American or African nations fit the description of simple barter. Modifications of simple barter include closed-end barter, in which a trading specialist finds a third-party buyer for the goods to be received before the contract is signed, and deferred barter, in which one party ships its set of goods before the other party. Actually, most barter transactions end up being deferred barter, since goods are seldom exchanged simultaneously despite the original intentions of the trading parties. In cases where one set of goods is deficient in quality or quantity, small amounts of cash may be used to settle the account. Barter is the oldest form of countertrade; however, in modern times it is relatively infrequent.

COUNTERPURCHASE

Counterpurchase (also called parallel barter) is the most common form of countertrade. It is an arrangement whereby each party agrees to buy goods and services from the other for hard currency over a specified period of time. Transactions are structured by two separate short-term sales agreements, one for the primary sale (seller company exports) and the other for the secondary sale (buyer country exports); there are separate delivery schedules and separate payment terms. Documentary letters of credit are usually used on both sides. The two transactions are usually linked by a third or side agreement called a protocol. The selling company's counterpurchase obligation is set out in the secondary contract; the obligation can range from 25% of the primary sale to several times its value.

The separation of the contracts theoretically protects both parties, because payments cannot be legally withheld if one party fails to execute its contract properly. In practice, however, the separation is usually more beneficial to the selling company, since disputes frequently arise over the quality of the goods provided under the secondary contract. Foreign purchasers are aware of this and accordingly will often try to have all of the sales obligations combined in one contract so that they can be assured of payment for the goods whether the selling company wants the goods or not.

The primary contract resembles a standard U.S. exporter's contract for a conventional export transaction, and ideally will avoid any reference to the counterpurchase obligation. The secondary contract sets out these obligations and should include some provisions to protect the U.S. exporter, primarily (1) that the U.S. exporter will be free to transfer its counterpurchase obligations to a third party, (2) that if the primary sale is canceled, the U.S. firm's counterpurchase obligations no longer exist, (3) that there will be no restrictions on resale of the counterdeliveries (where, to whom, at what price), and (4) that if penalty must be paid for nonperformance under the secondary contract, this will not affect any of the obligations of either party under the primary contract.

Counterpurchase arrangements used to be most common in transactions between Western exporters and Soviet bloc countries; however, today these arrangements are used everywhere, even in trade between developed countries. Counterpurchase is most often seen in nonmilitary countertrade, but it is becoming increasingly important in military offset trade.

REVERSE COUNTERTRADE

Reverse countertrade is an arrangement whereby the selling company makes anticipatory purchases from the buyer country. These purchases are contractually qualified for credits in the ensuing counterpurchase agreement. The credits may be sold to third parties, such as traders or other Western companies. A related practice is anticipatory countertrade, in which the company making a bid on a contract will make investments, set up joint ventures, or buy the country's products in the hope that these activities will help win the contract.

COMPENSATION/BUYBACK

Buyback is the fastest growing form of countertrade in terms of dollar value. Under a buyback arrangement, the selling company provides turnkey production facilities instead of taking counterdelivered goods from the buyer country. The exporter builds a plant in the buyer country, provides technology and equipment, and agrees to buy back all or a portion of the products produced. The transaction is accomplished through two separate contracts. Invoicing is in convertible currency, and third parties (such as trading houses) may participate in the sale of buyback products. Buybacks can be used for sourcing, thereby reducing the selling company's procurement costs. They can also be a means of producing nontraditional exports in the buyer country.

BILATERAL CLEARING AND SWITCH

This transaction is a bilateral soft currency agreement between two governments (rather than between a private exporter and a government) who agree to import a set volume of goods from the other over a specified period of time—usually a year. It is handled through a single contract. Payment for the goods is handled through nonconvertible clearing account units. The value of the goods traded is denominated in these units, which serve as lines of credit with participating banks in each country. Exporters in each country are paid by local banks in domestic currencies, and clearing units are credited to the importer's account. The contract specifies the type and volume of products to be traded, and usually requires that all trade exchanges stop if the trade imbalance reaches a specified maximum point, or "swing" (usually about 35% of the specified annual trade volume), until the deficit country decreases the imbalance below the level of swing. If the imbalance is not corrected by the end of the contract period, or if the accounts become seriously out of balance, settlement can be demanded in cash or by means of a switch trade. Since imbalances frequently occur, switch trade is often used; it is made possible by a stipulation in the bilateral agreement providing that the country with the trade surplus can make available to a third party all or a portion of its clearing account.

Rights to the surplus credits are transferred to switch traders for cash less a substantial discount (usually 2% to 12%). The switch traders then use the credits to purchase goods from the deficit country. Through a complex series of international trades, the switch traders eventually come up with goods that can be sold for hard currency. These deals are handled by specialty traders and trading houses.

EVIDENCE ACCOUNTS

These transactions occur between one or more private Western exporters and a government entity or entities, such as an FTO (foreign trade organization) or ministry of trade. Under an evidence account agreement, there are listings of purchases and sales that the buyer and seller conclude with each other, and an agreement on the ratio of sales to purchases. The trade flow is monitored and accounts must be partially or fully balanced at the end of the contract period, usually one to three years. Individual trade transactions do not have to be offset by counterdeliveries. The monitoring is done by the buyer country's foreign trade bank and a specified Western bank. The main advantage of an evidence account is that a mix of Western exporters and importers can trade with a similar group in the trading country on purely commercial considerations. In this way, each can get the products that they want, instead of undesirable or overpriced counterdeliveries. Evidence account trade is most often used in Soviet bloc countries and China.

OFFSET TRADE

The term "offset" is generally used to define compensatory practices in military trade, though it also applies to large civilian procurements. In the context of military trade, offset may be described as a range of industrial and commercial compensation practices required as a condition of purchase of military-related exports. Military offset consisted mostly of coproduction during the first twenty years after World War II; however, after the oil crisis and recession of the early 1970s, the objectives of the beneficiary countries changed. They now consider offsets as vehicles for employment, industrial development, and export development. Offset trade may be either government-to-government or private-to-government.

Offsets may be divided into two classes: direct and indirect. To put it very simply, direct offsets are those directly related to the original product sold to the country, while indirect offsets involve goods and services not related to the product. Arrangements under direct offsets include coproduction, licensed production, subcontractor production, foreign investment, and technology transfer. Arrangements under indirect offsets may include investment and technology transfer, but also include such things as counterpurchase, buyback, barter, tourism development, use of the country's air carriers and hotels, and so on.

Definitions of some of the more common military offset arrangements made by U.S. exporting companies are:

Coproduction. Overseas production based upon a government-to-government agreement that permits a foreign government or producers to acquire the technical information needed to manufacture all or part of a U.S.-origin defense article. It includes government-to-government licensed production. It excludes licensed production based upon direct commercial arrangements by U.S. manufacturers.

Licensed Production. Overseas production of a U.S.-origin defense article based upon transfer of technical information under direct commercial arrangements between a U.S. manufacturer and a foreign government or producer.

Subcontractor Production. Overseas production of a part or component of a U.S.-origin defense article. The subcontract does not necessarily involve license of technical information and is usually a direct commercial arrangement between the U.S. manufacturer and a foreign producer.

Overseas Investment. Investment arising from the offset agreement, taking the form of capital invested to establish or expand a subsidiary or joint venture in the foreign country.

Technology Transfer. Transfer of technology that occurs as a result of an offset agreement and that may take the form of research and development conducted abroad, technical assistance provided to the subsidiary or joint venture of overseas investment, or other activities under a direct commercial arrangement between the U.S. manufacturer and a foreign entity.*

Counterpurchase is becoming increasingly popular as a form of indirect offset, at least from the purchasing country's point of view. It is not always welcomed by the seller, since it often requires the seller to assist the buyer country in export development. The obligation may go far beyond simply taking title to, and disposing of, counterdelivered goods. The seller must undertake research to identify and evaluate target markets for the buyer

*U.S. Office of Management and Budget, *Impact of Offsets in Defense-Related Exports*, Washington, DC: U.S. Government Printing Office, 1985, pp. 5–6.

country's products (often this research must be done during the bidding process), and must work closely with the buyer government's export development agency. The seller may undertake establishment of trading companies or import houses in the target markets to facilitate the flow of goods from the buyer country. Other tasks may include promotion of the products—design and implementation of advertising campaigns, participation in trade fairs, organization of buyer groups to go to the country, and so on. Consideration must be given to the country's plans for industrial development and general economic development, as well as export development. Export development under an offset program can be very difficult, especially with nontraditional exports. As noted elsewhere in this chapter, the goods that the buyer country wants to export may be of inferior quality, overpriced, in low demand, or otherwise noncompetitive. There is also the frequent problem of restrictions on where the goods may be marketed.

Development of production facilities, under either direct or indirect offset, is often a better solution, since it can result in benefits for both the buyer and the seller. Production facilities may be desired by the buyer country for several reasons: to produce goods for increased export according to a development plan similar to the aforementioned one, to produce more competitive goods (better technology), to begin production of nontraditional exports, or for import substitution. These reasons are related to the goals of industrial development and employment. The seller may be interested in production facilities as a means of sourcing and as a means of having an increased presence in the buyer country. This can increase market share on both a short- and long-term basis, as the facility can continue in production long after the offset obligation is ended.

Offsets are highly competitive and require careful preparation, both in the bidding process and in the execution of the obligations. Sophisticated negotiation techniques on the part of the seller are crucially important, especially if the company's negotiation position is weak. The seller must be confident that it can meet all obligations satisfactorily, as nonperformance may result in heavy financial penalties; otherwise, the seller should try to negotiate the enforcement method as best efforts.

Offset percentages range from 25% of the value of the primary sale to several times its value. Most buyer countries will try to get at least 100% offset, while most sellers will try to keep it under 100%. In some cases, however, a seller will offer 200% or higher offset voluntarily just to beat the competition and win the contract. Offset implementation usually takes several years longer than the sales contract; it may be five, ten, or twenty years. The seller is usually paid for his exports on delivery or on other conventional terms, and thereafter accumulates offset credits to satisfy the contractual obligations to the seller. Most of the large offsets have been in trade between developed countries, although there have been a number of high value offsets with developing countries. [See the "Peace Shield Case Study," in Chapter 11 (the Boeing Company sale to Saudi Arabia) for an example of the latter.]

COUNTERTRADE LINKAGE

This is not exactly a form of countertrade; rather, it is a channeling method used by governments of developing countries to ensure timely delivery of products. It could be called a watchdog function. In many developing countries (and in many newly industrialized countries), suppliers and manufacturers may be unreliable; this is particularly true in the Soviet bloc countries (where low priority is given to manufacturing products for counterdelivery) and in the Republic of Korea. Countertrade linkage takes place when the government FTO or equivalent agency negotiates a counterpurchase agreement with the Western exporter, in which it is stipulated that the counterdeliveries will be supplied through the FTO, rather than the Western exporter obtaining them directly from the manufacturer. The FTO then takes the responsibility of pressuring the manufacturers to provide the counterdeliveries on time.

JOINT VENTURES

In some countries, notably China, countertrade is defined as a joint venture. These operations usually take the form of buyback countertrade, with some portion of the products resulting from the investment, technology transfer, new plant facilities, and so on going back to the original seller as full or partial payment.

2 The Developing World

Countertrade has become an established feature of international trade, and growing numbers of industrial countries' exporters now recognize its importance as a marketing tool. However, many exporters are confused and exasperated by the countertrade demands made by developing countries. Why are exporters asked to take back manufactured products which may be of poor quality, accept commodities which are already in oversupply, or transfer technology in order to make a sale? Why has countertrade continued to grow, although the 1982 debt crisis has passed? Why do some countries demand countertrade even though they do not have serious debt problems?

The effectiveness of a countertrade strategy depends on the strategist's understanding of the motivations behind trade management. The countries that require countertrade (either de facto or by legislation) have good reasons for their policies, and they also have justification for the types of products they offer for counterpurchase. Although strategy must eventually be tailored to the individual market, a general understanding of developing countries' economic problems is a necessary starting point.

Countertrade between developed and developing countries is in many ways an outcome of the economic clash between the First World and the Third World, known today as "North–South friction." The genesis of this friction has nothing to do with the 1982 debt crisis; its roots go back to at least the early nineteenth century, when the metropolitan powers supplied manufactured goods to the colonies and poor countries in exchange for primary products. These relationships were ostensibly transformed into a more equitable trading environment in the twentieth century, notably during the post-World War II period.

The trade liberalization movement, which began with the Bretton Woods arrangements, has had many benefits for the developing countries. World trade increased rapidly during the 1960s, growing by an average 8.4% per year. Output in both the industrial and developing countries grew by about 5% per year. Exports of manufactures from developing countries increased, and several developing countries graduated to the status of "newly industrialized countries," such as the Republic of Korea. Even when the effects of the oil price shocks and the debt crisis are taken into consideration, there has been overall progress in the export of manufactures from the developing countries.

However, there remains a sharp difference in attitude between the developed and developing countries as to the extent of this progress. The developing countries feel that they were shortchanged in the postwar industrialization process. The value of their commodity exports has not kept up with the increase in the cost of their manufactured imports, and their attempts to develop exports of high-value-added manufactured products have often been blocked by nontariff barriers in the desired industrial country markets.

COMMODITY PRICES

Low commodity prices have had a great effect on the movement toward trade management and countertrade, especially in countries dependent on one export product (coffee, bananas, bauxite, etc.). As recently as 1980, 72 developing countries still depended on primary products for over 50% of their exports; of this group, 34 are among the world's poorest countries, classified as LDCs (least developed countries). Price fluctuations and frequent cycles of low prices have hindered the economic development of developing countries by reducing their export income and causing their terms of trade to deteriorate. They have had to borrow money to afford increasingly costly imports, and when no more loans were available, they had to start countertrading. If the prices of their commodity exports had kept pace with the cost of their imports, the need for countertrade would have been greatly reduced.

The developing countries have been giving warning signs about commodity prices for a long time, complaining not only individually but as a group at sessions of the United Nations Conference on Trade and Development (UNCTAD). Their dissatisfaction was formalized at the 1974 session as a proposal for the New International Economic Order (NIEO). NIEO is an ambitious plan designed to bring about fundamental changes in the economic relations between developed and developing countries. It would also provide a mechanism through which the developing countries could exercise their collective bargaining power. Major areas covered under NIEO are: stabilization and increase of commodity prices, indexation of export prices to prices paid for imports of manufactures, extension of preferential treatment by industrial countries, and increased control of multinational corporations (i.e., enforced compliance with the host country's laws, regulations, and public policies).

The centerpiece of the NIEO is the Integrated Commodity Program, the mechanism designed to control commodity prices. The program is called integrated because it is intended to bring a wide range of commodities under one regulatory body, thus giving the producer countries strength in collective bargaining power as compared to the relative weakness of small groups of countries working on a single commodity basis. The ICP is very controversial, however. The developed countries, who are the major consumer countries, are unwilling to agree to a trade management scheme whose ultimate goal is not only to raise prices but keep the prices effectively divorced from free market forces. Although the stabilization of commodity prices would facilitate long-range industrial planning and protect against the harmful repercussions of sudden sharp price increases or declines, the developed countries are still apprehensive about unreasonably high prices. This opposition, together with some other negative factors—high start-up and maintenance costs, and some anticipated operational problems—will probably prevent the establishment of the ICP. However, the developing countries are not expected to abandon the idea, and will keep trying to form some sort of multi-commodity trade management organization.

Commodity countertrade is not a replacement for the ICP. Exporting commodities through countertrade does not increase prices; in fact, it often has the opposite effect. A country will usually push a commodity in countertrade because the product is in low demand on the world market—otherwise, the country could have sold the product for cash—and increasing the world supply of the commodity through countertrade will only depress the price. There is also the problem of the substantial discounts that third-party traders often demand for commodities, which further lowers the market price. Developing countries who are countertrading commodities benefit most by insisting on official prices, or in the case of a non-regulated product, the world reference price. The majority of countries follow this practice.

Although most developing countries would like to encourage the export of manufactures and other nontraditional products through countertrade, many are forced to provide commodities in exchange for imports, having little else to offer in sufficient quantities. Furthermore, the practice is often encouraged by trading partners of industrial countries, who prefer to take bulk commodities in countertrade, because the goods can be easily disposed of through established channels (commodity traders and trading houses). Western companies will usually resist accepting manufactured products if at all possible, due to apprehension about product quality and difficulty of resale. The commodities most frequently offered in countertrade are: coffee, cocoa, tea, sugar, bananas, vegetable oils, fish, fish meal, cotton, jute, and tobacco.

The countertrade strategist should determine the target country's attitude toward commodity countertrade before planning a proposal. Some developing countries refuse to offer cash-earning primary commodities in countertrade, since they need the income to make payments on their debts. Although this is a very reasonable position for them to take (also an obligatory position, if they are under heavy pressure from the IMF), it may prevent them from obtaining needed imports if they have nothing else suitable to offer the industrial country partner in payment. Other developing countries actively promote export of primary products in countertrade, either out of necessity or to maintain normal levels of production. Frequently, a country will require that additionality (exports above the usual level) result from the countertrade deal, and some countries also require that the commodity be sold in a new market. Since there are practically no *new* markets for most commodities, this usually means displacing the share of another supplier, a difficult task which the developing country exporter can transfer to the industrial country partner through countertrade.

In most cases, disposal of commodities received in countertrade cannot be handled in-house, as commodity trading is a "closed club" activity, requiring both expertise and appropriate contacts. Use of a commodity trading house, either as a third party or as a direct party to the negotiations, must be included in the company's countertrade strategy.

DEVELOPING COUNTRY EXPORTS OF MANUFACTURES

Development of exports of manufactures is a far more complex subject than commodity prices, as it involves industrial development, tariff barriers, and the issue of protectionism. However, it is a subject that should be thoroughly understood by the countertrade strategist. The chances for success in countertrade will be greater if the industrial country partner will agree to take manufactures rather than commodities as counterpurchases, and greatest if there is a joint venture arrangement in which the developing country can learn to make a new product, improve existing products, and penetrate new export markets.

The strategist must remember that export diversification is a primary goal in developing countries. These countries have learned that they cannot depend on income from commodity exports, due to the historic instability of commodity prices and the failure of commodity trade management efforts such as the ICP. Furthermore, all developing countries want to industrialize, and exports of manufactures are a major part of the industrialization process. One reason that countertrade has spread so rapidly is that many countries have realized the value of this form of trade management in overcoming protectionism; the developing countries are using countertrade as suasion to make the industrial countries take more of their exports. If developing countries try to build up exports of manufactures through conventional methods, they face various nontariff barriers. It is easier and faster to export the products through countertrade, although, for reasons detailed later in this chapter, countertrade does not necessarily result in the establishment of a market share.

Protectionism against manufactured exports from developing countries has contributed to the countertrade environment in two ways: by reinforcing trade management practices, and by diminishing export income of the developing countries, thereby contributing to their debt problems.

When a country practices trade management in the form of protectionism, the affected trading partners often retaliate by making their own markets less accessible to the offending country. Countertrade is certainly a form of restricting market access—"Buy from me or I won't buy from you"—and as such it is a reaction to protectionism, but does not itself constitute retaliatory protectionism. It is, rather, a form of retaliatory trade management. The developing country using countertrade this way is trying to promote exports, not keep out imports; the country sees countertrade as an orderly, "managed" way to become established as a supplier of manufactures to an industrial market where its exports have been heretofore blocked by protectionism. Evidence of this is found in the fact that many developing countries require that counterpurchased products be sold in specific major industrial markets.

The connection of protectionism to debt, and hence to countertrade, is more clearcut. If the developing countries had been able to earn more money through the export of value-added manufactures, they would not have needed to borrow so much. Though it is certainly true that the economic development programs of these countries could not possibly have been funded solely from export income (with the exception of OPEC countries), increased export earnings from the 1960s on would have left the Third World in a far stronger financial position in 1982.

Removal of tariffs by the EEC, Japan, and the United States on developing country exports would generate an estimated annual increase in their exports of $14.5 billion (4.6% increase) based on 1980 actual exports, according to the UNCTAD Trade Policy Simulation Model. If all nontariff barriers (i.e., protectionism) were eliminated as well, the gain in export earnings would be $34.8 billion (11.1% increase). Exports of developing countries in 1980 would thus have been $360.9 billion rather than the actual $311.6 billion. In current (1985) dollars, export value under this scenario would have been $695.2 billion for the year. The U.N. notes that this is approximately 85.5% of the developing countries' current external debt; thus these countries could, at least in theory, pay off a large portion of their debt if there were no barriers to their exports. (Of course, had the countries earned this extra income, they would presumably not have had to borrow so much in the first place.)

The composition of the increase is assumed to be 30% in apparel, 10.8% in six food products (fresh or frozen fish, vegetable oilseed and cake, crustacea and mollusks, preserved fish, sheep and goat meat, and prepared fruit and nuts), 5% in footwear, 4% in crude petroleum, and 3% in furniture, based on past export patterns. The remaining portion of the increase would be accounted for by exports of natural gas, coconut oil, printing paper, carpets, ferroalloys, synthetic fiber textiles, textile articles, iron and steel coils, cotton yarn and thread, telecommunications equipment, trucks, luggage, toys, and fur clothing.* Although UNCTAD made no reference to countertrade

*United Nations, *Trade and Development Report, 1985,* New York, 1986, pp. 123–125.

in the model, it is reasonable to assume that these products are popular items for export development through countertrade.

Protectionism continues to be a problem for the developing countries, preventing them from earning enough money to pay off their debt to private and official institutions. Ironically, though countertrade can circumvent protectionism and boost exports, it does not help a country pay debts; the exports are given in payment for imports and do not generate cash.

PROGRESS AND PROBLEMS IN EXPORT DIVERSIFICATION

The developing countries as a group have made considerable progress in the export of manufactures. Their collective world market share in exports of all products increased from 19.2% in 1973 to 24.8% in 1983, according to the IMF. Their share in manufactures went up from 6.9% to 11.6%, a proportionately greater increase than the 39.4% to 44.7% gain in share of primary product exports. Growth in the value of developing country exports of manufactures over the ten-year period, 17.7%, was greater than the industrial countries' growth in exports of the same products, 11.2%. Exports of manufactures have grown most quickly between developing countries, showing a 20.5% increase in value for the 1973–1983 period compared to 16.6% for their exports to the industrial countries. A breakdown of export activity for a slightly shorter period, 1973–1982, indicates the product areas in which the developing countries have made the most progress. Exports of manufactures of non-oil developing countries increased from $23.1 billion to $107.3 billion during this period, a gain of $84.2 billion. Engineering products (mostly office and telecommunications equipment, industrial machinery, and household appliances) accounted for 38.4% of the increase; clothing and textiles for 23.8%; miscellaneous consumer goods such as glassware, furniture, and footwear for 14.6%; chemicals for 9.5%; miscellaneous semimanufactures for 8.5%; and iron and steel for 4.9%.*

Unfortunately, the export gains were not spread evenly among the developing countries; a small group of countries accounts for the bulk of developing country exports of manufactures. Only a few developing countries have attained the status of newly industrialized countries, (NICs): these include Argentina, Brazil, Hong Kong, Mexico, the Republic of Korea, Singapore and Turkey, according to UNIDO definitions. The IMF classifies ten developing countries as "exporters of manufactures," (meaning that manufactures accounted for over 50% of exports in 1980): China, Hong Kong, Hungary, India, Israel, the Republic of Korea, Romania, Singapore, Vietnam, and Yugoslavia. Also counted by the IMF as "exporters of manufactures"

---

*Shailendra J. Anjaria, Naheed Kirmani, and Arne B. Petersen, *Trade Policy Issues and Developments* (Occasional Paper No. 38), Washington, DC, International Monetary Fund, 1985, p. 142.

(though not necessarily conforming to the 50% export breakdown) are Argentina, Brazil, Greece, Portugal and the Republic of South Africa. Of the hundred-plus countries classified as "developing," only these few are succeeding in export diversification.

TARIFF AND NONTARIFF BARRIERS AFFECTING DEVELOPING COUNTRY EXPORTS OF MANUFACTURES

Trade barriers have been a significant restraint to the growth of the developing countries' exports of manufactures (among other factors such as recessionary cycles and marketing strategy errors), and are increasingly cited by governments of developing countries as a justification for countertrade. Barriers to trade exist in all countries, but those in the industrial countries have the greatest impact, since these countries dominate world trade in manufactures. To the First World's credit, the developed countries have made several notable efforts to lower or eliminate the barriers and give preferential treatment to the developing countries. However, pressure from vulnerable domestic sectors has limited both the extent and the effectiveness of these efforts, and, in certain product categories, access to the industrial country markets has become even more difficult. Some restrictive measures are selectively applied against developing countries, such as the Multifiber Arrangement, while others have wider application but nevertheless affect products of particular importance to developing countries.

Tariff Barriers

There are substantial tariff barriers against several products in which the developing countries have an existing or potential comparative advantage. Although average nominal tariff rates for non-oil manufactured products have been reduced under successive GATT rounds to about 5%, the average rates are still about 19% for apparel, 13.5% on footwear and leather goods, and 12.5% on textiles. An additional tariff problem, one which affects all manufactures, is that the structure of tariffs in industrial countries tends to penalize products as the degree of processing goes up, thus making it difficult for the smaller countries to develop higher-value-added export industries.

The industrial countries have eased access to their markets through the Generalized System of Preferences (GSP). The GSP is a scheme of preferential tariff rates (varying from country to country) which allows imports of specified agricultural and manufactured products from developing countries to enter duty free or at reduced rates. A creation of the 1966 GATT Tokyo Round, the GSP provides an exception to GATT rules by allowing the developing countries the right to nonreciprocal privileges; their exports receive special preference in developed country markets, yet they are entitled to restrict foreign competition in their own markets. In 1980, eligible imports from beneficiary countries were valued at $55 billion, or 31% of dutiable imports (62% of non-oil dutiable imports), up from $4 billion, 27% of dutiable imports, in 1972.*

Although there is general agreement that the GSP has helped the developing countries penetrate the industrial markets, the developing countries are not satisfied with it. They feel that the GSP's impact is greatly lessened by the exclusion of some of the products they are most anxious to export in larger quantities, such as textiles. For example, the GSP of the United States excludes textiles, apparel, watches, import-sensitive electronic articles, import-sensitive steel articles, certain footwear articles, and certain glass products; the GSP of the EEC excludes textiles, steel, and import-sensitive industrial items; and the GSP of Japan excludes textiles, apparel, leather items, and footwear.

Nontariff Barriers

Although the exports of all countries are adversely affected by nontariff barriers (i.e., protectionism), the developing countries are most seriously hurt by such barriers, since protectionism impedes their economic development. Growth in export income is necessary not only for industrial and general economic development, but for servicing of external debt. Protectionism was an important factor in the accumulation of Third-World debt leading up to the 1982 crisis, and continues to affect debt repayment. Nontariff barriers affect one third to one half of all developing country exports to the industrial countries.

Forms of protectionism include quantitative restrictions (quotas, voluntary export restraints, etc.), surtaxes, surcharges, export subsidies, discretionary import licensing, countervailing duties, variable import levies, and outright prohibition of certain imports, as well as various other restrictive measures. The justifications given by countries (both developed and developing) for exercising restrictive measures which are contrary to the spirit, if not the letter, of the GATT, center on protection of employment, weak economic recovery, structural rigidities, trade or current account deficits, and exchange rate relationships.

Nontariff barriers (NTBs) in industrial countries are used more against products from developing countries than products from other industrial countries, and agricultural products are more heavily protected than manufactures, according to data compiled by the United Nations. A comparison of the shares of total 1980 imports subject to NTBs in seven industrial markets shows that in agricultural products, 46.2% of imports from developing countries face NTBs, compared to 34.0% for products originating in industrial countries. In manufactures, the proportion of products from developing countries subject to NTBs (19.9%), is over twice as high as that of products

*Anjaria, Kirmani, & Petersen, *Trade policy issues and developments*, p. 79.

from industrial countries (8.9%). The share of imports subject to NTBs from all countries averages 37.8% for agricultural products and 9.6% for manufactures.

In agricultural products, Switzerland and Japan are the most protectionist against developing countries. Switzerland places NTBs against 74.4% of agricultural products from developing countries, and Japan's rate is 71.4%; the U.S. rate is 19.6%.

Manufactures from developing countries have much easier entry into industrial markets than agricultural products, since the industrial countries are far more competitive in manufactures. Sweden is the most protectionist of the seven industrial countries surveyed, with 34.5% of imports from developing countries subject to NTBs, followed by the EEC, 32.0%; Norway, 23.9%; and the United States, 21.8%.*

In light of these statistics, it seems that manufactures are a better counterpurchase choice than agricultural items, since market access is better. Products received in countertrade and resold in industrial countries are not exempt from nontariff barriers, however; when the shipments cross the border, they are treated as ordinary imports. If industrial countries exempted all countertrade products from NTBs, countertrade would probably account for 90% of world trade in a very short time.

THE MULTIFIBER ARRANGEMENT

The Multifiber† Arrangement (MFA), a system of bilateral agreements regulating trade in textiles and apparel, is the classic example of protectionism by developed countries against exports of developing countries. It is one of the examples most often cited by economists, governments, international agencies, and the developing countries whenever the issue of protectionism is discussed. The MFA is a particularly sore point with the developing countries because textile industries are so important to them; in several Asian countries, the development of a textile and apparel industry has been the basis for the industrialization process as well as a source of export income.

The first MFA (MFA I) came into effect in 1974, though similar arrangements had existed since 1961 (The Short-Term Arrangement Regarding International Trade in Textiles, October 1961–September 1962, and The Long-Term Arrangement Regarding International Trade in Cotton Textiles, October 1962–1973). The justification given by the industrial countries for these arrangements was market disruption, a concept which would not violate GATT rules and which could be reasonably defended on economic grounds. Market

*United Nations, *Trade and Development Report, 1984,* New York, 1985, p. 208.
†"Multifiber" refers to the Arrangement's coverage of synthetic fiber textiles and apparel as well as those made of cotton and other natural fibers.

disruption was defined as having three elements: (1) a sharp and substantial increase, or potential increase, in imports of specific products from specific exporting countries; (2) prices for the imported products which are substantially lower than prevailing domestic prices for similar products; and (3) serious damage, or threat thereof, to domestic producers. The stated objective of the MFA is "to achieve the expansion and progressive liberalization of world trade in textile products," by functioning as a safeguard against disruption in both importing and exporting countries. In practice, the industrial countries set quotas on imports of textiles and apparel, and the developing exporting countries agree to voluntarily restrain exports so as not to exceed the quotas. Trade in textiles and apparel between industrial countries is not restricted under the MFA, presumably because these products do not meet the market disruption criteria of low prices.

As of 1984, 42 countries participated in the MFA. Hong Kong and the Republic of Korea, the major exporters of textiles and apparel, are the developing countries most affected by the Arrangement. Some of the other exporting country signatories to various bilateral agreements with importing countries are Bangladesh, Brazil, China, Colombia, Czechoslovakia, the Dominican Republic, Egypt, Guatemala, Hungary, India, Indonesia, Japan, Macao, Malaysia, Mexico, Pakistan, Peru, the Philippines, Poland, Romania, Singapore, Sri Lanka, Thailand, Uruguay, and Yugoslavia.

Arguments against the MFA, other than criticisms of its very nature as a protectionist mechanism, center on the fact that it has become progressively more restrictive instead of liberal—product coverage has expanded, and the number of developing country exporters included has increased—and that it appears to have become institutionalized, though it was introduced as a temporary measure. There is some grudging support for the MFA in developing countries, however, since they realize that in the absence of the MFA the importing countries might have resorted to severe unilateral restrictions. It is true that there has been considerable expansion in textile exports by developing countries under the MFA. The developing countries' share of world exports of textiles, already 34% in 1973, rose to 46% in 1982, and their share of apparel exports increased from 30% to 40% during the same period.*

Intra-developing country trade in textile products has always been restrictive, though there is no wide-ranging mechanism such as the MFA to control it. Imports are regulated on a country-by-country basis through measures such as high tariffs and quantitative restrictions, with the justification usually being protection of infant industries.

Viewed outside the context of trade in textiles and apparel, the MFA has had a profound effect on the trend towards trade management; the concept of "market disruption" was invented to justify the MFA, and this concept has since been used to defend various protectionist practices. Market disruption is used as a justification for protectionism by developed countries,

---

*Anjaria, Kirmani, & Petersen, *Trade policy issues and developments*, p. 11.

not only as a reaction to the emergence of comparative advantage industries in developing countries, but as a reaction to competition from other developed countries, particularly in product areas such as steel and automobiles.

TARIFF AND NONTARIFF BARRIERS IN DEVELOPING COUNTRIES

It comes as no surprise that developing countries favor countertrade when one understands how extensively they already practice trade management. Developing countries as a group are far more protectionist than developed countries; in fact, protectionism is built into the industrialization policies of many developing countries. Though tariffs are often prohibitively high in developing countries, nontariff volume controls are the predominant method of import restriction. UNCTAD estimates that such controls apply to as much as 71% of all product groups, compared to 23% for industrial countries.*

The prevailing attitude in the Third World is that protectionism imposed by developing countries is not as harmful to trade as that imposed by developed countries. The reasoning behind this is that the protectionism of industrial countries is directly restrictive to the developing countries' trade and economic development, since it reduces both their exports (earning capacity) and their ability to import; therefore, all trade between developed and developing nations suffers. In the context of the GATT goal of mutual reciprocity, the developing countries' protectionism is no more defensible than the industrial countries' protectionism; however, it seems impossible to reconcile the needs of the developing countries with the goal of the GATT.

Tariff Barriers

Tariff structure in developing countries is roughly similar to that in developed countries: above average rates apply to products such as tobacco, beverages, textile products, and certain food items, while rates are below average for fuels, chemicals, metals, and metal products. Statutory rates are generally higher, however, with maximum rates sometimes as high as 150%. Developing countries who are members of GATT can levy high tariffs without compensating their trading partners because of the high percentage of their tariff schedules which are not "bound," that is, included in the schedule of concessions. In the major industrial countries, up to 90% of the tariff schedules are bound, while in a sample group of developing countries surveyed by GATT the maximum proportion of tariffs bound was 35%.

Nontariff Barriers

Most developing countries rely on nontariff measures such as quotas and discretionary licensing to regulate imports. Total prohibition of imports of

*Anjaria, Kirmani, & Petersen, *Trade policy issues and developments,* pp. 73–74.

certain products—either because the item is produced domestically or for some other reason, such as classification of a product as a "luxury item"— is a fairly common practice. Exchange restrictions are often an important form of import control, especially in the period since 1982; in many countries, foreign exchange budgets are the basis for the central bank's approval of all import transactions.

Developing countries do not use nontariff barriers in quite the same way as industrial countries. Although the underlying motivation for their protectionism is the same—keeping the competition out—the developing countries' method of application of protectionist barriers represents a contingency planning approach to import trade. Tariff changes are time consuming, often requiring approval by the country's legislative assembly, and long-lasting once implemented. In contrast, quantitative restrictions can be quickly applied, adapted, or dissolved by a single agency in response to foreign exchange availability, domestic production levels, or other import requirements (including imports the country wishes to obtain through countertrade). However, for industrial countries attempting to export products to developing countries, it makes market access unpredictable and marketing planning difficult.

CONTINGENCY COUNTERTRADE IN DEVELOPING COUNTRIES

The contingency planning approach to imports is one of the reasons why so many countertrade deals fall through. Developing countries may appear eager to enter countertrade arrangements, or may even require countertrade by law; but if their needs change, they may abruptly back out of the negotiations, require various unwelcome changes in the type or amount of products available for counterpurchase, or simply let the deal die by deliberately sitting on it in bureaucratic channels.

On the other hand, contingency import planning can make it possible for exporters in industrial countries to play the developing countries' game: using countertrade to get around protectionism. Countertrade is often facilitated by the developing countries' attitude towards import regulation and by their ability to move quickly. Sometimes an import ban will be temporarily lifted, for example, if the country has the opportunity to export something which it could not otherwise sell easily in exchange for a desirable prohibited import. This kind of flexibility is rare in industrial countries.

OTHER PROBLEMS IN DEVELOPING COUNTRY EXPORTS OF MANUFACTURES: APPLICATIONS TO COUNTERTRADE

Protectionism is obviously a great impediment to the growth of developing country exports of manufactures. However, not all the problems that the developing countries have in export development are due to industrial country protectionism; there are several other factors, some of which are internal problems. Even the removal of all barriers to developing country exports would not solve these problems.

The countertrade strategist should determine which of these problems apply to the target country, and address the appropriate problems in the countertrade or offset proposal. Demonstrating understanding of the country's export difficulties will greatly strengthen the proposal.

Poor or Unacceptable Quality of Manufactured Products Destined for Industrial Markets. This is due to a number of problems, the most important of which are poor quality control and low standards of living. In the latter case, the manufacturer is producing a product which would be acceptable in the domestic market but unsalable in an industrial market. Can the Western company institute quality control procedures in the joint venture plant, provide training for managers or provide technical training for workers? Would it be feasible for the Western company to "loan" one of its managers to the foreign manufacturer for a specified period of time? Is the foreign manufacturer willing to make the effort to improve his product, or does he (or the state trading organization) insist that the product be accepted as is? (Demands for acceptance of an "as is" product usually mean that the country just wants to get rid of surplus production.) Will the foreign government or STO allow the Western company to work with the manufacturer on product improvement, or is direct contact with the manufacturer discouraged?

Outdated Technology in the Manufacturing Process. This outdated technology is related to product quality. Is the Western company willing to transfer technology?

High Cost of Energy Needed for Industrial Production. Energy costs may have constrained production of a sufficient or predictable quantity of manufactured items for export. The high cost of energy is probably at least as restrictive to export development as protectionism, though it is much more difficult to document. Can the Western company offer energy-saving equipment, or an energy-efficient industrial process?

Lack of Demand for Manufactured Products in Industrial Countries during Periods of Recession. Can the Western company help to create a demand for the developing country's product through a promotional campaign, product adaptations, new pricing structures, or other methods? If not, can the company persuade the developing country to offer a different product for counterpurchase?

Saturated Markets for Certain Manufactured Products in Industrial Countries. In this case, the Western company should try to convince the developing country that a different product should be offered; or that the original product be altered or updated to the point where it is accepted as a new, unique product by consumers.

Low Growth Rate for Imports of Manufactures in Industrial Countries. Low growth rate is due in part to the slow population growth in these countries. The Western company can try the aforementioned "saturated market" approach. Alternatively, the company could try to help the developing country target a segment of the population which is growing quickly or which is underserved by current marketing. In the United States, for example, these segments would include older people and minority groups.

Import Substitution Policies. Import substitution may divert manufactures to domestic use which might otherwise have been exported; also, concentration on import substitution weakens investment in export industries. This is a tough problem for the Western countertrader, since many developing countries are only interested in joint ventures because of the import substitution aspect. Can the Western company convince the developing country that setting aside a certain portion of production for export will be beneficial?

Shipping Problems. Shipping facilities may be inadequate or prohibitively expensive; ports may be so congested that shipments are seriously delayed. Also the shipping distance to the desired foreign market may be so great that the export products are competitive only on an f.o.b. basis. This is another tough problem; there is not much that the Western company can do to help, unless it is selling a shipping/port development project. Countries that are engaged in workable programs to improve shipping and port facilities may be good prospective countertrade partners in the long run, however.

Lack of International Marketing Skills. Exporters in many developing countries do not have the sophistication, training, or research facilities to promote their products effectively in foreign markets. Can the Western company provide promotional services or train the foreign exporter in product promotion?

Lack of Government Incentives to Export, or Restrictive Export Policies. In many countries, the official incentives to export (e.g., tax benefits, etc.) are not sufficient to encourage high growth of exports. Often there is excessive red tape—complicated licensing procedures, for example—and other disincentives such as unnecessarily strict exchange repatriation rules. The Western company can usually do nothing to change these policies. However, in a countertrade deal, the government will sometimes offer special export incentives that will make the deal workable.

Selection of the Wrong Products to Promote for Export. In some countries, the government decides more or less arbitrarily that certain manufactures should be targeted for export just because they look impressive—steel, automobiles, high-tech products, and so on—with little or no research into the possibility of getting a share in the desired market, projected growth in consumption of the product, or consideration of various aspects of the exporting country's competitive position. Can the Western company provide the necessary research to help the developing country find the best markets for its targeted products? Can the company find other good products made in the country, and convincingly demonstrate their export potential to the government?

Of the problems noted, product quality, technology, and marketing skills are the areas in which countertrade and offset programs can have the greatest impact. Technology transfer can often solve product quality problems, given that the root of the problem is not management or worker performance. Marketing skills can enable the developing country to participate successfully in conventional export trade after the countertrade transaction is completed.

Countertrade can be a significant stimulus to the export of manufactures. It can be a waste of time, though, if the developing country does not use the countertrade experience constructively to address its export problems. Sometimes, for example, a country will gladly export as long as the Western trading partner takes over the marketing of the products, but will not make an effort on its own to develop a share in the foreign market—research, marketing strategy, promotion, and so on—after the countertrade agreement terminates. In these situations, all that the Western company can do is meet the developing country's government halfway; the Western firm cannot be expected to function as a de facto export development agency, and really has no responsibility for export promotion once the countertrade agreement ends.

Buyback, the popular type of countertrade in which the Western company sets up a plant in the developing country and agrees to buy back all or part of the resultant production, may actually not be the best arrangement for the developing country. Buyback deals mean a guaranteed market for export of manufactures; but if the country becomes complacent with this guarantee and does not attempt to export some of the production to new markets, the gain in exports is temporary. There have been some successful cases of post-countertrade export development in industrial countries, however. Several companies which got their initial export opportunity as subcontractors in NATO military offsets are now competitive in the international marketplace.

Finally, the countertrade strategist must remember that a certain delicacy is required in the offer to help solve a developing country's export problems through countertrade arrangements. No one likes to have an outsider come in and tell him how to do his job, however enthusiastic that outsider may be. The Western company will score points at the negotiation table by being knowledgeable about the country's export situation and having a proposal ready, but it is best to present the project to government officials as a program of mutual benefit.

OPEC AND COUNTERTRADE

OPEC has had a far greater impact on countertrade than most people realize. The obvious contribution of OPEC to the countertrade environment is the damage the cartel did to the world economy; countertrade is one of the results of this general economic disorder. However, there are several specific areas in which OPEC has had less obvious but more pervasive effects on countertrade. The major area is the accumulation of developing country debt; OPEC indirectly made this debt worse by the powerful influence of its oil surplus money (liquidity supply) on the privatization of international finance. In other areas, OPEC increased North–South friction and strengthened the trade management trend, both of which have pushed countries toward countertrade. Finally, OPEC itself is directly responsible for about $70 billion worth of countertrade each year, in the form of oil barter conducted by various member countries. The following is a discussion of these areas of influence.

Strategists should understand OPEC's wide-ranging effect on countertrade whether or not they are participating in oil barter, for the world may not have seen the last of the oil price shocks. Another shock would likely cause a repeat of the 1974 and 1980 global economic recessions, which would intensify countertrade as the affected countries scrambled to maintain minimum import and export levels.

Debt: Private Bank Deposits

OPEC played an important supply side role in the accumulation of the developing countries' debt to private institutions. During the 1970s, the private capital markets became more important than the official lending institutions, which eventually worked to the detriment of the developing countries. One of the major supply-side factors in the growth of private capital markets was the great influx of OPEC money. OPEC preferred to keep its oil income surplus highly liquid, and deposited about $200 billion of the $500 billion surplus in commercial banks from 1974 through 1982. This provided the banks with an ample supply of money to loan. However, the flow of OPEC money was both unregulated and uncertain, and deposits tended to vary considerably from year to year.

The value of OPEC deposits in commercial banks from 1974 through 1981 totaled $162.9 billion. Most of this, $145.2 billion, consisted of Eurocurrency bank deposits. The deposits represented an average 35.5% per year of the OPEC surplus. The peak years were 1974, in which deposits were $28.6 billion or 50.9% of the year's surplus, and 1979, in which deposits were $40.4 billion or 65.2% of the surplus; these huge deposits reflected the two oil price increases. In 1981, the bottom fell out of OPEC liquidity. Only 3.8% of the surplus was deposited in commercial banks that year ($2.3 billion), although the surplus was still very large. Bank deposits for 1982 and 1983 were negative.*

OPEC helped the developing countries by fattening the private capital markets, which enabled the countries to get more loans than they could otherwise have obtained; however, OPEC deposits dried up at a crucial point. When combined with other problems that had been building up in the trade and financial systems, the sudden drop in the supply of OPEC money to commercial banks exacerbated the 1982 debt situation. The developing countries, unable to get new loans from commercial banks, turned to the official institutions; but these institutions had been so weakened by the private capital markets that their resources fell far short of meeting the urgent financial needs of the debtor countries. At this time many countries had to begin countertrading as an emergency measure, since they could not borrow more cash for imports.

Debt: Resource Transfers and Official Development Assistance

The shortage of official development assistance (ODA or foreign aid) has both contributed to countertrade, when countries must barter due to lack of funds, and obstructed it; official institutions such as the IMF often kill countertrade deals by demanding that the borrower countries sell exports for cash. OPEC was heavily involved in the events leading up to this situation.

One of the immediate results of the 1973 oil price increase was a massive transfer of resources from developed to (OPEC) developing countries. This transfer amounted to about $70 billion, an impressive figure compared to official aid flows at that time of $10 billion. Although only the OPEC nations were the beneficiaries of the transfer, the entire Third World was pleased. OPEC had accomplished in a few short months what the U.N. General Assembly had been unable to do over a period of years. The United Nations had been asking for a mere 0.7% of GNP as a target for official resource transfers, and could not get the developed countries to agree to donate this much. As late as 1983, only five OECD countries had met or exceeded this goal: Norway, the Netherlands, Sweden, France, and Denmark.

OPEC itself was quite generous in official development assistance, as long as the money lasted. The total OPEC contribution for the years 1975 through 1983 was $63.6 billion; OPEC donations accounted for 15% to 30% of ODA from all sources during this period. Additionally, the major OPEC countries contributed a far higher percentage of GNP than the OECD countries. In 1980, when OPEC ODA peaked at $9.5 billion, Saudi Arabia contributed 5.09% of GNP, Kuwait 3.52%, and the United Arab Emirates 3.30%. The largest OECD donations that year, in percentage terms, were the Netherlands'

---

*The World Bank, *World Development Report 1985*, New York, Oxford University Press, 1985, p. 89.

1.03%, Norway's 0.85%, and Sweden's 0.79%. The 1980 donations of the four richest OECD countries—the United States, France, the Federal Republic of Germany and Japan—were much lower, ranging from 0.27% to 0.64%.*

The negative aspects of OPEC assistance were that most of it went to Arab countries (about 80%) rather than being distributed evenly among all of the developing countries hurt by the oil price increases, and that it began to shrink drastically just when the developing countries needed it the most. It was in 1982, when the debt crunch came, that OPEC ODA suddenly fell. Today, only Saudi Arabia and Kuwait are still donating large percentages of GNP.

North–South Friction

In the context of North–South friction, OPEC has been one of the most divisive influences in postwar trade and economic relations between developed and developing countries. Although it is seldom mentioned today, the fact is that in the beginning the developing countries supported OPEC. They interpreted OPEC's 1973 action as the victory of a group of impoverished primary product exporters over the rich countries, and publicly defended OPEC at the sixth special session of the U.N. General Assembly. The OPEC countries at that time were no better off than other primary product exporters; of the countries who were members in 1973, 65% to 99% of their total exports consisted of petroleum and petroleum products. The Arab members had virtually no manufacturing industries that they could have built up into export industries, and there was little possibility of developing agriculture because of the region's unfavorable climate. The success of OPEC encouraged the other developing countries to push for the NIEO, especially for the ICP.

It took the developing countries a couple of years to see OPEC's price hike for what it was: a serious setback to world output and economic growth. The poorest countries could not even afford fertilizer to keep their agricultural sectors productive. The countries who were trying to export manufactures found the industrial markets shrinking due to depressed demand and protectionism. Oil-exporting developing countries that did not join OPEC, such as Mexico, did not become wealthy from oil sales; they had to manage as best they could in a market dominated by OPEC. The cartel pitted the North and the South against each other. Both sides lost, but the shared adversity did not improve their relationship. Instead, it has hardened their attitudes.

Countertrade demands made by a developing country to an industrial country trading partner are often tinged with North–South friction, especially when the demands are unreasonable. The developing country's negotiators may feel that the rich industrialist owes their country special consideration

*World Bank, *World Development Report*, pp. 208–209.

for past economic injustices, and will accordingly try to drive a very hard bargain. The contribution of OPEC to this attitude has been very significant.

Trade Management

OPEC has immensely strengthened the trade management trend, both by direct participation and by causing other countries to intensify their own trade management practices, thus indirectly encouraging the development of the countertrade sector. OPEC began to practice meta-trade-management in 1973, quadrupling oil prices that year and going on to increase prices by a total of 1,200% over the next seven years. This was a trade management nightmare, far worse in its repercussions than the Multifiber Arrangement and the NIEO combined could ever be. The ensuing economic disruption dealt a severe blow to world trade at the outset and hampered its growth for several years afterward, as the industrial countries tried to pull out of the recession. Growth of external trade among the developing countries was likewise slowed. Protectionism in the industrial countries has accelerated partly because of the economic problems caused by OPEC's price increases; and it is no coincidence that the developing countries say that they need countertrade to help overcome protectionism against their exports. The oil price shocks and the current volatility in oil prices have caused widespread uncertainty about energy availability, which has in turn led countries to depend increasingly on trade management.

Oil Barter

In hindsight, OPEC seems to have shot itself in the foot; for the OPEC countries themselves, collectively the richest developing countries in the world, are now reduced to countertrade. The 1973 and 1979 oil price increases not only caused a reduction in world output, but prompted major changes in patterns of production and consumption. In the early 1980s, OPEC oil revenues began to plummet as the effects of increased non-OPEC production, conservation, and fuel substitution began to be felt. In 1985, oil prices collapsed, and the official price structure was abandoned for practical purposes. The current trend in oil pricing is netback pricing, a system which is much more responsive to the market than official prices. Netback pricing is a market-related pricing system of on-arrival netback calculations which tie the crude contract price to spot product prices f.o.b. in major refining centers. At least 65% of crude oil is now traded under netback and other arrangements that are subject to current market prices. The loss of revenue has pressured OPEC to turn to oil barter. Oil is used as payment for essential imports such as food, major capital construction projects, and military hardware. OPEC countries also have numerous bilateral agreements with the centrally planned economies in which oil is traded for various products.

Oil barter began more as a method of maintaining production and market share than as a stark financial necessity, however. Several OPEC countries started countertrading oil when their production quotas were cut, and these countries frequently offered the oil to buyers at prices below the official OPEC price. This served to undermine the price structure. Other OPEC members offered oil at official prices, using countertrade to ensure exports of oil. OPEC has lost about half its world market share since 1973, and oil barter is a reflection of the effort the cartel is making to get its share back.

OPEC countries do not appear to be interested in using countertrade for export diversification or industrial development, with the exception of Saudi Arabia. For example, oil barter is used to support the war effort in Iran and Iraq, and for essential imports in Nigeria.

3 The Socialist Countries

The socialist countries of Eastern Europe have fundamentally different reasons for wanting countertrade as compared to the developing countries and socialist China. Some factors are shared with the developing countries, mainly hard currency shortage and the need for technology transfer, but others are not. The major difference is that Eastern Europe does not use countertrade for basic industrial and export development, or to assist in a modernization process. The USSR and the Eastern European countries were already industrialized countries at the time of World War II. Though their economies and infrastructures suffered heavy damage during the war, they were not "developing" countries in any sense of the word, and did not have the same priorities as the developing countries in the postwar restructuring and redevelopment of trade. They did not consider trade with the market economies to be a priority, preferring instead to strengthen trade within their group. Countertrade is used primarily to import technology and upgrade manufacturing facilities; the conservation of hard currency, the generation of foreign exchange through buyback exports, and the penetration of Western markets are secondary considerations.

The influence of the Eastern European centrally planned economies (particularly the USSR) on the development of countertrade cannot be overemphasized. In addition to accounting for a good deal of the volume of postwar countertrade, these countries have influenced the trade management policies and state trading systems of many non-socialist countries. When countertrade started to become popular in 1982, the developing countries often turned to Eastern European FTOs as models for their own countertrading entities, since the Eastern Europeans were the recognized countertrade experts. Some of the current confusion in national countertrade practices results from the developing countries' efforts to fit the socialist FTO model to their needs. The Eastern Europeans also promote bilateral trade, which fits neatly into the countertrade/trade balancing policies of certain developing countries.

Even more important, perhaps, is the influence that Eastern Europe has had on the strategies of industrial country exporters (multinationals) who participate in countertrade, and indeed, on these exporters' entire perception of countertrade. The development of the large countertrade service industries in Vienna and London is due to Eastern European countertrade. Many traders now operating in other parts of the world started out working in these service industries, "cutting their teeth" on countertrade with Eastern Europe. As a result, their negotiating strategies and those of their clients are often based on their experience with Eastern European countries, whether or not these strategies are appropriate for other countries. Thus Eastern European trading practices have played a great part in Western countertrade methodology.

China, which did not trade very much with the market economies until the late 1970s, has had far less influence on countertrade. Chinese FTOs were not very visible, and the volume of Chinese countertrade outside the centrally planned economies was insignificant until recently. This situation is changing rapidly as China becomes more and more involved in trade with the West. China's approach to reciprocal trade is very different from that of the other socialist countries, since its needs are different; it is more like a developing country in that countertrade is used to facilitate modernization, industrial development, and export development. (See Chapter 17 for detailed information.) The open trading attitude of the Chinese government and the attractiveness of the enormous Chinese market will probably make China the major force in countertrade by the end of the century. In that event, strategies for trading with China will supplant Eastern European trading strategies as the standard for countertrade operations.

THE DEVELOPMENT OF COUNTERTRADE IN EASTERN EUROPE

The Eastern European countries did not participate in the postwar Bretton Woods arrangements; rather, they became the responsibility of the USSR, which guided them in the evolution of a separate economic and trade system. Their mutual goal was self-sufficiency, with the mechanism designed to achieve this being the Council for Mutual Economic Assistance* (CMEA, formerly known as COMECON). The CMEA countries have never been very responsive to changes in the market economies, nor have they wanted to be. They adhere as closely as possible to their five-year economic plans and their policy of full employment. Although they are interested in trade with the market economies, both industrial and developing, their priority is to expand and strengthen trade among themselves.

This isolationist approach to economics and trade has been fairly successful, taking into account the relatively low standards of living in CMEA countries. However, there have been several problems that have induced the CMEA countries to seek countertrade with the market economies. One

---

*The current members of the CMEA are the USSR, Bulgaria, Czechoslovakia, the German Democratic Republic, Hungary, Poland, Romania, Cuba, Mongolia, and Vietnam. This discussion refers only to the European members.

problem is the availability of food. Severe weather combined with chronically low agricultural production has often made it necessary for the CMEA (especially the USSR) to import large amounts of food, either with cash payments to industrial countries or by bartering manufactured goods to developing country producers of wheat and other vital agricultural products. Another problem is currency inconvertibility. CMEA currencies have no value outside the bloc, leaving the USSR frequently in the position of literally having to pay for priority imports in gold. Obviously, countertrade is preferable to this kind of sacrifice. The major problem, though, is the availability of technology. The CMEA cannot get the latest industrial and agricultural technology if it avoids contact with the market economies. Nor can it independently develop all necessary technology on its own, if it cannot send large numbers of its young people to top foreign universities.

The USSR recognized the need for imported technology in the 1960s, and set about to obtain it through a reciprocal trade scheme called the Program of Industrial Collaboration with Industrial Countries. This program consists of a series of bilateral agreements with Western European countries and Japan for technology in the areas of electronics, chemicals, computers, and advanced assembly line production. Technology from the United States is also much in demand, but the flow of technology from the United States has been uneven due to shifting U.S./USSR political relations. When relations are good, technology transfer and other forms of countertrade proceed at a brisk pace and prove beneficial to both parties. There have also been many large-scale industrial projects, inside and outside the CMEA, in which U.S. and Soviet companies have cooperated; these projects too are vulnerable to political attack, though. The Siberian pipeline project is a notable example.

External debt, commonly cited as a major force behind countertrade, has not been a pressing motivation for countertrade in the CMEA countries. Their collective debt position is not nearly so desperate as that of the Third World. According to U.N. estimates, the net indebtedness of the CMEA countries fell by $14 billion between 1982 and 1984, declining from $25 billion to $11 billion. The decline was facilitated by exchange rate movements, especially by the appreciation of the U.S. dollar, since much of the debt of CMEA countries is denominated in currencies other than the dollar. This resulted in a decline in interest payments and in the ratio of interest payments to exports. Creditors have accordingly revised their assessment of the financial position of CMEA countries, causing the commercial banks to make considerable cuts in the spreads charged on CMEA institutional borrowers. Therefore, the CMEA countries, unlike the developing countries, have been able to get new commercial loans.*

There are several other areas in which the CMEA countries' motivations for managed trade/countertrade differ from those of the developing countries. Commodity prices are not an important factor, as the CMEA is not dependent

*United Nations, *Trade and Development Report, 1985*, pp. 57–58.

on commodities for export income. Export diversification from primary products to manufactures is also not an issue, since most CMEA exports are already manufactured products.

Protectionism is definitely a factor; there are substantial tariff and nontariff barriers against CMEA exports in industrial countries. (Only Hungary, Poland, and Romania are members of GATT.) However, it is not such an issue of contention in the CMEA as it is in the developing countries, since the CMEA has historically concentrated on mutual trade among members rather than the development of exports to industrial countries. Finally, there is nothing in the CMEA similar to North–South friction which would serve to fuel demands for reciprocity. East–West friction is based on differences in political ideologies rather than on financial and trade grievances.

One questionable point is the use of countertrade to overcome a lack of international marketing skills. Western analysts maintain that the CMEA does not know how to sell to Western markets, either in producing a desirable product or in the areas of packaging, promotion, distribution, and servicing, and therefore uses its Western countertrade partner as a marketing agent. It is true that such skills are not very evident in CMEA FTOs; however, this is not due to any absence of capability. Eastern Europeans, and Soviets in particular, are well-educated, disciplined people, noted for their negotiating expertise in trade arrangements. If they wanted to develop international marketing skills, they could do so easily. That they have not, despite some 40 years of trading with the West, demonstrates the CMEA's lack of interest in strong trade relations with the market economies rather than any sort of incompetence in exporting. From a strictly practical viewpoint, it would have been a waste of effort anyway for CMEA FTOs to train their staffs in international marketing when the export products are not up to the quality and technological standards of Western markets. If the CMEA countries ever decide to give the same priority to Western markets that they give to each other, they will not only dramatically improve the quality of export products, but will also produce a group of very astute marketing people.

EXTERNAL TRADE OF THE CENTRALLY PLANNED ECONOMIES

The external trade patterns of the centrally planned economies (the CMEA and China) demonstrate the closed nature of Eastern European trade, and highlight the wide-ranging aspects of Chinese trade. Both areas present marketing opportunities for Western exporters, although to date these exporters have shown relatively little interest in CPE markets.

The centrally planned economies as a group account for about 9% of world trade. CPE imports in 1985 totaled $210.5 billion (f.o.b.), and exports totaled $199.2 billion. About half of their trade is with each other: intra-CPE trade accounted for 47% of imports and 50% of exports in 1985. Of the remaining trade, statistics indicate that developed countries are more important as sources of CPE imports, accounting for 36% of 1985 imports, than developing countries, which accounted for only 17%. Developed and developing countries are of roughly equal importance as markets for CPE export products, though. In 1985, 27% of CPE exports went to developed countries and 22% to developing countries. The remaining small percentage of imports and exports represents CPE trade with OPEC countries. This trade does not amount to much because the CPEs do not need OPEC; both the USSR and China have ample energy resources.

CPE total figures represent mostly the trade patterns of the USSR and Eastern Europe, however. The trade of the Asian centrally planned economies (China, North Korea, Mongolia, and Vietnam) shows a quite different pattern. About 90% of the value of CPE Asia trade represents Chinese trade, and roughly 82% of CPE Europe trade represents Soviet trade; therefore, the two CPE trade patterns are largely the result of the differing external trade philosophies of China and the USSR.

Unlike CPE Europe, CPE Asia depends heavily on imports from the market economies: 65% of 1985 imports came from developed countries and 21% from developing countries. Only 13% of imports originated in other CPE countries. The market economies are also CPE Asia's most important export markets. In 1985, 43% of exports went to developed countries, 44% to developing countries, and 11% to other CPE countries.*

The CMEA countries' five-year plans through 1990 project an increase in annual import volume of 6.7% and an increase in exports of 5.6%, for the countries taken as a group. Emphasis is to be placed on high-technology products. All of the countries in the group, except Poland, have had trade surpluses since 1982; this is attributed largely to East–West trade.

Under China's 1986–1990 plan, imports are projected to increase by 6.1% annually and exports by 8%, with the total volume of foreign trade expected to increase by 40%. Emphasis will be on expansion of the energy and transportation sectors; upgrading of existing facilities; and the development of science, education, and technology. Chinese trade was fairly well balanced until 1985, showing only small deficits or surpluses; in that year, the deficit jumped to $13.8 billion. The government anticipates a deficit for the next few years.

These trade trends have great significance for companies interested in countertrade with the CMEA and China. China is reaching outward in its trade relationships and will be more receptive to countertrade proposals than the CMEA, which is still determined to maintain its closed trading system. Also, China will probably make more of an effort to provide quality export products as buybacks. In the CMEA, the member countries have first choice on the good export products, while Western countertraders must choose from whatever is left. Even then, the available counterpurchase products may suddenly disappear if a member country needs the products. This is

*United Nations, *Monthly Bulletin of Statistics*, New York, July 1986, pp. 284–285.

not to say that a company should necessarily choose China over the CMEA for countertrade, though. China may be a better potential market in the long run, but countertrade transactions run much more smoothly in the CMEA due to these countries' heavy experience with reciprocal East–West trade. The choice of a socialist market depends on the company's product and marketing plans.

Countertrade may stimulate Western interest in East–West trade. Thus far, the market economies have not responded to export opportunities in the CPEs. The United States and the EEC send only about 3.5% of their annual total exports to the CPEs, and the developing countries together export only 4% of total foreign sales to CPE markets. Japan sends about 7% of annual exports to the CPEs, but even this is a very small amount considering the size of the market group. Increased countertrade sales are the key to CPE market penetration, whether the target is China or the CMEA. Whatever differences the two may have in external trade objectives, they do agree on one thing: external trade should be reciprocal trade.

4 The Industrialized Nations

Most countertrade among industrial countries has been of the military offset type. Offset trade was an outgrowth of the Cold War, an environment of tension and hostility which led Western countries to share production of defense items for mutual security reasons. The United States, as the major Western world supplier of arms, was indirectly responsible for the rise in offsets; however, the USSR, as the major potential aggressor, probably had just as much indirect responsibility. Direct coproduction military offsets do not constitute discriminatory trade, under the Security Exceptions Article of the GATT. However, the status of indirect offsets is questionable. Additionally, some developed countries now require civilian as well as military offsets, which further stretches compliance with the GATT.

Today, offsets among developed countries are used as trade management tools; offsets are pursued more for employment, commercial, and industrial policy reasons than for defense capability considerations. Technology transfer, employment, and export development are the objectives of modern offsets.

This chapter covers the development of offsets in developed countries through discussion of military offsets, civilian offsets, buybacks, and other exports in developed country countertrade, and intra-developed-country protectionism as it is related to offset trade.

MILITARY OFFSETS

Military trade has always been a prime example of trade management. Free market forces have had little to do with arms trade, since the international arms market is governed largely by the objectives and policies of the purchasing and selling governments. Military offsets were originally only a small part of the larger trade management arena of the arms market; however, offset trade now has a life of its own as a trade management tool. The reasoning behind direct coproduction offsets—basically, the strengthening of mutual security through sharing of production and interoperability of defense systems, which has nothing to do with trade management—has not been abandoned by any of the trading parties, but it has been substantially altered by other considerations. Purchasing countries now use offsets for employment, technology transfer, industrial development, and export development. This is especially true of indirect offsets (those involving products or services unrelated to the defense items sold).

Military offset trade in the developed countries began shortly after World War II when there was an arms buildup resulting from Cold War tensions. The United States generated many of these offsets. The United States actively encouraged coproduction offsets for foreign policy and mutual defense capability reasons, especially in NATO countries. (It should be noted, however, that in U.S. government administrative usage coproduction is not offset.) The most important U.S. offset program was the 1974 purchase of the F-16 aircraft by the European Participating Governments (EPG), a consortium of four NATO countries. This program was valued at $2.8 billion in 1975 dollars.

The United States started having problems with offsets in 1975, when there were difficulties with the offset in Switzerland's purchase of 72 F-5 aircraft. The Swiss decided to limit participation in coproduction and demanded other types of offsets. The resulting difficulties led to a U.S. decision to place complete responsibility for offset commitments on the commercial firms making the sales (the Duncan Memorandum).

The European countries also had problems with offsets in U.S. defense sales, however. They had difficulty in establishing and maintaining efficient production lines for coproduction; thus offsets beyond coproduction were increasingly demanded to alleviate the economic problems associated with coproduction. These problems remain unresolved. The Europeans cannot possibly achieve the economies of scale of the U.S. defense firms, because they do not have the huge domestic demand of the United States. In the United States, about 75% of all military goods are produced for domestic use by the U.S. government. Moreover, the United States has a comparatively vast land area to protect, much larger than any single European country; in addition to the continental United States, there are the states of Alaska and Hawaii and the various territories. All of these areas must have well-equipped military bases.

Although offsets can be costly and inefficient for the beneficiary countries, the countries still want to have offsets. A 1981 Rand Corporation/U.S. Air Force study ("Multinational Coproduction of Military Aerospace Systems") projected that the F-16 fighter aircraft coproduced under the aforementioned U.S./EPG program could be approximately 35% more expensive for the EPGs than purchasing the aircraft directly from the U.S. manufacturer. The study also mentioned possible inefficiencies on the U.S. side, such as, costs to the U.S. government and private industry due to smaller production runs, lost R&D recoupment charges, and the procurement of subcomponents (10% of total U.S.-manufactured aircraft) from more expensive European subcontractors. Although the offset did turn out to be more expensive for the EPGs than a cash purchase, confirming the Rand projections, the extra costs on the U.S. side did not materialize. The projection was that the initial agreement with the EPG would have the effect of increasing the system cost of the 650 F-16s built for the USAF by 5%. The cost of offsets for U.S. follow-on orders (i.e., U.S. production of F-16's in excess of 650) was similarly estimated at 8% of the system cost. In fact, however, the unit fly-away cost (in constant 1975 dollars) showed a steady decline from $5.0 million in 1978 to $4.0 million for the last USAF F-16-A which was delivered in 1985. This represents a 20% reduction in the per unit cost to the U.S. government from 1978 to 1985.

The EPGs felt that the increased costs resulting from offsets were justified. They acknowledged that despite the expense, the F-16 program enhanced their industrial technology and development base, and improved their trade balances with the United States compared to what these balances might have been had they purchased the aircraft directly from the United States without coproduction. The program also indirectly created new defense export business for private industry in the EPG countries. For example, firms in the Netherlands and Norway have recently become competitive in the international arms market due partly to the technology and skills gained from participation in the program.*

Another example of a country's willing acceptance of the high cost of offsets versus conventional cash purchases is the new General Dynamics offset with Greece, involving the purchase of forty F-16s. (The contract was signed in 1985.) Greece could have saved $50 million on the aircraft, which are valued at about $1 billion, if it had made the purchase with concessionary FMS financing from the United States. However, the terms under this arrangement would reportedly have limited the direct offset portion and technology transfer. Greece chose to purchase the aircraft on commercial terms at a higher cost in order to get increased offset benefits. (See Chapter 20 for further information on the offset.)

Indirect offsets can give countries economic benefits they could not obtain from direct coproduction offset, given the extra costs of coproduction. The simplest form of indirect offset, counterpurchase, can result in incremental exports of various products and can increase the country's share in other developed country markets. Tourism not only brings in money, but introduces visitors to the country's products and may help to create a demand for the products in the tourists' home countries. Nonmilitary technology transfer (technology that can be used in the manufacture of nondefense items) is very valuable to the buyer countries. Investment and joint ventures are also highly desirable. All of these methods create opportunities for employment, which is one of the major considerations in offset for developed countries.

Most developed countries frown on countertrade, citing the GATT provisions against discriminatory trade. All GATT member countries that par-

*U.S. Office of Management and Budget, *Impact of Offsets in Defense-Related Exports*, Washington, DC, U.S. Government Printing Office, 1985, pp. 55–56.

ticipate in offsets, buyers and sellers alike, can state that they are not violating the GATT because of the Security Exceptions Article. Article XXI, among other things, exempts the actions taken by contracting parties with respect to "ammunition and implements of war . . . for the purpose of supplying a military establishment" from the obligations contained in the other articles. Given this fact, it is still questionable whether the types of indirect offsets used today fit the description of "security exceptions." Tourism and the counterpurchase of nondefense-related products such as agricultural commodities and textiles certainly do not fall under that classification. Developed countries cannot hide behind the GATT and criticize the countertrade practices of developing countries when they are practicing countertrade among themselves through indirect offsets.

CIVILIAN OFFSETS

Several developed countries require civilian offsets as well as military offsets for purchases exceeding a minimum value. These offsets are known as public procurement offsets or industrial benefits programs. Countries with such policies include Canada, Australia, New Zealand, and Greece. The civilian offset programs of these four countries have several features in common. The countries' export structures are more revealing than their public policies, however; three of the four have export structures which differ strikingly from those of other developed countries, while the fourth (Canada) has a serious problem with the diversification of export markets.

Technology transfer is the top priority in the offset programs of Canada and Australia, while Greece considers export promotion most important. Though all four countries give high priority to industrial development, only New Zealand ranks it first as a matter of public record. Employment is a major feature in the Canadian, Australian, and New Zealand programs; in Greece, however, employment is not mentioned in the public policy. (This may be because Greece has relatively high employment in the tourism service industry. Also, many Greek nationals have found employment as "guest workers" in other countries.) About 50% of Canadian employment in the aircraft industry is due to offsets, in some provinces, and in Australia offset provides 2,000 to 2,500 jobs annually.

Export development is a vital part of the offset programs in all four countries. Canada and Australia use their offsets to develop exports of high technology and high-value-added manufactured products; Australia, in fact, will not offer traditional exports (food, raw materials, etc.) in countertrade except to CMEA and developing countries. Canada is especially interested in finding new export markets (i.e., lessening its heavy dependence on the U.S. market). Greece and New Zealand, on the other hand, appear more interested in promoting traditional exports under their offset programs than developing new exports.

The Canadian and Australian offset programs seem to have been established partly as a response to the economic problems resulting from the 1973 oil crisis, as both countries instituted their programs shortly after 1973. The New Zealand program was established in 1980, at the onset of a recessionary period related to the 1979 oil crisis. The Greek program, which has been more or less in effect for many years, was tightened considerably in 1985; this possibly reflects Greece's interest in participating in the worldwide boom in countertrade. Of the four, Greece is the only country that openly approves of countertrade.

It is export structures, however, which demonstrate why these four countries have civilian offset programs and the other large industrial countries do not. One way of statistically identifying a developed country is to observe the total proportion of its exports which are in Standard International Trade Classification (SITC) aggregate group 7, machinery and transport equipment. The most technologically advanced and highest-value-added products are classified in this group: capital equipment, industrial machinery, engineering equipment, automobiles, aircraft, ships, electronics, and so on. A developed country usually has at least 30% of its exports in Group 7. Of the four countries discussed here, only Canada has machinery and transport equipment exports of that magnitude.

Only 3.4% of Greek exports, 4.0% of Australian exports, and 4.1% of New Zealand exports are machinery and transport equipment. (Table 4-1.) In comparison, of the total exports of the United Kingdom, 30.2% are machinery and transport equipment; Italy, 32.0%; France, 34.0%; Federal Republic of Germany, 45.4%; United States, 42.2%; and Japan, 63.7%. Canadian exports of Group 7 products represent 34.4% of total exports; however, most of these exports are automobiles manufactured in Canada by U.S. firms and shipped back to the United States.

The top exports of the four countries are not in high-value-added product categories, given the exception of Canada. Most Greek exports, 30.1%, are in Group 6, basic manufactures (wood, stone, glass, textiles, iron and steel, etc.). Group 6 is Canada's second most important export product area, accounting for 15.3% of the export total. (Note: when Canadian exports are considered outside SITC classifications, 70% of its exports are raw materials.) The major exports of Australia and New Zealand are food products, Group 0. Of total Australian exports, 23.9% are in Group 0, while 49.9% of New Zealand's exports are in this group. Mineral fuels, Group 3, are also an important export area for Australia; these exports (primarily coal) account for 22.8% of the export total. In the other large industrial countries, basic manufactures account for an average 17.1% of exports and food for an average 6.6% of the total.

These export structures show clearly that Canada, Australia, Greece, and New Zealand need to diversify and develop exports in order to keep up with the other industrialized countries; trade management practices such as offsets involving export development can help achieve this objective. It is not clear,

Table 4.1. Export Structure of Selected Developed Countries (by percentage of total exports, 1983)

Country	\multicolumn{9}{c}{SITC classification[a]}
	0	1	2	3	4	5	6	7	8
Australia	23.9	0.0	30.3	22.8	0.3	2.1	11.3	4.0	1.8
Canada	10.7	0.6	14.4	14.1	0.1	4.9	15.3	34.4	2.8
France	12.9	2.8	4.0	3.8	0.3	12.9	19.2	34.0	8.9
Germany, Fed. Rep.	4.3	0.6	1.8	3.3	0.3	13.1	18.5	45.4	9.3
Greece	22.0	5.3	6.6	6.9	5.7	4.2	30.1	3.4	14.5
Italy	5.1	1.3	1.6	5.3	0.0	8.4	23.1	32.0	22.1
Japan	0.8	0.0	0.8	0.3	0.0	4.6	19.7	63.7	8.5
New Zealand	49.9	0.2	21.8	0.0	0.8	4.1	12.0	4.1	3.2
United Kingdom	4.5	2.4	2.5	21.7	0.0	11.4	14.6	30.2	9.6
United States	12.1	1.4	9.3	4.8	0.7	9.9	8.0	42.2	7.8

[a]SITC codes:
0   Food and live animals
1   Beverages and tobacco
2   Crude materials
3   Mineral fuels
4   Animal and vegetable oils and fats
5   Chemicals and chemical products
6   Basic manufactures
7   Machinery and transport equipment
8   Miscellaneous manufactures
9   Commodities and transactions not classified by kind (not shown)
Source: Compiled from United Nations trade data.

though, how the four countries justify mandatory civilian offsets under the GATT.

See Chapters 14, 16, and 20 for detailed information on the offset programs of Australia, Canada, and Greece respectively.

SOURCING, BUYBACKS, AND OTHER EXPORTS IN DEVELOPED COUNTRY COUNTERTRADE

Buyback countertrade is just as popular in developed countries as it is in developing countries. This form of compensation, whether it results from a military or a civilian offset, provides a guaranteed export market for the term of the offset agreement. (It also guarantees a certain level of employment.) The purchasing countries are particularly interested in making buyback–sourcing arrangements. If the purchasing country can become established as a source for the seller country, it can count on a long-term share in the seller country market. Sourcing can also lead to investment, joint ventures, and technology transfer, if these were not features of the original offset agreement.

Product quality is much less of a problem in buybacks from developed countries than developing countries, due to the advanced manufacturing techniques and high standards of living in developed countries. Manufacturers in developed countries are generally able to judge whether a product will be marketable in another developed country. The only serious problem with buyback manufactured products from developed countries is that they are more expensive than products from developing countries, partly because of the higher wages in developed countries. If the product is a high-technology item, it will be even more expensive as producers try to recoup their R&D investments.

As noted in Chapter 3, promotion of exports through countertrade programs does not do the exporting country much good if it places responsibility for export development solely on the partner country instead of gaining marketing expertise. One would think that most manufacturers in developed countries already know a lot about export marketing (except in the United States), but in fact many companies need to learn how to export. Those who already have some expertise should use offset programs as an opportunity for further development of their marketing skills.

PROTECTIONISM AND OFFSET TRADE AMONG DEVELOPED COUNTRIES

Military and civilian offsets imposed by developed countries are in part a reaction to intra-developed country protectionism. There is a great deal of protectionism among developed countries; they do not constitute a united front against the Third World, often being as protectionist against each other as they are against developing countries in certain product areas. They have numerous mechanisms to regulate trade among themselves. There are trade tensions even within trade blocs, such as the EEC, and between countries who are mutual major trading partners, such as the United States and Canada. These tensions result in trade management practices.

To give a few examples: Steel is a highly protected product among developed countries. The EEC maintains bilateral agreements with a number of developed countries, as well as with developing countries, for the purpose of limiting steel imports. The United States and other countries limit steel imports from the EEC, in turn. Automobiles are another heavily protected item; the EEC, the United States, Canada, and other industrial countries have numerous restrictions on automobile imports, primarily those from Japan. Most industrial countries also restrict electronics imports from Japan. Japan itself has import restrictions on all manner of products. Agricultural protectionism by developed countries against other developed countries is even worse than protectionism against manufactured products; there are various subsidy programs and import restrictions. In general, Switzerland and Japan are the most protectionist against agricultural products from developed countries, while the EEC is most protectionist against manufactured products from these countries.

Antidumping and countervailing duty actions, which are one measurement of protectionism, occur most between developed countries. As noted in Chapter 3, the United Nations found in a survey of 1979–1984 actions that 80% of such actions were taken by developed countries against other developed countries.

Offsets cannot defeat specific areas of protectionism; for example, a NATO country in the EEC could not export unlimited amounts of steel to the United States on the strength of a military offset agreement. However, some "sensitive" exports can be increased significantly through offset if a sourcing arrangement can be made; furthermore, increases in any export category will help improve the beneficiary country's trade balance with the seller country.

PART **2** Corporate Countertrade Practices

This part examines various aspects of corporate countertrade practices: policy, strategy, organizing, selecting service organizations, market research, insurance, financing, and a case study. In most instances, the practices discussed are those of American corporations.

Chapter 5, "Countertrade Policies and Strategies," consists of a classification of the basic policies and strategies corporations use in countertrade/offset, frameworks for strategy formulation and evaluation, and a strategic process chart to aid in planning and implementing countertrade projects.

The two policies described are *company advantage*, in which countertrade is done primarily for the company's benefit, with the trade and economic needs of the buyer country being a secondary consideration; and *mutual advantage*, in which the company considers the buyer country's needs of equal importance with its own and designs mutually beneficial countertrade projects. Company advantage policies are usually associated with profit maximizers, while mutual advantage policies are generally found in socially responsible multinational corporations. This chapter also includes a discussion of how companies choose their countertrade policies.

Four countertrade strategies are described: defensive, passive, reactive, and proactive. Defensive companies will make reciprocal arrangements with buyer countries, although they studiously avoid formal countertrade obligations. Passive companies regard countertrade as a necessary evil and participate in it on a minimal level. Reactive companies see countertrade as a competitive tool; they will go further to cooperate with the buyer country than the defensive and passive companies, and consider countertrade a permanent feature of their international operations. Proactive companies have made a commitment to countertrade. They see trading as an opportunity for business expansion, and make every effort to satisfy the buyer country in order to establish a long-term business relationship. The proactive strategy generally goes with the mutual advantage policy, while the defensive, passive, and reactive strategies are outgrowths of the company advantage policy. Examples of American companies using the different policies and strategies are given. Although many of the company policy and strategy classifications are based on interviews with company officials, some are the result of the authors' observations and do not represent company policy statements.

In the final part of Chapter 5, the development of strategy and the matching of countertrade policy to strategy are discussed. This is followed by a countertrade synergy matrix, which illustrates how the choice of strategy affects the level of synergy and the financial position of the company's countertrade unit. The chapter concludes with a strategic process chart for countertrade/offset transactions. This chart shows a step-by-step approach to the transaction, from analysis of countertrade needs and cost–benefits up to fulfillment of the countertrade obligation.

Chapter 6, "Organizing for Countertrade," begins with an examination of the three options for handling countertrade: having an outside trading company handle all countertrade, handling all countertrade in-house, or using a combination approach. Rationales for the selection of an option are given, based on the volume of countertrade and the company's experience and resources.

The major portion of this chapter is devoted to the types of countertrade units existing within the four major organization structures: functional, product, territorial, and matrix. In functional organizations, countertrade is usually a departmental responsibility, while in product organizations the countertrade unit may be in a division, at the corporate office, or set up in a combination approach. Product organizations often have countertrade units in several different divisions. Countertrade in territorial (geographic) organizations is most often handled by a corporate countertrade unit or an in-house trading company. In matrix organizations, the countertrade unit is usually in the international operations division. There is also an extensive discussion of the in-house world trading company, which can be established under any organizational structure. The advantages and disadvantages of each approach are examined. Each approach is illustrated by examples of companies using that type of countertrade unit.

Chapter 6 concludes with a discussion of the major problems associated with in-house countertrade: the cost center status of most in-house units, how the soundness of particular countertrade deals will affect the unit, opposition of procurement officers to countertrade sourcing, inexperienced staff, intercompany conflict resulting from the efforts of divisions with countertrade obligations to have other divisions help them fulfill the obligations, and lack of communication in large companies concerning the availability of in-house countertrade services. Recommendations for improving the effectiveness of in-house countertrade units are given. These recommendations center on top management support of the countertrade unit and management of the unit by the MBO (management by objectives) method.

Chapter 7, "Service Organizations for Countertrade: Trading Companies and Other Service Providers," classifies the basic types of service providers, describes how each type of provider can help the company in its countertrade operations, and explains what factors the company should consider in choosing a service provider. The types of providers discussed are trading companies, bank export trading companies, brokers and consultants, and countertrade facilitators. Emphasis is placed on trading companies; their fees, how their business goals may or may not fit with those of the client, and the criteria to use to select the right trading company. In the section on bank export trading companies, there is an extensive discussion of the problems the banks have had with the Export Trading Company Act of 1982 and with the adaptation of their traditional financial management methods to the trading environment. Information is also provided on the major American countertrade associations, ALESA, DIOA, and ACA. The final portion of the chapter is a sample list of service providers in each category.

Chapter 8, "Market Research for Countertrade Products: Using Trade Data," covers an area unfamiliar to most executives: international trade statistics. It begins with a discussion of how the analysis of trade statistics can help the company find the best markets for products accepted in countertrade, as well as providing a good base for preparing the business plans of joint ventures and direct or indirect offset activities. Specific information is provided on the types of trade data available, followed by a discussion of the use of trade data in particular kinds of countertrade/offset transactions. Next is a section on overcoming limitations in data coverage. Chapter 8 concludes with a discussion of the establishment of an in-house data base (which is not recommended for smaller companies due to the cost and complexity of data base management) and a caveat concerning "countertrade data bases" (names of buyers and sellers of countertrade products). This chapter is written on a fairly technical level; manipulation of statistical data is a complicated process, and the detailed information is intended to help countertrade managers decide whether they have the human and hardware resources to analyze data in-house.

Chapter 9, "Countertrade Insurance," is intended to familiarize the reader with the countertrade insurance market. It provides a description of the countertrade insurance currently available in terms of insurable risks and exclusions. Countertrade insurance is largely the province of private insurance companies, and their coverage varies according to each company's assessment of risk in the particular types of countertrade transactions. The major risk in countertrade is that the buyer will not deliver the counterpurchase goods. There are also some serious political risks in countertrade, since so much countertrade is done with developing countries. Information is provided on how the seller can reduce risk by negotiating a good contract. Names of various insurance firms are given in connection with their practices in countertrade coverage; however, their coverage on specific transactions will vary, and exporters should not consider this to be firm information on what a given company will and will not underwrite in a given transaction.

Chapter 10, "Countertrade Financing," covers the major methods of financing countertrade transactions (excluding evidence accounts and bilateral clearing and switch, which are covered in Chapter 1, "Forms of Countertrade"). General information is given on financing transactions through bank guarantees, letters of credit, escrow accounts, and Parallel Technical Banking Agreements. Specific information is given on forfaiting, a European financing practice that is gaining acceptance in the United States and which is very useful in certain types of countertrade transactions. Areas covered include the advantages of forfaiting, forfait documentation, forfait procedure, and a sample forfait calculation, among other things. The information is presented on a technical level, but it should help interested parties understand forfaiting and decide whether it is applicable to their countertrade operations.

Chapter 11, "Case Study: the Peace Shield Offset," describes the formulation of offset proposals by the three bidders on the billion-dollar defense contract (Boeing, Litton, and Hughes) in considerable detail. The offset proposal process is emphasized in order to help companies bidding on similar contracts be forewarned about buyer country expectations, and help them avoid making the same mistakes in their offset proposals. The chapter concludes with a description of Boeing's projects under the offset.

5 Countertrade Policies and Strategies

Many companies have no specific policy or strategy concerning countertrade. Some deliberately downplay countertrade, feeling that it is only a small part of their international operations and thus is not worth the trouble of special policy and strategy formulation. Others are interested in countertrade, perhaps even enthusiastic about its possibilities as a marketing tool, but have not been able to develop an effective strategy due to inexperience, confusion, intercompany conflict, or lack of intercompany coordination. The basic policies and strategies outlined in this chapter represent an attempt to classify and compare the countertrade practices of selected American companies, with the aim of helping companies to evaluate their own countertrade practices. Frameworks for strategy formulation and the strategic process in countertrade are also provided.

The terms "policy" and "strategy" are often used interchangeably. In the context of this discussion, however, distinctions are made between the two terms. Countertrade policy is defined here as the company's attitude toward countertrade, while countertrade strategy is defined as the approach the company takes to countertrade planning and transactions.

COUNTERTRADE POLICIES

There are two basic types of countertrade policies: *company advantage* and *mutual advantage*. Under a company advantage policy, countertrade/offset is used primarily for the company's benefit (to make a sale, to maintain market share, etc.), with the needs of the buyer country being met at the minimum possible levels. Most companies follow this policy. The effectiveness of the company advantage policy varies. At best, it results in a satisfactory arrangement for both seller and buyer. At worst, it can be a disaster; companies may try to get out of their obligations once the sales contract is signed, on the theory that it will be easier to pay the penalty than carry out the offset, and then get into a lot of trouble with the buyer country. In contrast, companies with a mutual advantage policy give the needs of the buyer country equal weight with their own. Under this policy, the company is concerned with the goals of the buyer country (i.e., modernization, industrialization, balancing trade, increasing living standards, etc.) and how the countertrade transaction will help achieve these goals. These companies are willing to meet the challenge of achieving mutual benefit through countertrade, and in most cases their efforts are successful.

The choice of a countertrade policy may be an early and deliberate decision on the part of the company president. More often, however, the policy evolves slowly, growing out of the company's experiences in trading with different countries. If the company trades with "good" countries (i.e., countries in which the state trading officials are well-intentioned, straightforward, and efficient in carrying out their side of the deal), it will probably develop a mutual advantage policy. There are also some cases in which the company begins to follow a mutual advantage policy in a particular country because of a foreign-born executive's loyalty to that country, and then expands the policy to include trade with other countries.

Companies which have countertraded with "problem" countries usually hate countertrade; depending on how difficult their experiences are, they will either approach countertrade with extreme caution or wish it would disappear. If the company has encountered corrupt foreign officials, slow delivery or nondelivery of counterpurchase products, poor quality products, sudden changes in product availability, demands for the moon (secret product formulas, proprietary technology, etc.), or other aggravations, it can hardly be blamed for following a company advantage policy. On the other hand, some companies whose countertrade transactions run relatively smoothly still resent having to countertrade. This resentment may be due to something concrete, such as lowered profits, or to something intangible, such as a belief in the pure forms of free trade and fair competition. Sometimes the company is simply new to countertrade, and wants to move cautiously until it builds up expertise.

Countertrade policies may change over time, due to many factors; these include changes in corporate leadership, the weight of accumulated countertrade experiences, profit levels, and the overall international trade and financial environment. Generally the policy moves from the lower form, company advantage, to the higher form, mutual advantage, although sometimes a singularly bad countertrade experience can push the policy backward to company advantage. Dual policies may exist within the same company, with some divisions believing in company advantage and others in mutual advantage; this reflects ambivalent leadership. Some companies are in a state of flux concerning countertrade policy. For these reasons, the policies of individual companies are somewhat difficult to identify, but they can be roughly classified. The following examples of the two policies given reflect the authors' observations of companies' countertrade activities rather than policy statements of the companies themselves.

The Cyrus Eaton Company and Armand Hammer's Occidental Petroleum Corporation are the classic examples of companies with mutual advantage policies. Both companies have been trading and countertrading with socialist countries since the 1950s. Each company has exceeded $50 billion in trade and investment. They are heavily involved in infrastructure projects for economic development and modernization. These projects include agricultural and dairy technology, mining and chemicals, energy and transport, and high technology. Cyrus Eaton and Armand Hammer have been powerful positive forces in the promotion of East–West trade.

The Coca-Cola Company operates under a mutual advantage policy through the Coca-Cola Trading Company. In most countries, Coca-Cola goes much further than simply selling syrup and taking back local products; the company transfers food and beverage technology and assists in developing foreign marketing programs. Most of these programs are designed to help the countries penetrate the American market. Coca-Cola assisted Yugoslavia and Romania in the production of wine for the American market, advising them on American taste in wines and appropriate package designs, as well as making agreements with American wine distributors. In Turkey, Coca-Cola set up a joint venture to produce tomato paste for the American market and other markets, providing management and technology for the plant. Coca-Cola generally tries to set up a partnership with customer countries.

Avon, Colt Industries, and Grumman International are examples of companies following a company advantage policy. Avon uses countertrade to release blocked funds; they build plants in various countries and export part of the production in order to generate hard currency. Avon products made in developing countries are exported to other developing countries, rather than to industrial countries. (Unlike most other products, 80% of the cost of cosmetics is promotion; thus there is no cost advantage in making cosmetics in low-wage countries for export to industrial markets.) Avon does not accept counterpurchase products. Colt's defense divisions do a small amount of countertrade in order to compete with foreign defense firms. They usually limit their countertrade obligations to sourcing or counterpurchase; they do not buy back or export products related to the original sale. Counterpurchases are liquidated through trading companies. The defense divisions of Grumman handle substantial amounts of countertrade. Their countertrade methods include sourcing, counterpurchase, and subcontracting. Grumman uses trading companies to liquidate indirect offset obligations.

Boeing and McDonnell Douglas are examples of companies with dual countertrade policies; their military and commercial divisions each follow different policies. Boeing Commercial Aircraft Company follows the company advantage policy. In the sale of the 747 and other civilian transport aircraft, they will accept only minimal countertrade obligations, and will then liquidate these obligations through outside trading companies. In some cases, they will handle direct offsets such as aircraft maintenance facilities. Boeing's defense divisions operate under the mutual advantage policy, however. This is best illustrated by the Boeing Peace Shield offset with Saudi Arabia, in which Boeing is helping the Saudis develop a number of high-technology projects.

In contrast to Boeing, the commercial company of McDonnell-Douglas follows the mutual advantage policy, while the military follows the company advantage policy. The Douglas Company (civilian aircraft) was one of the first companies to market civilian aircraft through countertrade. They emphasize export development in the buyer countries, helping the countries market nontraditional as well as traditional exports. A recent large project is the offset with China for the sale of MD-82 jetliners. The offset includes subcontracting of components to the Shanghai Aviation International Corporation, manufacture of landing gear doors in China, technical training, and participation of Chinese engineers in the design of new generation McDonnell-Douglas aircraft. The military aircraft company, the McDonnell Company, has a small countertrade staff to fulfill direct offset obligations, and liquidates other obligations through a New York trading company which it helped to establish.

DEFINITIONS OF COUNTERTRADE STRATEGIES

The countertrade strategies of American companies may be divided into four general types: defensive, passive, reactive, and proactive. Defensive, passive, and reactive strategies correspond to the company advantage policy, while proactive strategy is derived from the mutual benefits policy. (Again, the identification of strategies for individual companies is based on the authors' observations.)

Defensive Strategy

Companies with a defensive countertrade strategy ostensibly do not countertrade at all; however, they make many countertrade-type arrangements with buyer countries. These companies will avoid any contractual countertrade obligations, but they make it clear to the country that they will reciprocate in some way for their sale. Some companies will sell their products at rock-bottom prices and promise to help the country with export development. Others participate in barter deals by having an intermediary such as an independent trader take title to the goods on each side, therefore making the transaction appear to be conventional import and export rather than a swap. No matter what kind of deal is made, however, these companies will insist that they do not countertrade. They seldom have in-house countertrade units. A variation of the defensive strategy is that of companies who say that they do not countertrade, although they do it openly and regularly with the Eastern European countries and China. They seem to think that this trade does not count, offering the excuse that "it's the only way to do business in socialist countries." They may also be defining countertrade as a practice restricted to developing countries. Incidentally, most industrial country governments that practice military offset among themselves follow a defensive countertrade strategy. The beneficiary countries call their requirements "industrial benefits" and swear that they are against countertrade; the partner countries go along with this by refusing to include military offset in the definition of countertrade.

Examples of companies following a defensive countertrade strategy are Bell Helicopter, Textron, EBASCO, Gould and Borden.

Passive Strategy

Companies with passive countertrade strategies regard countertrade as a necessary evil. They participate in countertrade at a minimal level, on an ad hoc basis. Some companies operate this way because they have product leverage (i.e., little or no competition), while others follow the passive strategy because of disinterest in countertrade. These companies will accept contractual offset and countertrade obligations, but only on their own terms. They will rarely obligate themselves to export development or indirect offsets such as counterpurchases. However, they will use countertrade for sourcing, which is a form of export development. Passive companies regard countertrade primarily as a method of export financing. They will not initiate countertrade or offer it as a sales incentive; rather, they will wait until the buyer country requests countertrade. Some of these companies have small in-house countertrade units.

Most chemical companies and manufacturers of chemical products have passive countertrade strategies. These include DuPont, Dow Chemical, Cyanamid, Smith-Kline, and the chemical divisions of Amoco and the Ethyl Corporation. Some of the defense companies with product leverage have passive strategies, such as Lockheed-Georgia, Martin Marietta Aerospace, Texas Instruments, Sperry Corporation, and the Singer Company. Other companies using passive countertrade strategies are Alcoa, Polaroid, S. C. Johnson & Sons, and Nabisco.

Reactive Strategy

This is the most common strategy among American companies. Companies with reactive strategies will cooperate with the buyer country in offset/countertrade requirements. They use countertrade strictly as a competitive tool, on the theory that they cannot make the sale unless they agree to do countertrade. Although they may consider countertrade as a permanent feature of their international operations, they do not see it as a marketing tool for expansion. Reactive companies often have large in-house countertrade units, and use outside trading companies when necessary. They rarely have in-house world trading companies.

Most defense companies have reactive strategies; among these are the defense divisions of Litton, Grumman International, Garrett, BMY, TRW, Perkin-Elmer, Emerson Electric, General Dynamics, Northrop, Allied Signal, McDonnell, Motorola, ITT, Raytheon, and LTV Aerospace and Defense Company. Nondefense companies with reactive countertrade strategies include Kodak, Xerox, Dresser Industries, Chrysler, Burroughs, and IBM.

Proactive Strategy

Companies with proactive strategies have made a commitment to countertrade. They use countertrade aggressively as a marketing tool, and are interested in making trading an active and profitable part of their business. They regard indirect offset and counterpurchase as an opportunity to make money through trading rather than as an inconvenience. Proactive companies participate in all kinds of countertrade, including global sourcing, releasing of blocked funds, trade development, and trade financing. They often have in-house world trading companies, and will sometimes liquidate countertrade obligations for other companies.

Examples of companies with proactive countertrade strategies include Cyrus Eaton, Armand Hammer, Continental Grain, Caterpillar, Monsanto, General Foods, Goodyear, Rockwell, General Electric, FMC, Westinghouse, Tenneco, 3M, General Motors, Ford, Coca-Cola, United Technologies, Pepsi-Cola, and the civilian product divisions of McDonnell-Douglas and Lockheed.

DEVELOPMENT OF COUNTERTRADE STRATEGY

The company's strategy should be guided by the policy it has formulated to achieve its goals. Unfortunately, the guidelines derived from company policy are not always specific; this can result in either the wrong strategy or multiple and conflicting strategies within one company.

When a company has an ambiguous countertrade policy, the divisions are left to interpret the policy as they see fit, and they will develop strategies on a trial and error basis. Sometimes one division will take the initiative in countertrade/offset; the manager of that division becomes the company countertrade expert by default, and other divisions will follow his strategy. This at least results in a consistent strategy, even if it happens to be the wrong one. In other cases, the divisions handle countertrade independently, with each division following its own strategy or adopting various contingency strategies. The entire company's countertrade-related sales performance suffers because of a lack of coordination and teamwork.

The first step the company must take in developing a countertrade strategy is to define its policy clearly to its divisions. It should then make periodic reviews and evaluations to ensure that the strategy being used is consistent with the policy. However, the divisions should have the flexibility to use contingency strategies, as long as these strategies are within the framework of company policy. Finally, it is important that the divisions coordinate their countertrade operations, in order to minimize conflict and improve cost-effectiveness.

The countertrade policies discussed here are mutual advantage and company advantage. As noted earlier, proactive strategy is usually associated with the mutual advantage policy, while the defensive, passive, and reactive strategies fit the company advantage policy. (In rare cases, proactive strategy may be used by a firm pursuing the company advantage policy.)

The mutual advantage countertrade policy is the appropriate policy for socially responsible multinational corporations. MNCs are expected to contribute to the economic development of developing countries through the transfer of management, marketing, finance, and technology. Countertrade is a part of this effort, and is treated as a developmental activity. In industrial countries, MNCs are expected to provide technology and employment. Many U.S. corporations agree with this policy in theory, but cannot afford to follow it. American business is geared to short-term profit because of the structure of financial markets. Only the largest corporations can afford to undertake socially responsible projects; such projects are usually oriented to long-term profit. Large-scale countertrade operations involving economic and trade development usually fall into this category. Under the proactive strategy of a company following a mutual advantage policy, the major task is to design a countertrade/offset project that will be profitable for both parties. The objective is to get continued and expanded business in the country (market growth) through the establishment of a long-term relationship with the country, even if it means losing money for the first few years.

Companies following a company advantage policy are more entrepreneurial and opportunistic than socially responsible. They are usually profit maximizers. The most effective strategy under a company advantage policy is the reactive strategy. The major objective of the reactive strategy is to make the sale through cooperation with the buyer country. The goal is not so much long-term business as it is satisfaction of the buyer country in a particular countertrade/offset deal. The objective of passive strategy is either sourcing or export financing; cooperative arrangements with the buyer country are not very important. The least effective strategy is the defensive strategy. Companies using this strategy are the "sneaky countertraders"; they want the benefits of countertrade (making the sale, export financing, etc.) without the responsibility of contractual countertrade obligations. This is a short-term strategy.

COUNTERTRADE SYNERGY AND STRATEGY

Synergy, in the context of countertrade, means the benefits accruing to the company from the cooperative activities of the countertrade unit and the

Synergy level	1.1	1.2	1.3
HIGH	PROACTIVE	PROACTIVE	REACTIVE
	2.1	2.2	2.3
MEDIUM	PROACTIVE	REACTIVE	PASSIVE
	3.1	3.2	3.3
LOW	REACTIVE	PASSIVE	PASSIVE
	PROFIT	BREAK-EVEN	LOSS

Cost-benefit index of the countertrade unit

Figure 5.1. Countertrade synergy matrix

divisions. The choice of strategy directly affects the level of synergy, as well as the financial position of the countertrade unit.

Figure 5-1 shows a matrix in which countertrade strategies are classified by levels of synergy and cost–benefits of the countertrade unit to the company. The nine cells position three of the four basic strategies according to their relative proportions of costs and benefits: proactive, reactive, and passive. The defensive strategy is not included in the matrix because companies using that strategy usually do not have a countertrade unit.

The optimum position in the matrix is cell 1,1, which represents the maximum in synergy and benefits. The lowest position is cell 3,3, where synergy is low and costs are high. The median position is 2,2, where synergy is median and costs are at break-even.

Some companies may find that their strategy does not correspond with one particular cell because of the varying practices of the divisions, each of which may have its own countertrade offices and strategies.

THE STRATEGIC PROCESS IN COUNTERTRADE

Many companies do not have a clear strategic process for countertrade/offset bids and transactions, although they may have a well-defined overall strategy such as reactive or proactive. The strategic process in countertrade is not

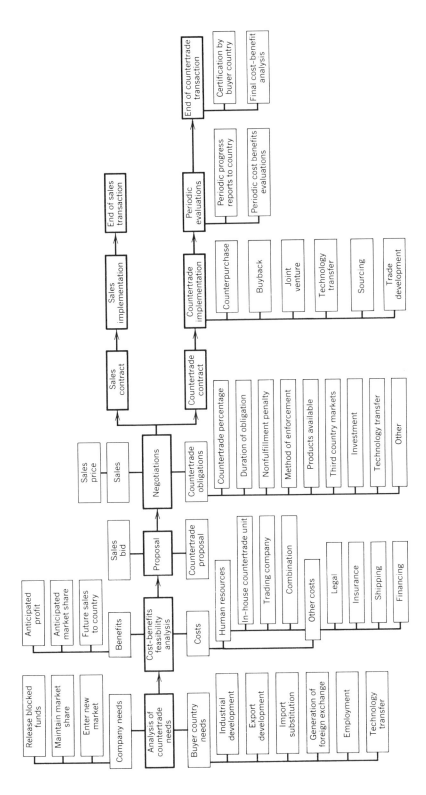

Figure 5.2. Strategic process chart for countertrade/offset

59

directly related to the type of strategy used; rather, it is a series of steps that companies should follow in countertrade operations. These steps are illustrated in Figure 5-2.

The first step is to analyze the countertrade/offset needs of both the company and the buyer country. The company's needs may include entering a new market, maintaining market share, or releasing blocked funds. Some typical needs of buyer countries are industrial development, export development, import substitution, employment, and the generation of foreign exchange. In analyzing these factors, the company must decide how it can match its needs with those of the buyer country.

The second step is the cost–benefit feasibility analysis. The company should estimate the cost of: (1) human resources, which is the cost of doing the entire transaction in-house, versus giving it to a trading company or other service provider, or a combination approach and (2) other costs such as legal, insurance, shipping, and financing. These costs must then be weighed against the anticipated benefits in terms of profit, market share, and future sales to the country (market growth).

When the countertrade needs and cost–benefits have been analyzed, the company is ready to prepare its sales bid and accompanying countertrade proposal. (Some portion of the countertrade cost is usually factored into the sales bid; although this practice is routinely prohibited by buyer country governments, it is necessary.) After the proposals are submitted, the company enters into negotiations with the buyer country.

Areas covered in the countertrade/offset proposal negotiations may include the offset percentage, amount and type of technology to be transferred, amount of investment in joint ventures, degree of technical and management training to be provided, duration of the obligation, level of nonperformance penalty, method of enforcement of the obligation (best efforts, liquidated damages, etc.), and details about the counterpurchases (products available, quantities available, delivery dates, etc.). In some countries, the countertrade regulations may specify such things as additionality (exports above the usual level), specific markets for exports, or prohibition of the use of third-party traders. These points must also be negotiated, if the company feels unable to carry out the proposed obligations under specific restrictions.

Two contracts will be signed when the negotiations are completed: one for the sale and one for the countertrade. In sales implementation, the company should adhere to the promised delivery schedules. In the implementation of the countertrade/offset obligation (which may include counterpurchase, buyback, technology transfer, joint ventures, or sourcing), the company should make periodic progress reports to the buyer country. Throughout the countertrade implementation period, the company should make periodic cost–benefits evaluations.

An authorized agency of the buyer country will issue a certification when the countertrade obligations have been fulfilled. At this point, the company should do a cost–benefits analysis. The analysis should be used as a guide for improving future countertrade transactions.

6 Organizing for Countertrade

Corporations have three main options in organizing for countertrade: having an outside firm handle all countertrade, handling all countertrade in-house, or a combination of the two. The selection of an option depends on the volume of countertrade, the frequency of transactions, and the requirements of the foreign government, as well as the company's experience with countertrade. A company new to countertrade may need to depend on an outside firm during the learning period. The size of the company is also a consideration; small companies usually do not have the resources to handle countertrade in-house.

If the volume of countertrade is small and transactions are infrequent, there is no point in setting up an in-house countertrade unit. In this case, companies are better off conducting their countertrade business through outside trading companies, banks, brokers, or consultants. Companies with large amounts of countertrade should handle it in-house, although in practice almost all companies with in-house countertrade units use outside services for part of their operations. (A good example is commodity trading, which is best done by specialist commodity trading houses.) However, in cases where the foreign government frowns upon the use of third party traders (such as South Korea), countertrade will have to be handled in-house regardless of the company's resources and trading volume.

There are four major reasons for doing countertrade in-house: capability, control, confidentiality, and cost. Capability is the most important. If the company develops in-house countertrade expertise, these people can then be called upon to assist any division in countertrade. They can also generate new business by handling countertrade for outside companies. In-house countertrade allows the company control over all aspects of the transactions, from negotiations to fulfillment of the obligations; the company will also concentrate on its own countertrade deal, giving it more time and attention than the deal would get from an outside trader who is servicing several other clients.

Confidentiality is assured when countertrade is done in-house. Trading companies do their best to maintain confidentiality, but sometimes information leaks to competitors. Finally, the cost of using outside assistance is an important consideration. Trading companies' fees range from 1% to 7% of the total transaction value, and sometimes go to 15% or higher depending on the country or product risk.

When countertrade is handled in-house, the design and placement of the countertrade unit depends on the existing organizational structure as well as the types of products countertraded. The four traditional corporate organizational structures are *functional, product, territorial,* and *matrix.* Appropriate countertrade organizational designs and examples for each structure follow. Following this is a discussion of corporate world trading companies and common problems with in-house countertrade units.

COUNTERTRADE UNITS WITHIN ORGANIZATIONAL STRUCTURES

Functional

The functional organizational structure consists of departments organized according to major function (production, marketing, finance, procurement, etc.) rather than by product or other areas. Countertrade operations in a functional structure are assigned to the department with the greatest stake in the countertrade deal; for example, if countertrade is used primarily as a method of global sourcing, it will be the responsibility of the procurement department. The advantage of this approach is the leverage of the functional department handling the countertrade. The countertrade operation will receive more attention when concentrated in one department. The disadvantage is that a countertrade operation usually impacts more than one department; thus the interests of the other departments are not well served by the department handling the countertrade.

Most functional organizations that handle countertrade in-house put countertrade under the procurement office, although some put it in finance or marketing. Global sourcing is the main justification for placing countertrade under the procurement department. When countertrade is used for releasing blocked funds or generating foreign exchange, it becomes the responsibility of the finance department. The marketing department can handle countertrade most effectively when countertrade is used to penetrate new markets or increase market share.

Functional corporations that prefer to have trading companies handle their countertrade obligations often let the marketing department deal with the trading company, since the marketing people are familiar with the trading company's activities. However, many corporations use a combination of in-house and outside approaches because of the size and complexity of their countertrade transactions.

Lockheed is an example of a functional organization handling countertrade in-house, though it is a somewhat unusual example since countertrade is handled by two different departments. This dual setup exists because of product considerations. Lockheed-Georgia has countertrade under the Finance Department, where it is handled by a staff of four persons. The product that Lockheed-Georgia sells, the C-130 Hercules military transport aircraft, has little competition in the world market. Therefore, the main countertrade-related consideration in selling the C-130 is financing the export. At Lockheed-California, on the other hand, the product, the L-1011 commercial airliner, is less competitive. Countertrade for the L-1011 must be used as an incentive for buyer countries, and is therefore handled by a staff of 14 persons in the Materials (procurement) Department. The Materials Department can also supervise the countertrade obligations of the subcontractors, since the department already deals with them in procurement.

Product

Under this organizational structure, the activities of the company are divided by product. Each product division is responsible for procurement, production, marketing, and financing of its product(s). Many companies that make a multitude of products group the divisions by type of product; for example, the automobile group might include the engine, body, and parts divisions. When these groups operate as profit centers, they are commonly called strategic business units (SBUs). Most American manufacturing companies use the product organizational structure because it facilitates growth, promotes entrepreneurial attitudes, enhances teamwork, and strengthens commitment to the company. It is the most effective of the organizational structures. However, it is also more costly because of the duplication of functions among divisions.

Countertrade units in product structure organizations are set up under individual product divisions. The divisional marketing department usually initiates countertrade deals as a part of its marketing package. Responsibility for carrying out the countertrade transaction may remain with the marketing department, or it may be assigned to the procurement or finance offices. There are three basic forms of countertrade units in product organizations: the divisional countertrade unit, the corporate countertrade office, and the combined divisional/corporate countertrade office.

The divisional countertrade unit is the most simple structure. Each corporate division is responsible for handling its own bids, negotiations, contracting, and implementation of offset/countertrade obligations. These divisions are not required to share information with each other or with the corporate office. This approach is workable as long as the obligation is a direct offset, since each division has the necessary expertise to fulfill the obligation. However, when there is an indirect offset—which is becoming increasingly common—the divisions are out of their areas and do not know what to do. The support of other divisions is often needed for an indirect offset, but under this type of structure there is no mechanism for communication and information sharing.

Emerson Electric Corporation established a divisional offset office in 1983. This office services the offset needs of the Electronics and Space Division. At the present time this is the only division with offset activities, but Emerson anticipates that other divisions will have offset/countertrade responsibilities in the future. The Electronics and Space Division has deliberately kept its countertrade staff small (a manager with two assistants) for cost purposes. They will increase the staff as countertrade business expands. The countertrade unit's responsibilities include global sourcing. The method of handling indirect offset is to liquidate the obligation through outside trading companies.

Many organizations use the corporate countertrade office structure; a corporate officer coordinates the offset/countertrade activities of the product divisions. This officer has the authority to participate in negotiations, prepare contracts, report to foreign buyers on the progress of offset implementation, and enter into agreements with outside trading companies to discharge obligations. The advantages of this approach are efficient use of company resources, access to external sources of expertise, and strength of the corporate presence in prospective markets. It is especially helpful in indirect offset, since the divisions can get all the outside support they need. The shortcoming of the corporate countertrade office structure is that there is still a heavy reliance on outside parties such as trading companies, which cuts into the corporation's profits and also may displease the buyer countries.

Litton Industries uses a corporate countertrade office structure. Their countertrade office was established in 1983 to monitor the offset and countertrade activities of the divisions. The office has established a network of trading contacts and a data base of trading companies, consultants, and government sources. This information is available to all Litton product divisions.

A refinement of the corporate countertrade office structure is the combined structure, which consists of a corporate countertrade office and the divisional countertrade offices. It reflects corporate support of the activities of the operational divisions. Under this arrangement, it is still the responsibility of each division to implement countertrade/offset obligations. This structure combines the advantages of the divisional office and corporate office structures; it is more effective than the simpler structures because the countertrade office takes an active role. Its disadvantage is that there is no separate legal entity to take full responsibility for a complete countertrade/offset obligation, and there is still considerable reliance on outside sources.

The FMC Corporation uses the combined structure. The corporate countertrade office was established in 1985 under Corporate International. Its responsibility is to assist the divisions in offset (both direct and indirect) and countertrade by finding ways to liquidate obligations, although some of the divisions have their own offset offices. The countertrade office is also responsible for global sourcing. FMC has countertrade operations in fourteen countries.

Westinghouse Corporation is now using a corporate countertrade office to service its twenty-eight strategic business units. Westinghouse began its countertrade operations in 1982 with an in-house world trading company, but changed to the corporate office approach in 1986 for cost-effectiveness. There are seven people working on countertrade at Westinghouse, three at the corporate countertrade office and four in the SBUs. The defense specialists in the SBUs actually carry out offset transactions, with the support of the corporate staff; their expertise complements the function of the corporate people.

Territorial (geographic)

Companies with a territorial structure are organized by geographic regions; the geographic divisions may be organized by either function or product. This structure is most often used by multinational corporations. Territorial organizations usually handle countertrade through a corporate countertrade office or an in-house trading company. They seldom have a countertrade unit in each territory because of the expense and the shortage of experienced countertraders, although they may have countertrade representatives in the geographic regions.

The relative importance of the corporate countertrade office depends to some extent on whether the territorial division presidents operate from corporate headquarters or from the overseas divisions. If all of the presidents are at headquarters, the corporate countertrade office has direct access to them; if they are scattered about the world, the countertrade office will not be able to work with them as effectively.

The task of the corporate countertrade office in a territorial organization is to coordinate or monitor the company's countertrade activities worldwide. The staff functions in an advisory capacity rather than participating actively in negotiations and implementation of contracts.

Kodak set up a corporate countertrade office in 1985 at its headquarters in Rochester, New York. Their countertrade office is a service and support unit, featuring a computer network connecting Kodak offices worldwide to facilitate countertrade through global sourcing. Three people work on countertrade at the corporate marketing support office; their task is to assist the 18 geographic SBUs in countertrade.

A world trading company (WTC) in a territorial organization, on the other hand, can take an active role in countertrade transactions. The WTC can handle the complete transaction on behalf of the territorial division or it can simply provide advice and support as needed. The major advantage of the WTC is that it is in close touch with the territorial divisions through its offices in the territories.

Caterpillar established the Caterpillar World Trading Corporation in 1984 under its international division. CWTC has offices in Peoria, Geneva, Hong Kong, and Miami; each office has a staff of about five persons. CWTC aggressively pursues countertrade on behalf of Caterpillar divisions.

Matrix

The matrix organization combines two or more of the other structures (functional, product, territorial). The advantages of the matrix structure are flexibility and cost-efficiency; for example, the finance office can be centralized, and able to service all divisions. Matrix structures are not common, however, because of their complex design. The countertrade office in a matrix structure is usually in the international operations division. This is a very strong position for a countertrade office, since the office has the authority to initiate and execute countertrade transactions. Some matrix organizations have WTCs, although in this type of organization a WTC is not as effective as a divisional countertrade office.

Monsanto International's Countertrade Department is under the International Development and Administration Division of the Monsanto Chemical Company. The Countertrade Department was established in 1982 under the corporate office; it was later moved to the Monsanto Chemical Company because this company had the most countertrade obligations. The Countertrade Department services all other Monsanto divisions. Monsanto uses countertrade primarily for marketing purposes. The company countertrades in 12 countries, including Brazil, China, the Soviet Union, and Yugoslavia. Some of the products accepted in countertrade are petrochemicals, vegetables, and wood products.

The Coca-Cola Company (which is regarded as a matrix structure because it combines product, territorial, and functional activities) handles its countertrade through the Coca-Cola Trading Company, which was established in 1979 under the corporate finance office. There are 24 persons on the staff; of these, two are corporate officers and six are traders. The primary task of the trading company is to release blocked funds in fifteen countries, including China, the Republic of Korea, Romania, Turkey, and Yugoslavia. The trading company buys products in these countries with local currency and sells them in hard currency markets. Some of the products the trading company buys are wine, beer, toys, furniture, and juice concentrates.

THE WORLD TRADING COMPANY

The ultimate form of in-house countertrade operations is the WTC. Any corporation, regardless of organizational structure, can establish a WTC. The WTC is a separate legal entity which can negotiate and carry out entire countertrade transactions, including the indirect offset portions of contracts. Some WTCs will handle noncompetitive products of other companies and act as brokers for companies who need countertrade services. The establishment of a WTC signifies a commitment to countertrade by the corporation. Depending on the degree of commitment, the WTC can range from a corporate trading company to one with overseas offices, or to a general trading company.

Synergy is the major feature of the WTC. A WTC brings together specialists in the functional fields of countertrade, drawing them from both inside and outside the company. The team can be developed into a flexible and innovative unit. However, the head of the WTC should be a member of the corporation rather than someone from outside the company. Although the outsider may be highly qualified, the corporate member will usually receive more support from the corporate divisions. There are some other important advantages to the WTC. First, a WTC is easy to evaluate on a cost–benefit basis, since it has its own budget. Also, when a corporation has a WTC, it makes a very good impression on the buyer government, since one of the WTCs functions is to assist the buyer in export development. Finally, the WTC gives the corporation a competitive edge in international marketing.

The major disadvantage is the cost factor. As a rule, WTCs have to be cost centers rather than profit centers, since they are handling products which may not always be profitable. Some of the products may be of poor quality, in low demand, or otherwise difficult to market. There is also a tendency for WTCs to grow in staff size but not in volume of business, which has caused many to fail. A related cost factor is that it is very expensive to keep trading specialists (such as commodity specialists) on the staff. They may not be needed on an ongoing basis if the particular commodity in which they specialize is traded in only a few countertrade deals. Furthermore, since companies must pay benefits to employees, it is usually more economical to use outside help when necessary.

Specific functions of a WTC may include finding ways of releasing blocked funds, dealing with the foreign country's central bank, setting up and staffing an offset office in the foreign country, global sourcing, monitoring the performance of subcontractors, and coordinating the company's activities in fulfilling offset obligations. In a large offset program, the WTC's responsibilities may include developing a comprehensive trade program tailored to the country's needs, providing technical coordination between corporate divisions and foreign subcontractors, and developing a system to report offset implementation activities to the foreign government.

The best way to establish a WTC is through an incremental approach. Ideally, the WTC should start small and add staff as necessary. It is not a good idea to set up a large WTC in anticipation of winning a bid; if the corporation loses the bid, the large WTC must then be disbanded or severely reduced in size.

The Rockwell International Trading Company (RITC) is a corporate international trading company. It was established in 1978 under the corporate international vice president (a position which focuses corporate attention on offset and countertrade), and has the support of the Rockwell corporate offices throughout the world, although the trading company itself does not have overseas offices. It can assist any Rockwell division in negotiating and implementing offset and countertrade programs.

Rockwell's rationale for establishing a trading company instead of a corporate countertrade office was to set up a separate legal entity which could, if required, negotiate an entire offset or countertrade transaction on its own. Also Rockwell feels that customers will take their trading activities more seriously because they have a separate trading company.

The staff of RITC consists of ten persons with expertise in different areas relating to countertrade. The functions of the staff are: (1) participate in the development, structure, and estimating of cost proposals; (2) negotiate and sign agreements; (3) organize trade missions; (4) implement actions; and (5) report to the foreign government on Rockwell's offset and countertrade performance.

RITC maintains close contact with the procurement offices of the corporation, which have an annual purchasing budget of $3 billion for 250 plants in 28 countries. This worldwide purchasing function offers opportunities to buy from countries to satisfy countertrade commitments. In special cases, RITC will retain other trading companies to dispose of products in which they have limited experience.

Caterpillar's trading entity, the Caterpillar World Trading Company, is currently operating as a service center and is scheduled to become a profit center. CWTC's main function is to finance exports of CAT equipment through counterpurchase of minerals, agricultural commodities and raw materials. It also handles licensing and technology transfers, does global sourcing, and releases blocked funds. CWTC will handle products of other companies, as long as the product has a CAT component, such as an engine. Small size countertrade deals and highly specialized commodity deals are given to outside trading companies.

CWTC has been most successful in countertrade with China. Through countertrade, it was able to displace Komatsu of Japan as the major supplier of earthmoving equipment to China, and now sells equipment valued at $100 million per year. Most of these sales require counterpurchases of minerals, such as phosphate rock. CWTC has one joint venture in China and plans to establish others.

The philosophy of CWTC is to be proactive in countertrade and to take full advantage of countertrade as a competitive tool. The major reasons for its success are an expert staff and wide-ranging support from within the company.

The General Electric Trading Company (GETC) was established in 1982 as a general trading company to assist General Electric in international trade and countertrade. Originally, GETC was also intended to handle countertrade for noncompeting companies in the traditional product areas of General Electric, but the break-even requirement of a General Electric strategic business unit precluded this. At the present time, GETC handles most of General Electric's countertrade and offset obligations.

In offset programs, GETC will participate in negotiations, develop a trade program for the client country, act as technical liasion between divisions and subcontractors, and monitor offset implementation. GETC is also very active in global sourcing, whether or not it is related to offset programs.

Since General Electric has operations in so many parts of the world, GETC does not have overseas representatives; instead, it works with the appropriate people in the General Electric overseas offices.

GETC was instrumental in helping General Electric win contracts for the sale of aircraft engines to Spain, Turkey, and Greece and the sale of locomotive engines to China. These are examples where countertrade capability gave a company the necessary competitive edge.

COMMON PROBLEMS WITH IN-HOUSE COUNTERTRADE UNITS

There are various problems associated with in-house countertrade. Most of these are management problems rather than problems created by countertrade, however, and can be addressed by the application of good management methods. A few of the most common problems are: the cost center status of in-house countertrade units, poor planning in countertrade transactions, procurement conflicts, staffing, intercompany conflict, and lack of communication from the top down.

Most in-house countertrade units are cost centers; they charge their expenses to the operational divisions as a service cost. The problem with this system is that the countertrade unit cost center has no clear budgetary control and reporting mechanisms (with the exception of the WTC). The ideal arrangement, of course, is to develop the countertrade unit into a profit center. However, it is very hard to turn a countertrade operation into a profit center; the best that most companies can do with a countertrade unit is break even. The most effective way to run a cost center is to use the management by objectives (MBO) method. Under MBO, the company sets clear and measurable goals that are communicated to all members of the organization, and solicits the input of the members. The most important features of MBO are training and development, evaluation and review, and rewards and sanctions. For the countertrade unit specifically, the company sets a break-even point and establishes accounting controls to protect against losses. Periodic evaluations of the unit's performance will help to make it "lean and mean" rather than allowing it to become an unwieldy, uneconomical, and ineffective group.

The company must do thorough advance planning to ensure that all countertrade deals are sound; a bad deal will lose money no matter what management method is used in the countertrade unit. This involves careful attention to negotiations, contract terms, insurance coverage, pricing of both the company's product and the counterpurchase products, and the identification of good potential markets for the counterpurchases. The company must be reasonably certain that it can fulfill all countertrade/offset obligations, to avoid paying penalties. Care must also be taken in the selection of the buyer country. Companies should not try to countertrade with countries that have a poor reputation for supplying counterpurchase items (slow delivery, substitution of other products for the original counterpurchase products, etc.)

or are otherwise known to be difficult partners in countertrade. If outside trading firms are used to liquidate some of the obligations, the company should be sure to select a reputable firm which can do the job efficiently and economically.

Companies that use countertrade for sourcing often run into opposition from procurement officers in divisions not involved in the countertrade transactions. For example, if division A has a countertrade obligation but cannot use the products the country is offering for counterpurchase, the countertrade unit will try to route the products to division B, which is not participating in the countertrade transaction but routinely buys the same types of products. The procurement officer in division B will usually resent being told to source from a certain country in order to satisfy division A's countertrade obligations, feeling that countertrade is division A's problem, not his. Procurement officers are also used to the leverage they get in paying their foreign suppliers with dollars; if they must pay in local currency according to the terms of the countertrade deal, they are not in such a good bargaining position. Sometimes the problem is that the procurement officers are using domestic sources of supply and are reluctant to break off their longstanding relationships with domestic suppliers in order to do foreign sourcing. They may also be apprehensive about product quality, product specifications, delivery time, and the like, from a new supplier. The opposition of procurement officers can often be overcome by offering them better terms on the new sourcing.

Staffing is an acute problem with in-house countertrade units, since people drawn from within the company will seldom have countertrade skills. Countertrade is such a new and fluid field that even people brought in from the company's international operations division will usually not know much about it. Trading is a specialized field requiring not only experience but contacts. The director of the countertrade unit, a member of the corporation, should hire people from outside the company who have the necessary qualifications. Since one of the objectives of a good countertrade unit is to develop in-house resources, though, the director should also have the new staff members assist in training people recruited from inside the company. This is the ideal approach, but it may not always be possible due to budgetary restraints. Companies with limited budgets can help the existing countertrade staff develop trading skills and contacts by sending them to countertrade seminars, or by having consultants give such seminars in-house. It is also helpful to build up a library of countertrade books and periodicals.

Intercompany conflict is sometimes a problem with in-house countertrade. Most conflicts arise because the operational divisions are so independent that they will either avoid cooperating with the central countertrade unit or will simply ignore it. There are two sides to this problem. One is the fact that many divisions are headed by engineers, whose characteristic attitude is that they are capable of handling any transaction for their divisions without help from elsewhere in the company. Furthermore, they frequently have their own countertrade/offset offices. The other side of the problem is the ineffectiveness of many corporate countertrade units; if the unit has no real authority and no staff with countertrade expertise, no one will pay attention to it, and the divisions will always bypass it when they are involved in countertrade transactions. The solution, like the problem, is twofold. Division heads must be directed to cooperate with the central countertrade unit; however, they must have something substantial to cooperate with. The company must build up the countertrade unit's capability by developing or hiring expertise and adding attractive features such as data bases. What the company has to do, in other words, is make the countertrade unit so valuable that the divisions will want to use it.

At the other extreme, the divisions may be anxious for countertrade assistance but cannot find it due to bureaucracy at the corporate office level. In some of the larger companies, there is such a lack of communication that the divisions are not even aware that there is a corporate countertrade unit available to help them, or that sister divisions have countertrade expertise. To prevent this problem, the company's countertrade services and activities should be publicized internally through memos, meetings, in-house trade journals, newsletters, and other communications tools. Intercompany countertrade contacts should be established.

GENERAL RECOMMENDATIONS FOR MAKING IN-HOUSE COUNTERTRADE UNITS MORE EFFECTIVE

1. Top management support of countertrade units is vital. Countertrade/offset is a staff/advisory function rather than a line function in most cases; therefore, the staff has little authority. The countertrade unit will be far more effective if it has line authority. It should be located in the international division; if there is no such division, the unit should be at the corporate level.

2. Countertrade operations should be coordinated, especially if the company has more than one countertrade unit. A corporate office with executive authority, rather than a staff office, should be the coordinator of countertrade activities.

3. Countertrade activities should be integrated with other international operations such as licensing, joint ventures, and procurement.

4. The company should establish a network of contacts with traders, service providers (consultants, brokers, lawyers, bankers, insurance companies, etc.), and other companies participating in countertrade.

5. A systems approach to countertrade should be developed, so that the company can respond quickly to external changes in the international business environment.

7 Countertrade Service Organizations

Most corporations involved in countertrade use outside services to some extent. The outside services available include trading companies, bank export trading companies, consultants, brokers, and countertrade facilitators, whose functions range from advisory capability to complete handling of countertrade transactions. Service in the form of general advice and information sharing is also available from industry countertrade associations. This chapter provides guidelines for choosing a service organization, and examples of such organizations.

TRADING COMPANIES

A large, established trading company will be capable of taking the entire countertrade deal off the corporation's hands. These companies will arrange financing and take title to the counterpurchase goods, thus assuming all risk for their resale. Smaller trading companies will have a less comprehensive line of services, but they can still be of great value in liquidating countertrade obligations. There are two problems in dealing with trading companies (assuming that their performance in liquidating obligations is satisfactory): their cost and their need for more business.

There is no set fee scale by which trading companies can be compared. Even within one company, fees vary according to the product and the country involved (risk). Fees range from 1 to 5% of the countertrade transaction value on the low end, and from 5 to 10% on the high end. Occasionally, fees will be as high as 50%, if the country or the product is an especially hard case. Most corporations shop around for the best fees in particular transactions.

A certain amount of conflict may arise concerning the trading company's desire for additional business from the corporation. Few trading companies operate exclusively in countertrade, with the exception of European switch traders; most of them are in the conventional import and export business. Countertrade is not very profitable for them, unless they can land a lucrative offset deal. Thus they generally use countertrade services as a means of getting other business from the client. Ideally, they would like to handle the corporation's exports to current and new markets, and its imports (sourcing) on a long-term basis. Trading companies can hardly be faulted for following this strategy. Unfortunately, it is often inappropriate in the American countertrade environment. Most American corporations participating in countertrade are multinationals. MNC's are usually not interested in extensive relationships with trading companies, since they already have their own international divisions, distribution channels, and procurement offices. There is nothing left for the outside trading company to do except handle countertrade. Some trading companies, realizing this, may try to hang on to the countertrade business by discouraging the MNC from forming an in-house countertrade unit.

In selecting a trading company, the corporation must first decide exactly what it wants from the trading company: limited services, such as the disposal of counterpurchases, or more complete services, such as assistance in finding financing and handling of the entire transaction. Then the corporation must find the trading company with the right qualifications at the right price. Criteria for selecting a trading company include:

Whether the trading company will assume title to the goods, or will work only on a "best efforts" basis

Fee schedule for the product and country

Product and country experience and specialization

Availability of a package including financing, shipping and insurance

Global network of contacts

Reputation and years of experience

Many corporations use different trading companies for each transaction, depending on the country and the product involved. The trading company would prefer to handle all of the corporation's countertrade business, and may pressure the corporation to let it handle a deal in a new country (a country in which the trading company has little experience). The corporation should resist this pressure and go to another trader with expertise in the country in question. Sometimes trading companies will refer the corporation to other trading companies with the necessary expertise, but most often the corporation will be left on its own to decide. The corporation should be wary of trading companies that claim to be able to handle any product in any country (unless it is a very old and very large trading company), companies that are vague about their services or their fees, and inexperienced companies. If the corporation has any doubts about a trading company, the company should be checked out through banks, association members, corporate peers, and other reliable sources. The corporation can also request a written proposal and bank references.

BANK EXPORT TRADING COMPANIES

Bank export trading companies became possible through Title II of the Export Trading Company Act of 1982, a legislative attempt to facilitate American exports. (The Act also provided for the establishment of nonbank ETCs.) Banks were initially enthusiastic about the Act, expecting to get new business by serving both the financial and trading needs of their clients, and by 1984 about 40 bank ETCs had been formed.

Unfortunately, the experiment has not been very successful. Only a few bank ETCs are still active. The others have either dissolved their ETCs or retrenched, retaining the legal entity of the ETC in the event that they wish to resume trading operations in the future. This situation is attributable in part to constraints in the law itself, but it is due mostly to American banking mentality and practices.

The most restrictive element of the Act is the "51/49 rule," which requires the bank ETCs to export more (at least 51%) than they import into the United States. The figure used by the government to determine the 51% is net revenues from export sales compared to gross revenues from the ETC's other business; the banks feel that it would be more fair to measure export activity by gross profits on export sales. More troublesome, though, is the fact that the 51/49 rule effectively penalizes bank ETCs for participating in countertrade. The export part of the transaction is not credited toward the ETC's export sales, but the import portion is counted *against* export sales even if the import products (counterpurchases) are not sold in the United States.

Other problems with the Act are the audit requirement and the Federal Reserve regulations. Under the audit requirement, bank ETCs are audited every two years to ensure compliance with the 51/49 rule, while nonbank ETCs are simply required to file an annual report confirming compliance and are not audited. Also, the Act does not exempt banks from Rule 23A of the Federal Reserve Act, which limits the amount of credit the bank can extend to its ETC relative to the ETC's collateral; this makes it very difficult for bank ETCs to secure joint venture partners. The banks maintain that these restraints prevent them from having the flexibility necessary to participate in trade, and that the law favors nonbank ETCs. Due to the volume of complaints, the government will probably revise the law, but it will be a slow process.

Problems originating in the banks rather than the law are conservatism, the desire for short-term profits, and overenthusiasm. The banks have been unable to develop the risk mentality of traders; they want safe deals, a sure thing, and pass up many potentially good countertrade deals that involve risk. Concerning profit, American banks have not yet learned that countertrade units should be allowed a two-year start-up period before evaluation. Countertrade deals usually move fairly slowly, not only because of the inexperience of new countertrade staff but because of delays in production or shipping of counterpurchase products. Offset programs, joint ventures, and other large projects can take several years to show a meaningful profit. The banks still insist on short-term profits, though, and because of this some banks have even shut down ETCs that were doing a lot of business. European and Japanese banks, in contrast, trust in the ability of their trading units to show a profit eventually. Finally, many of the larger banks were overconfident about the new business their ETCs could generate through trade and countertrade. They hired large staffs, waited for big deals to come in, and then folded the ETCs when the expected business did not materialize. In this, they should have learned from the example of Sears World Trade, which started out with a huge number of employees (300) and was gradually cut down to nothing. The trading company was disbanded in 1987.

The few bank ETCs that have survived this shakeout are those which started small and used a step-by-step approach to achieve incremental growth. Most of them limit their countertrade services to financing the transactions, but a few provide a full range of countertrade services. Though the standard practice is to provide these services only for the bank's customers, some bank ETCs will take outside clients.

There are many advantages to handling countertrade through a bank ETC. Corporations trust them, since they are familiar with the bank's international services and know that they have a global network of contacts. Banks also have excellent research staffs. The level of risk in a countertrade deal handled by a bank is usually considerably reduced because of the conservative way in which banks do business. Fees are usually lower than those charged by a nonbank trading company. Finally, a bank ETC will have more leverage than its nonbank counterpart in dealing with foreign entities.

BROKERS AND CONSULTANTS

In small countertrade deals the corporation may wish to use a freelance broker. These are often one-person operations, though they may have incorporated themselves as trading companies. Brokers often have intense country and product specialization, and a good network of contacts; many are heavily experienced, having worked many years for MNC's or big trading companies. They can move quickly, and are frequently more flexible and innovative than traders at large established companies. Reputation and references are important in the selection of a broker.

Consultants provide a variety of services; they may or may not also be brokers. The services of independent consultants may include advice on countertrade practices, market research, and global contacts in exporting and sourcing. Although many consultants have trading expertise in particular products and countries, their value is mainly in advisory and research capacities. They are especially useful in the preparation of offset and countertrade proposals and feasibility studies for countertrade programs. They can also provide political risk analysis. Consulting firms can provide a broader range of services, but they usually charge much higher fees than independent consultants.

COUNTERTRADE FACILITATORS

There is also a group of service providers classifiable as countertrade facilitators, for lack of a more precise term. They may offer some of the same services of trading companies, brokers, and consultants, or a combination of such services. Countertrade facilitators usually assist in setting up deals in countries where market access is difficult (such as China) or in countries that are otherwise problematic. Some countertrade facilitators will simply use their connections to arrange meetings with the appropriate foreign trade officials, and then let the corporation take it from there. Others will arrange travel to the foreign country for individual companies or business groups; set up conferences, meetings, and tours of plant facilities; and stick with the company through all aspects of the transaction in an advisory capacity. Countertrade facilitators can be a great help to companies that are inexperienced in countertrade or new to the market.

ASSOCIATIONS

The three major American countertrade associations are the American League for Exports and Security Assistance (ALESA), the Defense Industry Offset Association (DIOA), and the American Countertrade Association (ACA).

ALESA was founded in 1977 as a nonprofit organization. It is one of the few industry associations that include both corporate and union members; membership includes 30 corporations and five unions. ALESA's objective is to encourage the export of defense goods and services consistent with American security requirements. The association has an impressive list of lobbying activities on behalf of its members, such as helping to bring about changes in restrictive regulations on the export of defense equipment, the adoption of the Export Trading Company Act, support of Eximbank funding, and the implementation of the Tokyo Round MTN trade codes.

DIOA is a nonprofit organization formally established in 1985, after three years of informal meetings. Its membership is limited to companies in the defense equipment and service industry. DIOA's objectives are to promote the exports of American defense companies and to advance professionalism in the management of offset requirements. The association meets twice yearly in April and October. The agenda for the meetings consists primarily of member presentations on offset developments in foreign countries. Occasionally, experts from major trading companies, banks, insurance companies, and law firms are invited to make presentations. Officials from federal government departments and agencies and from Congress are also invited, for the purpose of dialogues with association members. Most DIOA members are also members of ALESA.

ACA was established in 1986 to serve the interests of nondefense companies involved in countertrade. Its purpose is to provide a meeting place and network for its members. It also serves as an educational forum by inviting specialists to discuss various aspects of countertrade.

In addition to these associations, there are countertrade roundtable associations (patterned after the New York Countertrade Roundtable) in major American cities such as Pittsburgh and Atlanta. The major members of the World Trade Center Association provide seminars and publications on countertrade. Some other organizations providing these services are the American Management Association, the American Marketing Association, the Academy of Management, and the Academy of International Business.

Some associations also function as countertrade facilitators. These include the trading company of the New York World Trade Center, which can take title to goods and assist in countertrade operations in selected product areas and countries; the Virginia Port Authority, whose trading company can assist in export trade and countertrade; and Mass Port (Massachusetts), which can arrange trade missions and seminars, as well as providing consultation and publications. Companies interested in countertrade should check with their state port authorities to see what services are available.

SELECTED LIST OF SERVICE PROVIDERS

The following is a sample list of trading companies, bank trading companies, and other service organizations, with brief descriptions of the services provided. The purpose of the list is to familiarize readers with the different types of services available and not to recommend these companies over others. An extensive listing of trading companies and other service providers, with addresses, is given in the Appendix.

Trading Companies

Contitrade Services Corp. Contitrade provides international trade finance to multinationals and exporters, using countertrade techniques such as barter, bilateral clearing, and buyback. The company specializes in agricultural products traded in socialist countries, especially the Soviet Union and China, and in South America and Mexico. (They do not operate in Central America or Africa.) Contitrade handles bulk commodities: all grains, tobacco, cotton, and animal and vegetable oils. They also handle textiles and yarn. They operate in 50 countries through the 200 offices of Continental Grain, the parent company. Contitrade will take title to counterpurchase goods.

Cyrus Eaton World Trade, Ltd. CEWT was formed in 1985 as part of the Eaton Group, which has participated in over 140 East–West trade projects since 1954. The Eaton Group has an extensive network of longstanding contacts in socialist countries and has generated a total of $1.5 billion in trade. CEWT's objective is to expand the Eaton Group's trading activities. Services include arranging financing; matching of American companies with potential partners in the USSR, Eastern Europe, and China; marketing of countertrade products and services; targeting of markets; and negotiating and drafting contracts. CEWT acts as principal in all transactions. Products handled include agricultural items, beverages, petroleum, natural gas, metal ores, chemicals, fertilizer, pulp, paper, rubber, building materials, textiles, and apparel. Services handled include construction, hotels, television and films, and transportation, as well as technology transfer in any of these areas.

MG Services. MG Services is a global group of countertrade specialists based in New York, with offices in Toronto, London, Frankfurt, and Paris. MG Services handles all aspects of countertrade transactions, including barter, offset, switch trading, debt and blocked funds settlements. Additionally, MG Services offers integrated project finance services through FB/MG, a joint venture with the First Boston Corporation. MG Services will structure the programs, negotiate documentation, underwrite the obligation, and fulfill the export obligations on a non-recourse basis. MG handles a full range of manufactured and semi-manufactured products, as well as commodities traded by the two parent companies. Annual trade volume exceeds $40 billion. MG is currently handling transactions in twenty countries.

Prudential-Bache Trade Corp. PBTC operates a global network of trading and finance subsidiaries, with offices in ten countries. The company negotiates and structures countertrade and offset transactions, acting as either principal, agent or partner in the deal. PBTC is also active in international leasing and trade receivables financing. The PBTC International Bank, a wholly owned subsidiary, provides pre-export financing, full trade documentation, factoring and forfait discounting, foreign exchange trading, and clearing account administration, as well as traditional trade finance facilities. PBTC specializes in metals, minerals, capital goods, and soft commodities.

Bank Export Trading Companies

Chase Trade, Inc. (Chase Manhattan Bank). Chase Trade is a full-service countertrade unit which can structure and implement transactions as well as provide financing. They will also provide export promotion for buyer countries by identifying markets for countertrade products. Chase Trade's approach to countertrade is secured lending (title-linked financing), in which they follow Chase Manhattan's credit policy guidelines. They will take title to counterpurchase goods, on the condition that each purchase is covered by a binding repurchase commitment. Chase Trade has fifteen trade specialists (including four countertrade specialists) and has access to Chase Manhattan's 72-country network of subsidiaries and affiliates. The areas in which Chase Trade handles countertrade are the Western Hemisphere, southern Europe, Asia (China, Israel, India and Pakistan) and Africa (Algeria, Morocco, Tanzania, and Zimbabwe). Chase Trade is the only bank ETC operating in Africa. Products handled are value-added manufactured items; in China, the products include chemicals and rare metals. They do not handle commodities. Chase Trade will accept clients who are not Chase Manhattan customers.

Manufacturers Hanover World Trade Corp. The Manufacturers Hanover WTC will handle all aspects of countertrade transactions and will take title to the goods. (Financing is handled by the Manufacturers Hanover World Trade Group.) They have ten countertrade specialists in New York, one in London, and one in Hong Kong. Areas covered are Latin America, Eastern Europe (Poland and Romania), and China. The products handled include metals, coal, agricultural commodities, textiles, and fishing industry products (the latter in Latin America). They also handle services such as tourism, hotel accommodations, and cruises. The average size of countertrade transactions is $10–$15 million. They will accept clients who are not Manufacturers Hanover customers.

Brokers

International Countertrade, Inc. IC was established in 1985 in Dayton, Ohio by Patricia Ballard. Her previous trading experience includes five years as the President of Countertrade Operations for the Cheney Group. She has countertraded in oil, food, tires, aluminum, copper, and art products. IC is interested in long-term countertrade relationships with the United States and foreign companies. Areas of primary interest are Latin America and the Caribbean, the Middle East, and the Far East.

Countertrade Facilitators

China/Tech, Ltd. China/Tech is a cooperative joint venture between the Chinese Association of Science and Technology (CAST, a professional Chinese organization whose membership consists of virtually all of China's technicians, engineers, factory managers, and scientists) and a group of American private firms and individuals operating under the guidance of the Advanced Technology Development Center of the Georgia Institute of

Technology. China/Tech is headquartered in Beijing and is managed from its Atlanta office on the Georgia Tech campus. Its purpose is to provide services to American and Chinese parties in the formation of joint ventures in technology-related enterprises. China/Tech's services include brokerage services, feasibility studies, marketing surveys, translating and interpreting services, and assistance in meeting countertrade requirements. They also provide training and education for American and Chinese business people by sponsoring trade shows and exhibits, conducting business seminars, and supporting exchanges of scholars in technical fields. China/Tech will provide consulting services for the duration of the project.

8 Using Trade Statistics in Countertrade

Counterpurchase products are often disposed of through networking and personal contacts. This approach may be satisfactory for one-time deals, but in a longer term countertrade or offset transaction, it is necessary to base marketing plans on hard data (i.e., trade statistics).

Trade statistics are especially useful in carrying out indirect offset programs of the type in which the company has agreed to assist the buyer country in export development. The country may wish to expand exports of traditional products by selling them to new markets, or it may wish to begin exporting nontraditional products. In either case, the company will be expected to find world markets for the products. Since indirect offset concerns products unrelated to the original sale, the company often has no idea where these markets might be. Analysis of trade statistics will identify the best markets in terms of size, growth potential, and projected value; the company can then do some meaningful work with the country offset officials in formulating export plans.

Statistical analysis of world markets is also useful in direct offsets and joint ventures. Although the usual arrangement is sourcing or buyback (the company uses the foreign-made products in-house), the country will often want to reserve some portion of production for export to new markets. This will enable the country to continue its export business after the offset or countertrade agreement ends. The company will have some degree of expertise in locating international markets for familiar or component products, but it will need hard data to demonstrate to the buyer country that good potential markets exist. Also it is important to include trade data in the initial business plans for the joint venture if the country plans to export the products on its own eventually.

Some countries do not particularly care where the counterpurchase products are sold, as long as they can get the company to take the products in payment for their import. However, the company will have to sell these products *somewhere* in order to get offset credit and/or hard currency. Trade data will turn *somewhere* into a market.

Trade data can also be used to analyze just one country: identify its top value and growth imports and exports (import and export product ranks), its major trading partners by product, and its balance of trade by industry sector. This type of analysis is useful in helping a country plan its trade program through identification of its strengths and weaknesses. On the other hand, the country may be interested in only one export market, and will ask the company to help it plan its penetration of that market with a variety of products; the desired market will usually be the United States or one of the other OECD countries. Trade statistics can be used to evaluate the possibility of establishing a share in the target market.

In this chapter, we identify the major sources of trade data, give brief examples of the use of the data in countertrade and offset situations, explain data limitations, and discuss the feasibility of in-house data bases.

TRADE DATA AND DATA PUBLICATIONS AVAILABLE

The sole source of comprehensive world trade data is the United Nations; no other agency collects data on such a massive scale. The U.N. sells this data both in raw form (from the New York office) and in manipulated hard copy form (Geneva), and permits anyone to use and publish it, on the condition that they do not resell it in raw data form; printouts are copyrighted and may not be reproduced without permission. Almost all government and private world trade data services, including the International Market Information System, use U.N. data as part of their bases. Few corporations buy their own U.N. data, however, as it is hard to program. (See "In-house data bases versus outside services," later in this chapter.)

United Nations trade data is organized by the SITC, a system of five-digit commodity classifications covering approximately 1830 commodities. (All products, whether or not they are manufactures, are called "commodities" in the context of the SITC.) Over 200 countries, territories, and areas are covered in the data. Country data is available on Series D magnetic tapes by year; extracted data by commodity is also available. Charges for raw data are based on the number of records. The data is available from the U.N. Statistical Office in New York.

The United Nations has a number of useful statistical publications. The most valuable is the *International Trade Statistics Yearbook*, which is published annually. This two-volume set (trade by commodity/trade by country) shows trade in the major product classifications and the rank of importers and exporters of each product for a period of four years, in the first volume, and trade by country showing major import and export partners and products in the second volume. Though the yearbook does not provide the information necessary to identify market shares by product in individual countries, it is very useful for constructing a quick trade matrix. Other publications of special interest are the *Monthly Bulletin of Statistics* and the alpha/numeric indexes to the SITC. These publications are available by mail or may be purchased directly from the bookshop at the United Nations in New York. Most university libraries carry U.N. publications.

The U.S. Department of Commerce has an extensive data base of U.S. imports and exports. This is very valuable data; however, since it is restricted to U.S. trade it does not contain data on total market size or international competition. Many researchers prefer to use USDOC data wherever possible, however, because the product classifications are more detailed than the SITC. The four most useful sets of USDOC data are: (1) FT410 data, seven-digit Schedule E classifications covering U.S. exports by product; (2) FT135 data, seven-digit Schedule A classifications covering U.S. imports by product; (3) FT155 data, four-digit Schedule A classifications covering U.S. imports by country; and (4) the Foreign Traders Index (FTI), a file of importers, agents, and distributors worldwide for all products as defined by the Standard Industrial Classification (SIC). Unfortunately, none of the data are available in raw data form; the FT410, FT135, and FT155 data are available in book form, and the FTI, though available on tape, is a "print tape" (i.e., the data cannot be manipulated, only formatted and printed). Most USDOC data is available in hard copy printout form by country or product. Printouts may be ordered from the USDOC in Washington; FTI printouts are available from Washington or through the Lockheed Dialog data base. Most USDOC regional offices have current issues of the FT410, FT135, and FT155 books, although for back years it will be necessary to go to a library.

A limited amount of data in the six-digit NIMEXE classification (a system based on the BTN or Brussels Tariff Nomenclature) is available in book or microfiche form from the European Community office in Washington. NIMEXE data covers EC imports and exports of approximately 5,000 commodities. This data has the same limitation as USDOC data, however, in that coverage is restricted to trade between the EC countries.

USING TRADE DATA

The following are three simplified examples of the use of trade data in countertrade and offset programs. The data referred to in these examples would be SITC data obtained from the United Nations and processed by the company or its consultant.

In the first example, the company accepts an unfamiliar product as a counterpurchase from Country A, cannot use the product in-house, and must find somewhere to sell it. To find a market, the company researcher will collect five years of SITC commodity data on worldwide trade in the product. Next, the researcher will rank the import markets by five-year total value (ranking markets by the most recent year alone can be very misleading) and determine which of the top value markets have good and stable growth rates. This results in a group of potential markets with both high value and promising growth. The researcher will then compare market shares of the major suppliers with Country A's share; if Country A has only a tiny share or a declining share, the chances of market penetration are not good. The markets in which Country A has a decent share will be the target markets. The researcher will then locate names of buyers in the target markets, and contact them about importing the product. Of course, the researcher could skip the trade research entirely and just go down a worldwide list of buyers; however, identifying the appropriate markets first will save a great deal of time.

The second example is a medium-term (five years or less) indirect offset with Country B. The research method outlined previously is usable, but in this case the research must be tied into an export development program for Country B. Trade data can be used to create an export rank of Country B's products; this procedure will identify the products with the best export potential. The researcher should obtain *country data*, rather than commodity data, for the first part of this task: five years of Country B's complete export records. These five country data files will then be transformed into 45 aggregate commodity files (i.e., records for each of the nine major SITC product divisions for each of the five years). (The tenth SITC division, "unclassified commodities," is not useful in trade analysis.) Next, the researcher will rank the disaggregate products within each SITC division (food, chemicals, fuels, etc.) by five-year total export value and growth rate; this results in 18 files, value and growth ranks for the products in each of the nine divisions. The top export potential products are now easily identified, and the researcher can obtain commodity data for these products and proceed to a target market analysis.

The third example is a long-term offset with Country C, which may involve both direct and indirect portions. Here the research methods include export product ranks and targeting of export markets, but it can also include the planning of import substitution programs and the development of new products for export, as well as the evaluation of business plans for possible joint ventures in terms of the export potential of resultant products. Researching import substitution requires the construction of an import rank, which is developed in the same manner as an export rank. Identifying new products for export is more difficult, since they will not show up on either an export rank or a world market commodity analysis (Country C will have no share). The researcher must still collect export data on countries similar to Country C—countries which are at the same level of economic development, are in the same world region, and have similar materials resources and labor forces—and proceed on the assumption that if these countries can export the product, so can Country C. Then, the researcher can identify the markets where the other countries are selling the product, evaluate those markets, and advise Country C accordingly. This procedure can also be used to determine the export potential of joint venture products. Data projections, if done properly, are usually accurate for about five years into the future, and will help the company and Country C to decide how much of production they should allocate for export.

In both of the examples given for offset programs, data from the USDOC can be used to augment U.N. SITC data in pricing the product. It is very difficult to calculate import and export prices per unit from SITC data, because in most cases the quantity information is useless; quantity trade in computers, for example, is reported in metric tons rather than number of computers. The USDOC has printouts showing unit prices of Schedule E export products, and since Schedule E is based on the SITC, it is fairly easy to match the information with SITC data. Of course, the prices will be U.S. prices, but this information is relevant if a U.S. company is Country C's joint venture partner. NIMEXE data from the EC can also be used to calculate prices for some products.

OVERCOMING LIMITATIONS IN DATA COVERAGE

The two most common complaints about SITC data are that the classifications are too broad, and that the data is always a year or two behind. Another complaint is that the data on some developing countries, such as China, is not available. However, all of these limitations can be partially overcome.

The main reason for the broadness of SITC classifications is that the SITC is based on a tariff nomenclature, the BTN. Market researchers may be anxious to find the exact statistics on canned tomatoes and canned peas, for example, and become frustrated upon finding these two products dumped in a statistical "basket" along with all other canned vegetables; however, for tariff purposes all canned vegetables are subject to the same duty rate; thus the SITC offers no further breakdown. For some product classifications, it is not possible to determine what portion of the total SITC value was accounted for by a specific item, while in other classifications one can extrapolate the value by using the more detailed USDOC classifications and estimating the shares of the United States and other suppliers. For electrical machinery or mining machinery, one can also make estimates based on the country's electrical production and mining indexes. However, a broad data classification is still far better than nothing, because the researcher will be able to eliminate unsuitable markets. If research shows that the market in question is a poor market for canned vegetables in general, then it will certainly not be a good market for canned tomatoes.

Many people feel that the U.N. should change the SITC to make it more specific. In fact, it is updated every few years; it is now in its third revision. However, it will never be extremely detailed, partly because of its tariff code orientation and partly because some countries refuse to report detailed trade information on particular products. Even now, countries such as the United States, Canada, Switzerland, and Austria often will not report trade in some high-tech and machinery products on any useful level of detail. Trade in sensitive products can usually be extrapolated from other countries' records ("created data"); if the United States does not report exports of a certain product, for example, checking the import records for that product in the EEC countries and other major markets will reveal most of the U.S. sales.

SITC data is never up-to-the-minute simply because not all countries report trade promptly; some of the developing countries are years behind. Most industrial countries are prompt in reporting, though a complete set of data for one year's trade will usually not be available until July of the following year at the earliest. This is a data processing problem; some of the larger countries' files contain nearly a million records per year. The solution to this is to make projections based on either the last few years' data or on this data plus the most recent quarterly data.

Obtaining trade data for nonreporting countries, slow-reporting countries, or countries whose reporting is unreliable is fairly easy in theory; however, as with making projections, it is a difficult programming task. The researcher must work backward, searching the records of other countries to find records of trade with the country in question; this is basically the same process previously described for tracking trade in sensitive products. For example, all records of all reporting countries' imports from China would be reclassified as Chinese exports, and records of their exports to China would be reclassified as Chinese imports (import value of the new records would be f.o.b. country of origin, which may make the value appear to be a little low). If the research objective is to develop a rank of all the country's import or export products rather than identifying its trade in a single commodity, this task will involve a massive search and file-building procedure. The United Nations performs this "created data" procedure for its own research purposes, and will sometimes make the resultant data available. The International Market Information System (IMIS) uses the procedure routinely.

IN-HOUSE DATA BASES VERSUS OUTSIDE SERVICES

Generally speaking, it is not a good idea to attempt to develop an in-house trade data base from scratch. Development, programming, and maintenance of a large trade data base is expensive and difficult. The start-up cost is high; several years of SITC raw data must be purchased, tape or disc storage space allotted, CPU time allocated, and staff hired or trained. Comprehensive trade data bases containing millions of records require a mainframe computer. Though small files can be downloaded on a PC, the data base itself requires a system with a large amount of memory. Operating costs can also be very high, especially if the data base is on-line. Programming trade data is difficult if the programmer knows nothing about U.N. data. The programmer may assume that some records are missing or inaccurate, when actually the problem lies with some quirk of the reporting country which can be resolved through additional manipulation of the records. There are no software packages (canned programs) for U.N. data. In addition to the programmer, there must be someone on the staff who can analyze the data, that is, interpret the printouts so that anyone in the company could comprehend the information.

The only companies which should seriously consider undertaking data base management on the scale described here are large corporations involved in long-term or multiple offset programs, shipping companies, and large export trading companies handling a variety of products. Smaller firms (or any firm which cannot commit the funding and resources to data base management) have the options of using a data service, hiring a consultant, or purchasing hard copy printouts and training an employee to analyze them. Firms that can afford the data and CPU time but do not have the programming resources can buy raw data and hire a consultant to develop the software for the system.

Hard copy data is available from government and private sources. In general, printouts from government sources such as the USDOC are less expensive than printouts from private sources, but they are often hard to read due to poor formatting and insufficient descriptions of products. Printouts from private data services vary in quality (depending on the staff's experience with programming and analyzing trade data) and on the degree of manipulation of the data. These printouts may range from simple trade matrices to full analysis printouts. Some services (such as IMIS) also provide a "plain English" written analysis of the printout. Most data services, government or private, will provide custom printouts for a fee. Charges for standard printouts are usually a certain amount per product or per country, rather than by number of records, as for raw data.

WORLD BUYER DATA

Several private agencies have attempted to develop "countertrade data bases," that is, files of buyer names worldwide. Most of these data bases fail due to their high operating costs. Customers want the data on line, but the agency is usually unable to get enough subscribers to support an on-line service. In addition, no buyer data base can ever be complete, because no single private agency can discover all buyers for all products, or get permission to reproduce confidential data from competitors' data bases. Private buyer data bases can be valuable, but users should be aware of their limitations.

The best approach to collecting buyer data is to use government sources These data bases are usually very large, since they are subsidized operations, and are often on line as well. They are not "countertrade" data bases per se, but are intended to facilitate exports, and are thus useful for marketing various products. The USDOC buyer data base is the FTI, noted earlier. The FTI contains approximately 175,000 names of importers, agents, and distributors in 150 countries. This information is collected by American commercial officers worldwide, and the file is updated continuously as new data come in. Most governments in other industrial countries have similar data files or publications containing buyer names.

9 Countertrade Insurance

The insurance market for countertrade is in a developmental stage. However, more and more companies are offering new or expanded countertrade coverage because the demand is so great. The problem with countertrade coverage is that the import side of the transaction is considered very risky, especially when there is a time lag between delivery of the original export and payment. Therefore, the premiums for the import contract coverage can be quite high, sometimes up to 12% of the contract value. Export contract coverage (export credit insurance) is far less troublesome. Insurance policies are normally written separately for the import and export contacts.

This chapter covers sources of countertrade insurance, the relationship of good negotiating and contracting to insurance coverage, insurance risks in countertrade, insurable risks, exclusions, and the prospects for countertrade insurance in the coming years.

WHERE TO GET COUNTERTRADE INSURANCE

Insurance coverage for countertrade transactions is generally available only from private companies. National scheme insurers such as the United States' Foreign Credit Insurance Association (FCIA) and the United Kingdom's Export Credit Guarantee Department (ECGD) will not cover a complete countertrade transaction, not because they disapprove of countertrade or are unwilling to take the risk, but because their business is promoting national exports rather than imports. Also, their charters prevent them from becoming involved in third country trade (disposal of counterpurchased goods). National schemes will sometimes cover the export part of the transaction if there is a separate contract providing for hard currency payment, but even this activity is rare, and they will not cover a barter contract at all.

The private insurance market has responded to the need for countertrade coverage. Lloyd's of London, the industry leader, was the first company to offer countertrade insurance. This coverage is now widely provided by American firms as well, primarily by American International Group (AIG) and by a number of other groups, including CIGNA/INA/AFIA and Chubb. At the present time, the private insurance market for countertrade is in a developmental, unstructured stage. Standards for risk, losses, rates, and so on have not yet been established because of the diversity of countertrade transactions.

Many exporters prefer to use private rather than government insurers, regardless of the type of transaction, because of the advantages offered by the private sector. Foremost among these is flexibility in the risks covered and in the use of limits, deductibles, and so on; policies can be formulated on an individual basis. The larger private firms, such as Lloyd's and AIG, can also provide *combined programs*—the underwriter who provides the political risk or export cover can also provide insurance for the marine cargo, property and liability. A complete program of this type will cover "all risks," warehouse-to-warehouse (coverage protecting the cargo from origin through final destination), interruptions in transit, work in process, construction, inland transit, warehousing, physical assets and direct and contingent corporate/ product liabilities. Cover can be obtained for all aspects of a countertrade deal in a single comprehensive policy.

Private insurance coverage has several disadvantages compared to government insurance, though for practical purposes these drawbacks must be accepted if the exporter needs countertrade coverage. In general, private insurance is more expensive: rates for premiums range from 0.125% to 12% of the contract value. This applies especially to coverage of countertrade transactions, which can be highly risky and, therefore, costly to insure. Private coverage is also more restrictive and offers fewer guarantees than national schemes. For instance, private insurance will not cover "full war"; there is an exclusion which precludes loss if there is a war between the countries of buyer and seller. Loss in the event of a *five great powers war* (war between any of the following: the United States, United Kingdom, France, China, and the USSR) is also precluded. National schemes will cover these war risks. Additionally, national schemes will usually provide coverage for five years, while private insurance coverage is normally limited to three years. The three-year limitation can be a serious problem in the type of countertrade where the counterpurchased goods will not be available for three or four years (e.g., semiprocessesd materials from a new mine or manufactures from a new factory, which involves long-term technology transfer and training of workers). Some private insurers will roll over the policy after three years, but this is not usual. The maximum indemnity available from private insurers is 90%, whereas national schemes will often provide higher indemnity; the FCIA, for example, indemnifies an exporter 100% for a political loss and 90% to 95% for a commercial loss. In general, the disadvantage of private firms is that their decisions are based on purely commercial considerations, whereas national schemes have a mandate to promote exports.

International insurance brokers (specialist export credit brokers) can manage the corporation's export credit insurance program. Some of these brokers have experience in countertrade transactions. A full service broker will select the appropriate private insurance firm, provide political risk intelligence, review sales contracts for exposure, draft and design coverage, handle claims, and restructure contracts in order to help the exporter obtain financing. Brokers familiar with countertrade will go to the negotiating table with the exporter; in fact, the presence of a broker during the negotiations is strongly advised. The broker will be able to help the exporter minimize risk through good contracting, thus leaving less risk for the underwriter to cover.

THE IMPORTANCE OF A GOOD CONTRACT

Many insurance coverage problems in countertrade are directly related to holes in the contract. It is true that countertrade is inherently risky because of its noncash, delayed payment aspect, and because so much of this type of trade is done with politically unstable or heavily indebted countries. However, according to the consensus of underwriters, it is often the exporter, not the buyer country, who makes life difficult for the insurance community. The common complaint is that the exporter signs the contract first and seeks insurance later. Exporters new to countertrade are usually apprehensive and confused, and do not realize that the best way to minimize risk in countertrade, as in conventional trade, is through good negotiation and contracting. Instead, they tend to think that countertrade is different and that an insurance policy can somehow salvage a bad contract. The fact is that if the contract is all that bad, no underwriter will touch it. This is why the insurance sector urges exporters considering countertrade to have a broker or other insurance expert present at the negotiations (preferably, this person should be consulted as early as the tender stage) and have him assist in the drafting of the contract. In the event that problems arise during the transaction, contractual solutions (arbitration, standby letters of credit, etc.) should be the first recourse, with insurance being the second phase.

Aside from being poor strategy, failure to negotiate a good contract can be an expensive mistake. The cost of insurance coverage for countertrade is higher than that for conventional exports to begin with, due to the higher risk involved, and laying extra risk on the underwriter because of a poor contract will only further increase the premiums. Failure to consider insurance in the early stages of a countertrade arrangement can also eat into profits, even with a good contract. If the cost of insurance coverage has not been taken into account prior to tendering of the bid, there may be no room left for it in the final contract price.

The import and export contracts should be separate. Though coverage for the entire transaction can be provided in a single policy, underwriters generally view a countertrade arrangement as two completely separate transactions, mainly because the level of risk is different. The import contract will require the heaviest coverage, since nondelivery of counterpurchased goods is a frequent problem.

In relation to the import contract, the exporter must think about disposal of the goods. A disposal contract should be made with the end user of the goods (if the exporter is not sourcing for his own use) at the time that the original import and export contracts are framed. Insurance coverage of this third contract will offer some protection to the exporter if the goods are not delivered or are delivered late.

INSURANCE RISKS IN COUNTERTRADE*

The major risk in countertrade is that the buyer will not deliver the counterpurchased goods for either commercial or political reasons; this will prevent the exporter from getting paid and result in a large loss to the underwriter. The next most serious area of concern is political risk. Political risk is high in many countries that demand countertrade, due to unstable governments, civil disorder, terrorism, and debt, to name just a few of the problems. According to underwriters, political risk is highest in oil barter deals.

Most commercial and political risks can be covered by private insurance companies, though the cost of the premiums will vary considerably depending on the level of perceived risk in a particular country. The problem is often in the definition of commercial and political risk; each underwriter seems to have a slightly different set of rules. Some general definitions are given in the following discussion.

"Political risks" are those incurred due to a political or government action, regardless of whether the buyer is private or sovereign, according to Cook & Miller International of New York. Hogg Robinson & Gardner Mountain Ltd. defines it as any act of a political nature which adversely affects a contract. Other companies, such as Lloyd's and some of the American underwriters, apparently do not define any risk as political unless the buyer is a government entity, and their definitions of a government entity vary. Some underwriters define it as any organization "acting with the full faith and credit of the government," while others consider any organization financially controlled by the government to be a government entity.

Definitions of "government entity" may include a central government, ministry, department, or agency thereof; a regional or local authority (city councils, utility authorities, fire departments, etc.); a nationalized corporation; a state trading organization; and so on.

Cook and Miller International categorizes political risk as confiscation, nationalization, expropriation, deprivation, war, strikes, riots, civil com-

---

*The definitions and lists of insurable risks provided in this chapter are not intended to be a representation of coverage available from any specific company. Exporters should consult their own brokers and underwriters for specific information.

motion, boycott, embargo, currency inconvertibility, and export/import license cancellation. Commercial risks ("caused solely by the buyer's action") are categorized by the company as contract frustration, buyer default, and buyer bankruptcy. With some exceptions, most other companies make the same basic distinctions.

Factors considered in political risk analysis include the following: expropriation, nationalization, foreign currency policy, joint venture analysis, import/export laws, foreign policy analysis, opposition to the government, terrorism, "law and order" and bribery. Other factors are GNP, inflation, external debt, debt service ratio, unemployment, trade balance, balance of payments, and reserves.

Insurance Risks (Private Companies)

In general, the insurable risks on the export contract are insolvency of buyer, payment default of buyer, currency inconvertibility, import/export restrictions (such as cancellation of licenses) imposed by either the exporter's or buyer's government, unfair calling of bonds and force majeure. Insurable risks on the import contract are insolvency or default of supplier, repudiation of contract by supplier, nonperformance in terms of availability or quality of goods, import/export restrictions imposed by the government of either party, unfair calling of bonds and force majeure. Lloyd's syndicates (about 430 underwriters) will cover pure barter contracts, provided that an exchange monetary value is established and agreed to between the contracting parties. Coverage is for the following risks: laws, decrees, and the like, anywhere outside the control of the insured, which prevent export, import, or shipment; cancellation of import/export licenses; repudiation of contract by the buyer where the insured is not at fault; continued refusal by the buyer to perform for more than six months, where the insured is not at fault; and termination of contract by either party due to war, revolution, and the like, preventing performance by more than six months.

Cover is normally for an exporter's accounts receivable, out-of-pocket expenses, or profit foregone if the contract is frustrated for reasons beyond his control. The maximum possible exposure is the contract value itself. Indemnity is normally 90% of losses/extra costs up to an agreed maximum liability on each policy.

Exclusions

Private companies will not cover war risks, defined as a *five great powers war* or war between the countries of buyer and seller. Some companies will not cover insolvency or financial default on the part of either government or private buyers, loss due to currency fluctuations/devaluations, or material default of the insured, their agent, or sub- or co-contractors.

Underwriters will evaluate the exporter as well as the buyer. Factors that they consider include the financial structure of the exporting company, the company's experience and competence in fulfilling countertrade contracts, and worldwide export/import activities. It will help if the exporter has been trading in the buyer country for many years without problems. Underwriters will also bear in mind the volume of business placed with them by the exporter and their relationship with the exporters.

COUNTERTRADE INSURANCE IN THE FUTURE

It should be easier and cheaper to obtain countertrade insurance in the future, partly because insurance firms will gain experience and establish standards for policies and partly because countertrade is becoming institutionalized. More and more countries are using countertrade as a trade management tool rather than a financial necessity, seeing it as a way to obtain technology, build up industrial sectors and promote nontraditional exports. This trend will make countertrade much more formal and predictable, which will in turn make the insurance community feel more comfortable with it.

References

Cooke, Henry, "Lloyd's of London," *Countertrade and Barter Quarterly*, No. 4, Winter 1984, pp. 38–39.

Edwards, Burt, "Credit Insurance Solutions to Countertrade Risks," *Countertrade and Barter Quarterly*, No. 4, Winter 1984, pp. 27–31.

Higgins, Tom, "Mitigating Risks in Countertrade Transactions," *Countertrade and Barter Quarterly*, No. 4, Winter 1984, pp. 32–33.

Jeffries, Francis M., "Political Risk Analysis: What's in it for Exporters?" *Export Today*, Vol. 1, No. 2, Summer 1985, pp. 61–64.

Milone, Michele A., "Export Credit Insurance: Government vs. Private Sources," *Export Today*, Vol. 1, No. 2, Summer 1985, pp. 59–60.

Mountain, Georgina, "Political Risk Insurance," *Countertrade and Barter Quarterly*, No. 8, Winter 1985/1986, pp. 30–34.

Oscroft, Allan, "Countertrade: Political and Credit Risk Management," *Countertrade and Barter Quarterly*, No. 4, Winter 1984, pp. 24–26.

Roberts, J. Peter, W. Roberts, and Francis X. Boylan, "The Insurance-Banking Bridge," *Countertrade and Barter Quarterly*, No. 4, Winter 1984, pp. 35–37.

10 Countertrade Financing

Conventional trade financing is done through export credit agencies, government aid funds, commercial banks, supplier credit, buyer credit, trade credit, and preexport finance. Unconventional financing methods are necessary for countertrade. Two of these methods, evidence accounts and bilateral clearing and switch, are described in Chapter 1. In this chapter the remaining major methods of countertrade financing are covered, including two complex methods which are gaining in popularity: parallel technical banking agreements and forfaiting.

BANK GUARANTEES, LETTERS OF CREDIT, AND ESCROW ACCOUNTS

In barter trade, the exporter often uses bank guarantees; this is a simple system that is especially suitable for short-term transactions. Compensation products are handed over against issue of a letter of guarantee made out by the exporter's bank in favor of the supplier of the compensation products. This document stipulates that the bank will pay cash for the compensation products even if the exporter fails to deliver his own goods within a specified period of time. The value of the bank guarantee is gradually reduced as the exporter makes his deliveries and forwards the relevant despatch documents to the bank.

Alternatively, export and compensation products can both be made payable by letters of credit. The letter of credit made out in favor of the exporter is funded with assets gained through the purchase of compensation products.

Escrow accounts are also common in countertrade. Under this arrangement, the exporter and the trading partner open a joint account at a Western bank. The account is credited with funds paid by the purchaser of the compensation products, and debited in favor of the exporter when he has fulfilled his obligations. Escrow funds are handed over by the bank that manages the

---

Information on forfaiting was provided courtesy of Frederick N. Schnurr.

account, and interest is divided between the exporter and the trading partner under the terms stipulated in the trust agreement.*

PARALLEL TECHNICAL BANKING AGREEMENTS

Parallel technical banking agreements (PTBAs) are technical banking agreements that regulate accounting operations under commercial trading agreements. They are similar to evidence accounts. PTBAs are used mostly in high-value countertrade agreements between Western exporters and Eastern European FTOs, although they are beginning to be used in countertrade with developing countries. They are considered feasible only for agreements with two-way trade in excess of $10 million annually; in fact most active PTBAs cover trade valued over $50 million.

The PTBA constitutes a current account maintained by a foreign trade bank on behalf of the FTO and a private Western bank. The two banks agree on a formal interbank basis to handle jointly all payments and process documentary credits necessary to carry out countertrade transactions under the agreement. This arrangement actually functions as a joint trust account, since each bank opens a trust account on behalf of its partner. They jointly book the debits and credits in their respective accounts ("mirror accounts"). As a rule, the accounts established under a PTBA do not pay interest.†

FORFAITING

The procedure known as forfaiting or *A Forfait* arose in Europe in the late 1950s and early 1960s as a means of financing trade with Eastern Europe. The term is derived from the French word for "to forfeit" and refers to the nonrecourse nature of the financing. The purchaser of the paper forfaits his claims against the exporter.

The forfaiting market has grown considerably in recent years. It is now estimated that approximately $15 billion in paper is outstanding and roughly $5 billion in new paper is issued each year. The principal market is London and secondary markets exist in Zurich and Geneva, where forfaiting originated. A number of U.S. financial institutions are now engaged in the business. The main sources of paper are European exporters—chiefly West German and Italian, but more recently, British and French exporters have taken to the vehicle as official export credit agencies (Export Credit Guarantee Department (ECGD) and Coface) have cut back on their coverages.

Although Eastern Europe remains the largest single source of forfait paper (perhaps a third of the total), other areas are gaining in importance. The Far

*Association for Compensatory Trade. *Practical Guide to Countertrade.* 1985, pp. 27–28.
†*Countertrade Outlook,* "Parallel Technical Bank Agreements Spreading Beyond E. Europe to LDC's," Vol. 3, No. 40, October 21, 1985, p. 2.

East is perhaps the most important growth area as a source of paper, and the Middle East and southern Europe are also important sources. Latin America has been reduced in importance because of the debt crisis, but about a half dozen countries can be financed for reduced terms (up to two or three years). Several African countries are also manageable.

Definition of Forfaiting

Forfaiting is the discounting of debt without recourse to the seller. Among its usual features are the following:

Medium term: 1–10 years

Fixed interest rate

Almost always trade related (about 90% of the time)

Uses the straight discount mechanism (the alternative discount to yield method, however, is gaining in importance)

Use of a local bank guarantee or Aval (a sovereign guarantee is also occasionally used)

Secondary markets in London and Switzerland

Denominated in one of several hard currencies

Use of promissory notes or bills of exchange

Semiannual repayments of principal and interest based on a 360-day year and actual days elapsed plus grace days, weekends, and holidays

Advantages of Forfaiting

For the issuer:

1. *Fixed Rate Financing.* The importer knows his future interest costs exactly.
2. *Lower Costs.* Because of the secondary market, a purchaser of the paper will not require as high a rate of return as with other forms of fixed rate financing.
3. *Flexibility of Currency.* The market routinely accepts dollars, Swiss francs, and deutsche marks. Sterling and yen may also be possible.
4. *Flexible Grace Periods and Commitment Periods.* Occasionally commitment periods as long as 18 months may be possible, and grace periods as long as 8 years have been offered.

For the exporter:

1. *Nonrecourse Financing.* The exporter need not concern himself with the future balance of payments problems, the importer's financial situation, and so on.

2. *Freedom from National Content Requirements.* All official export credit agencies require a certain amount of national content in order to finance an export. Forfait is an exception to these rules.

3. *Speed and Simplicity of Transaction.* A forfait transaction can be arranged in as little as two days. Eximbank approvals may take months and involve considerable effort on the part of the exporter.

For the purchaser of the paper:

1. *Little or No Credit Risk.* The forfait market requires a local bank guarantee, usually in the form of an Aval. Thus the purchaser of the paper need only be concerned with the transfer risk, the political risk, and (optionally) the interest rate fluctuation risk.

2. *Liquidity.* Because a secondary market exists for forfait paper, the holder of the paper can be reasonably assured that he can unload his paper at some price. Of course, if a country involved in the transaction experiences payment difficulties, the price could be at a large discount.

3. *Attractive Return.* Although the return on forfait paper is somewhat lower than on a straight fixed rate loan, it is considerably higher than on a floating rate loan for the same risk and maturity. At present the most desirable countries are yielding ½ to ¾% over the average life cost of funds. Less desirable countries may yield 10% over cost, or more.

Assumption of Risks and Responsibilities

The forfaiter or investor accepts:

Risk	Means of dealing with risk
Credit risk	Local bank guarantee or Aval
Political risk	No practical way—built into price (in Italy paper is often guaranteed by SACE)
Transfer risk	Same as preceding items
Foreign exchange risk	Funding in same currency
Interest rate fluctuation risk	Match funding, annual funding, or portfolio management (i.e., funding short in more or less equal amounts throughout the interest rate cycle)
Collection responsibility	Forecast transfer delay days—built into the price

The exporter accepts:

The responsibility for the legality of the claim for payment.

The responsibility for ensuring the authenticity of the trade documents. The issuing bank (i.e., the original forfaiter) will check the authenticity of the local bank guarantee or Aval.

The responsibility for the satisfactory performance of the trade contract with his buyer (usually covered by a performance bond, warranty, or standby letter of credit).

Typical Forfait Documentation

Always required:

1. Evidence of debt are usually promissory notes or, less commonly, commercial bills of exchange. The promissory notes should follow an international format showing the borrower, creditor, amount (principal and interest), maturity date, and place of payment. The notes will be signed by an authorized signatory of the borrower (i.e., the importer).
2. Signing authority of the borrower—Director's resolutions, and so forth.

Usually required:

1. Bank guarantee, Aval, or sovereign guarantee. An Aval is preferred because it is stamped right on the paper. It carries the unconditional irrevocable promise to pay on the part of the financial institution that provides it. It is governed by Article 30 of the Geneva Convention and is recognized throughout continental Europe and many other parts of the world. Although it is not officially recognized in English common law or in the United States, there has never been an instance where this has caused a problem in British or U.S. courts in the forfait business.
2. Signature authority and signature card for the Aval or guarantee.
3. Commercial invoice.
4. Bill of lading.

Sometimes required:

1. Import license
2. Transfer authorizations from the central bank
3. Stamp duty payment voucher (all forfait payments must be net of withholding or any other type of tax. Tax absorption cannot be considered because different holders of the paper will have different absorption capabilities).

4. Correspondent or branch bank of avalizing bank's attestation of the authenticity of documention.

Typical Forfait Procedure

1. Buyer requires trade credit.
2. The exporter and forfaiter (bank) agree on forfaiting terms on an indication basis. Forfaiter sends indication telex.
3. The exporter presents terms to the importer.
4. The importer contacts the local avalizing bank. The forfaiter has indicated which local banks would be acceptable.
5. Importer accepts terms, and later signs commercial contract.
6. The exporter and forfaiter commit to terms. The forfaiter sends a commitment telex. The exporter begins paying a commitment fee, usually paid quarterly in advance.
7. The forfaiter may or may not fund his fixed rate commitment at the time, depending on his near term view of future interest rate movements.
8. The exporter ships the goods.
9. The importer delivers the promissory notes and other relevant documentation to the avalizing bank (invoice Bill of lading, license, etc.).
10. The avalizing bank studies the documents, places the Aval and sends the notes, signature cards, and copies of other documents to the exporter. The importer pays the Aval fee to the avalizing bank.
11. The exporter delivers the relevant documents to the forfaiter along with his endorsement.
12. The forfaiter studies the documentation, and may get an attestation of the exporter's signatures from the exporter's lead bank.
13. The forfaiter pays the exporter the discounted proceeds.
14. On each maturity, the forfaiter presents the notes to the avalizing bank, either directly or through a prenegotiated third bank. The avalizing bank presents the note to the importer. The importer pays the avalizing bank in local currency, and the avalizing bank purchases the foreign exchange to pay the forfaiter.

How Forfait Pricing Works

The forfait pricing mechanism usually causes the most difficulty for those new to the procedure. In fact, it is somewhat complicated, and for that reason all the practitioners in Europe possess special software for this purpose. Forfaiters will either purchase this software from vendors or develop their own software tailored to their specific needs. Basically there are two ways to structure notes: the straight discount method and the discount to yield method. The former uses as the denominator the gross notes (i.e., with the interest included) while the latter uses the discounted proceeds as the denominator. Thus the straight discount is always lower than the discount to yield. While the straight discount method is still the most common way of structuring notes, the discount to yield method is growing in importance. For financing with long maturies (over six or seven years) the discount to yield method is usually used, because as maturities lengthen the same straight discount is equivalent to a large increase in the yield. In the interbank market, prices are always quoted on a yield basis and usually as a spread over average life cost of funds, that is, London Interbank Offered Rate (LIBOR).

The Straight Discount Method. The straight discount method is the rate from which interest is deducted in advance on a compound basis. The note must be grossed up to include this interest. This mechanism has two attractions:

1. Cosmetics. The lower quoted rate appeals to Eastern European officials concerned about appearances. These countries have often had legal ceilings on the amount of interest they could pay.
2. An automatically increasing yield curve; for example, straight discount of 10%, internal interest of 7.5%.

Maturity Years	Discount to Yield Paid (Compounded Semiannually)
3	11.25%
4	12.03%
5	12.56%
6	13.15%
7	13.80%

Finally, there is a third interest rate called the nominal or internal interest rate. This interest rate is used when the importer agrees to pay a certain rate of interest that is lower than the market rate (or perhaps higher). If the notes bear a lower rate than the forfait rate, the exporter's price will have to be grossed up so that he will receive the original amount. This is accomplished by the multiplier which is produced in the forfait calculation. The multiplier can be calculated manually with considerable effort, or easily by means of a computer program. Changes in the internal interest rate will cause only minor changes in the discount to yield for the same straight discount.

In forfait, the calculation is always done on the basis of a 360-day year (denominator). The numerator consists of the actual days plus weekends, holidays, and grace days to cover expected collection delays. The standard number of grace days is five, however, in some countries, such as Egypt, the market may require several months in transfer delay days. At the end of this discussion, there is an example of a calculation using the straight discount method.

The Discount to Yield Method. The discount to yield method is the nominal interest first grossed up on the notes, in the standard method using a calendar year (365/366-day) basis. Then a series of *discount factors* are calculated for each note and applied to them as follows:

Where a = days to maturity (including grace days, etc.) starting from last maturity
b = annual discount to yield rate
c = reciprocal of discount factor
$d1$ = the first discount factor; $d2$ = second discount factor, and so on.

$$\frac{1}{\frac{(a \times b)}{360} + 100b} \times 100 = \frac{1}{c} \times 100 = d1$$

Then, all factors are multiplied together ($d1 \times d2 \times d3$, etc.) to get the final factor dN. The face value of each note is multiplied by the final factor for that maturity. The final factor for the first maturity will be $d1$. For the second maturity it will be $d1 \times d2$, and so on.

The Forfait Market in the United States

The forfait market has been slow to catch on in the United States, but this appears to be changing now as its advantages become more known to the American exporting community. Some of the reasons that forfait has not grown faster are:

1. No U.S. banks were involved in forfaiting until approximately 1980. Even today, only a few U.S. banks are making a major effort in this area.
2. Lack of trade ties to Eastern Europe, the traditional forfait market. However, forfait is fast expanding out of this traditional area.
3. The damage to U.S. exports in general, due to the strong dollar.
4. A general lack of appreciation of the importance of trade finance, except among a few major U.S. exporters.

Why Forfaiting Should Increase in Popularity

1. Eximbank cutbacks.
2. Increased awareness, as more banks enter the field. This is especially important for small- and medium-size exporters, who can use forfait very effectively.

3. Lack of national content requirements. As firms increasingly go to multi-sourcing of intermediate parts, the Eximbank national content requirements will pose greater difficulties.
4. Lack of alternatives. Banks are increasingly seeking to avoid exposure in high risk countries. Forfait, with its liquid secondary market, can deal with country risks that banks alone will no longer accept.
5. Simplicity and speed of the procedure. The exporter need not be familiar with any of the aforementioned mathematics. He can simply get a quote, and in three days close a deal with his client, bypassing the red tape of the export credit agencies.

When Forfaiting Is Especially Appropriate

1. Down payments on Eximbank financing. The forfait structure allows for fixed rate financing at the same rate as Eximbank financing, usually with little additional cost to the exporter.
2. When speed is of the essence.
3. When the foreign content in the export exceeds that permitted by Eximbank.
4. When the product exported is not usually covered by Eximbank, or Commodity Credit Corporation (CCC).
5. When the country is not open to Eximbank coverage (e.g., the Soviet Union).
6. When the transaction involves countertrade. Credit agencies and the World Bank will often avoid financing deals with countertrade.
7. When the rate and/or terms are better. This can often happen, especially for attractive transactions in European and Asian countries.
8. When another currency is required. The Eximbank procedure is not as flexible.

Sample Calculation

Inputs

1. Amount to be received by exporter: $1,000,000.00
2. Term: 2 years—4 semiannual repayments
3. Drawdown: November 1, 1985
4. Last payment: November 1, 1987
5. Transfer days grace period: 5 days
6. Nominal interest rate: 6% p.a.
7. Straight discount rate: 8%
8. Down payment: None

Straight Discount Method

AI. CALENDAR COUNTER

Nov. 1, 1985 =	Friday	0 days
May 1, 1986 =	Wednesday	181 days + 5 grace = 186 tenor days
Nov. 1, 1986 =	Saturday, advance to	
Nov. 3, 1986 =	Monday	186 days + 5 grace = 191 tenor days
May 1, 1987 =	Friday,	179 days + grace = 184 tenor days
May 1, 1987 =	Advance to	
May 4, 1987 =	Monday	185 days + 5 grace = 190 tenor days

Total days

11/1/85– 5/1/86 = 181 days + 5 = 186 tenor
11/1/85–11/3/86 = 367 days + 5 = 372 tenor
11/1/85– 5/1/87 = 546 days + 5 = 551 tenor
11/1/85–11/2/87 = 731 days + 5 = 736 tenor

A2. CALCULATION OF THE AVERAGE LIFE OF THE BILLS (ALB)

Capital	Simple Interest at 6% p.a.	Nominal Bills (V)
250,000	30,000	280,000
250,000	22,500	272,500
250,000	15,000	265,000
250,000	7,500	257,500
1,000,000	75,000	1,075,000

$$\text{Calculation of discount numbers } \frac{V \times t}{100} = N$$

Nominal Value of Bill	Tenor Days	Discount Numbers (N)
280,000	186	520,800
272,500	372	1,013,700
265,000	551	1,460,150
257,500	736	1,891,520
1,075,000		4,886,170

$$\text{ALB} = \frac{(N \times 100)}{(V \times 360)} = 1.263527$$

A3. CALCULATION OF THE MULTIPLIER

$$X = \frac{1}{\left(1 + \dfrac{P \times \text{ALC}}{100}\right) \times \left(1 - \dfrac{d \times \text{ALB}}{100}\right)}$$

Where X = multiplier
   P = nominal interest rate (6%)
   ALC = average life of the credit (1.25 years or (.5 + 1 + 1.5 + 2) /4)
   d = discount rate (8%)
   ALB = average life of the bills

$$X = \frac{1}{\left(1 + \dfrac{6 \times 1.25}{100}\right) \times \left(1 - \dfrac{1.263527}{100}\right)}$$

$$= \frac{1}{(1.075) \times (.89891784)}$$

$$= 1.0348359$$

Invoice price to importer: 1,034,835.90

Capital	Interest at 6%	Total
258,708.97	31,045.08	289,754.05
258,708.98	23,283.81	281,992.79
258,708.98	15,522.54	274,231,52
258,708.97	7,761.27	266,470.24
1,034,835.90	77,612.70	1,112,448.60

Internal rate of return: 4.47%
Discount to yield compounded semiannually: 8.94%
Discount to yield compounded annually: 9.14%

11 Case Study: The Peace Shield Offset

The Saudi Arabian Peace Shield is one of the largest offsets in recent history. The total contract is valued at about $1.3 billion; the offset is 35%, or roughly $350 million. The offset program instituted by the Boeing Company went into operation in 1985 and will last ten years. It includes both direct and indirect offsets, and has an export component, although its focus is import substitution. The Peace Shield program is of great interest not only because of its value and complexity but because of the change it seems to have brought about in the Saudi government's policy on countertrade.

Prior to the Peace Shield, Saudi Arabia had not done much countertrade; the only notable transaction was an oil barter deal, used to finance the purchase of aircraft. When the Peace Shield RFP was first issued, in fact, there was no mention of offset. Today, Saudi Arabia has a permanent Economic Offset Committee and is aggressively promoting nonmilitary countertrade as well as offset. The government's position is that industrial country exporters can no longer market their products in developing countries through licensing and training programs alone; there must be an investment of capital and management, and technology must be shared. The major objective of the Saudi offset/countertrade strategy is import substitution, which they plan to extend to all sectors of the economy. (This is understandable; Saudi Arabia, as a rich oil exporter with almost no manufacturing base, has had to import heavily for many years to modernize and meet domestic demand.) The Saudis see countertrade as part of their economic development program.

This case study describes the bidding process for the Peace Shield in terms of the offset program, addressing both Saudi Arabia's needs and the methods used by the bidders in their attempts to win the contract. Boeing's competitors for the contract were Litton Industries and Hughes Aircraft. In summary, the process was hectic. None of the bidders anticipated an offset requirement, although they knew that many military contracts included offsets. When they were informed of the requirement, they resorted to crisis management, and all three were severely criticized for their poor offset proposals by the Saudi government at one point in the bidding process. One of the major lessons to be learned from this case is that companies must take the foreign government's offset requirements very seriously; the Peace Shield bidders thought the offset was relatively unimportant, an attitude which caused them much grief. We hope that the detailed analysis given here will help other companies avoid mistakes in offset proposals and encourage them to plan offsets carefully.

THE PEACE SHIELD DEFENSE SYSTEM

Saudi Arabia's RFP for the Peace Shield Defense System was issued in 1982. The Peace Shield is a ground-to-AWACS (airborne warning and control system) electronic communication system, to be used in conjunction with the AWACS for surveillance aircraft and its C31 (Command, Control, Communications, and Intelligence). General Electric Corporation had already been designated as the sole source for the FPS-117 radar. The technical component of the Peace Shield consisted of five items related to the C31: equipment, software, system tests and evaluation, systems project management, and data. The value of the contract was originally set at close to $4 billion; however, the value had been cut to a little over $1 billion by the time the contract was awarded, due to a reduction in Saudi oil revenues over the 1982–1984 period.

The U.S. Air Force acted as the agent for the Peace Shield; they administered and evaluated the bids. The USAF's tasks were to make sure that the bidders met the minimum requirements of the specifications, and to work with the companies in bringing the bids up to standard prior to submission to Saudi Arabia. The companies bidding were Boeing, with subcontractors ITT (International Telephone and Telegraph), Westinghouse Corporation, CSC (Computer Sciences Corporation), and Frank E. Basil, Inc.; Hughes Aircraft, with subcontractor Rockwell; and Litton Industries, with subcontractors ATT (American Telephone and Telegraph) and Bechtel. Final bids were to be submitted in December 1984, thus allowing about three years for the companies to develop their Peace Shield proposals.

THE PEACE SHIELD OFFSET PROGRAM: SAUDI REQUIREMENTS AND THE ROLE OF LEHMAN BROTHERS

The Peace Shield offset requirement was not included in the original RFP put out by the Saudi government. The bidding companies were surprised when they learned of it; since countertrade had been rare in Saudi Arabia, no one was prepared for the announcement of an offset requirement. In retrospect, the possibility of offset should have been anticipated, since offsets had long been a common feature of military sales. The companies learned

of the offset in late 1983. A representative of the Saudi government met with
the bidding companies in Washington, DC in September to give the requirements orally, and written guidelines were issued in November. The companies
had about one year to prepare offset proposals.

Saudi Motivation for the Offset Requirement

According to the "General Guidelines for Peace Shield Investment Offset
Program" issued by Saudi Arabia, the Saudi government wished to "increase
the rate of diversification of the economy by stimulating the establishment
of private commercial activities which are not directly related to petroleum."
The principal objectives specified were:

(1) to diversify national income by broadening the Kingdom's economic base;

(2) to provide increased opportunities for Saudi Arabian managerial and technical personnel in the private sector to develop their expertise and gain access
to sources of technology; and

(3) to provide an opportunity for middle income Saudi Arabian investors to
share more fully in the Kingdom's economic prosperity.

These objectives were to be achieved through the establishment of joint ventures in high-technology areas, with 50% Saudi ownership.

In simpler terms, Saudi Arabia, like any other country dependent on a
single product for most of its export earnings, wanted industrialization in
areas not related to its principal export. The Saudis wanted the joint ventures
to be industries that had good export growth potential. Although in practice
the export markets evaluated were the neighboring Arab countries (since it
would take some time for product quality to reach a level acceptable in developed countries), the Saudis expressed a particular interest in buyback
arrangements with American joint venture partners; this would provide market entry into the United States at a fairly early stage. Import substitution
in Saudi Arabia was also a factor.

The desire for the development of a high-technology sector is common
to all developing countries. In the case of Saudi Arabia, the expressed desire
that joint ventures should also be "capital and/or energy intensive," rather
than labor intensive, reflects both Arab culture and the particular situation
in Saudi Arabia. The new jobs desired were management level positions,
not the type of factory jobs against which there is a cultural bias. Additionally,
Saudi Arabia did not want projects which might require bringing in even
more guest workers, as one of their goals is to eliminate guest workers insofar
as is possible.

The statements concerning opportunities and income diversification refer
to the fact that, although Saudi's per capita income is statistically very high,
most of the wealth is concentrated in the royal family; the government wished

to spread some of this wealth to the middle class through business opportunities. American business partners were preferred because it was felt that Americans would provide the best business training.

Other possible motivations included the economic need for countertrade in view of diminishing oil revenues and follow-the-leader behavior in imitation of other countries' offset/countertrade requirements.

Saudi Organization for the Offset: The Role of Lehman Brothers

The Saudi Offset Committee was chaired by the Ministry of Defense and Aviation (as represented by the Royal Saudi Air Force), with members selected from the Ministries of Finance and National Economy, Planning, Commerce, Industry, and Electricity. In practice, the "working offset committee" turned out to be Lehman Brothers, the international investment firm which the Saudis selected as the "advisory staff" for the offset committee. Lehman's assistance to the committee was to consist of further refinement of the offset guidelines; stimulation of foreign and Saudi investment; evaluation of the offset program proposals; and monitoring of the establishment and implementation of the joint ventures. In assisting in the formulation of the guidelines, Lehman developed, changed, and refined some parts; they also made a number of changes after the guidelines had gone out. A list of prospective products suitable for the joint ventures was prepared by Lehman in cooperation with the Saudi offset committee; this list was amended from time to time. Lehman's responsibilities to the bidding companies were to write the offset requirements and assist the bidders in formulating programs consistent with the requirements.

Offset Requirements

The selected contractor(s) were to enter into an agreement with the Saudi government to invest and participate in joint venture industries that would involve high-tech related processes and/or products. The objective investment by the U.S. contractor was set at 35% of the Peace Shield LOA (Letter of Agreement) cost of technically related products and services required for execution of the LOA (the C31 items), resulting in a 65% offset. Although a 50% equity was preferred, the Saudis stated in their Guidelines that they were willing to accept a different ownership structure in special cases, with the limitation that the American contractor and associated investors maintain an ownership of at least 40% in the joint venture during the first five years after its formation, and at least 30% for the following five years. Equal ownership was preferred because it was felt that this would provide an opportunity for a large number of Saudi investors to profit from new commercial ventures, and would assure long-term foreign commitment to the success of the ventures.

There were four general requirements for the joint ventures. First, all ventures were to stress high-tech transfer and the continuous updating of the transfer in order to maintain the ventures' competitiveness. Second, each venture had to have a detailed plan for both domestic and international markets, with buyback being of special interest. Third, the contract had to bring in an outside company as a partner for ventures in which the contractor had no prior operating experience. Finally, employment and training of Saudi technical and managerial personnel were to be considered a priority in each joint venture. The overall offset program had to be of sufficient size to contribute significantly to the growth and diversification of the Saudi economy.

Offset Proposal Content

Each company's proposal was to include a reaffirmation of the company's intent to fulfill the requirements of its offset program, information about the joint ventures, and a summary of the entire offset program, with specific reference to how it would meet the guidelines. A draft MOA (Memorandum of Agreement) was to be submitted with each proposal. The information to be provided about the joint ventures consisted of:

1. Detailed description of the proposed joint venture, including intended site location.
2. Review of markets for the output of the joint venture (current market size, expected growth rate, and price projections).
3. Review of all essential technical aspects.
4. Preliminary management and employee plan (staffing levels, skill requirements, training programs, etc.)
5. Financial plan, including preliminary capitalization, capital expenditures, working capital needs, projected cash flow, and return on investment analyses.
6. Identification of anticipated sources of equity and debt capital.
7. Detailed summary of the anticipated investment incentives, approvals, marketing arrangements, and the like, required from or obtained with the government.
8. Summary of the credit anticipated toward that contractor's offset program obligation as a result of the particular joint venture.

Offset Proposal Time Schedule

A preliminary review of the general content of the offset programs was held about three months after the guidelines were issued. After six months, the written preliminary proposals were submitted, and there was a meeting in Riyadh four weeks later between the companies and the Saudi Offset Committee (July 1984). Final proposals were submitted along with the sealed bids in December 1984. The decision was scheduled for announcement in February 1985, though it actually did not occur until March of that year.

Offset Proposal Evaluation

According to the Guidelines, evaluation of the proposals was based in particular on (1) the level of commitment of the contractor to the offset program, as judged by the overall quality of the program; (2) the profitability prospects of each joint venture; (3) the degree of sophistication and quality of the technology proposed; and (4) the extent of the transfer of skills and technology to be achieved through the proposed joint venture. In general, the bidding companies were expected to adhere to both the spirit and the provisions of the guidelines in their proposals.

PREPARATION OF OFFSET PROGRAMS
BY THE BIDDING COMPANIES

All three companies made the same mistake in their offset proposals—they considered the offset of minor importance relative to their Peace Shield bids, and did not do much work on it until chastised by the Saudi Offset Committee. The offset proposals, such as they were, were submitted in June 1984, and in July, representatives of the three firms went to meet with the Saudi committee in Riyadh.

Things went very badly. The Saudi committee was exasperated with all of the offset proposals, complaining that they were not relevant, not well thought out, and inadequately detailed; in the words of one participant, "everybody got chewed out." The Saudis made it clear that the offset proposals would have to improve drastically, and that furthermore, these proposals would carry great weight in the decision to award the contract. This brought on an attack of crisis management in the three companies; frantic activity on the offset proposals began. At Litton, for example, a task force was hastily assembled and several consulting teams were brought in. This group began to collect and analyze data on various new joint venture projects, as well as searching for and evaluating new joint venture partners.

The final bids and proposals were submitted in December 1984. Litton's offset proposal contained 28 joint ventures, divided into four general areas: basic electronics industry, including manufacturing plants for silicon wafers and microelectronic circuits, as well as a polycrystalline silicon plant and a metallurgical and ferrosilicon plant; defense and aviation industry, including an avionics overhaul facility; industrial manufacturing, which included plants for telecommunications and float glass; and agricultural genetics, including a pure line chicken industry and a seed-breeding production industry. Boeing's proposal contained four projects: aircraft maintenance, repair, and support; advanced electronics engineering, manufacturing, and repair; computer services; and digital telecommunications design, manufacture, installation, and service. The proposal submitted by Hughes covered two projects, aircraft maintenance and global communications networks.

Litton's Peace Shield bid was the most expensive; originally priced in excess of $3 billion, it was regarded as a "Cadillac" and the company was advised early on to cut the price drastically. The price had been adjusted to $1.4 billion by the time the final bid was made. The Hughes bid was the next most expensive at $1.3 billion, while Boeing's was the least expensive at $1.2 billion. Boeing was awarded the Peace Shield contract in March 1985.

ANALYSIS

Why did Boeing win the contract, and what could Hughes and Litton have done to strengthen their proposals? In some respects, much could have been done by Hughes and Litton to improve their chances; in others, it seems that no matter how hard they had tried, Boeing would have won the contract, anyway.

Company commitment is one area where there might have been improvement. Boeing's strength in the offset proposal was total company commitment, as opposed to Litton's approach of giving all responsibility for the offset to a single division (Data Systems) and assigning all of the joint ventures to outside companies. However, it must be said in Litton's defense that it could hardly have spread the offset over its 90 divisions, many of which had nothing to do with the products being considered for the offset program. Even if Litton had been able to somehow group and mobilize the applicable divisions on short notice, there would have been formidable management problems. This scenario also does not account for the failure of Hughes which, like Boeing, had a total company approach.

Thus the content of the proposals must be examined. Litton's offset proposal was generally considered to be the strongest, most comprehensive, and the one that adhered most closely to the Saudi guidelines; in its final form it was an excellent program. Hughes' program was comparatively weak, as the concentration on telecommunications projects did not sufficiently address Saudi Arabia's offset objectives. Boeing was in the middle as far as program content went. Hughes could certainly have improved; but what of Boeing, the winner?

Boeing started out with two advantages over its competitors: a good track record in Saudi Arabia with the AWACS system, and the friendship of the president of Boeing with the Saudi king. A third advantage, gained in mid-1984, was Boeing's acceptance of oil as payment for ten 747 aircraft sold to Saudi Arabia; this demonstration of willingness to countertrade may have influenced the Saudis in Boeing's favor.

Taking these preexisting advantages into account, it seems that the final determination of the winning bid depended on price. The recommendation of the U.S. Air Force carried considerable weight, of course, but as far as can be determined the USAF felt that the Peace Shield equipment and software were of roughly the same quality for each of the three bidders; thus, price emerged as the most important factor. Any reasonably good offset program would have been acceptable when combined with the lowest price for the Peace Shield. Interestingly, this negates the Saudi position that the quality of the offset proposal would carry great weight in their decision, as it can be argued that Litton had the best proposal. In conclusion, therefore, Boeing's price was the clincher in its winning combination: a good reputation, personal contacts, company commitment, a good offset proposal, and the low bid.

What lessons can be learned from the Peace Shield experience? In hindsight it is easy to say that Boeing started out with advantages and ended by underselling its competitors. It is also easy to become cynical and say that having the best product and the best offset proposal cannot ensure success against such odds. However, in viewing the entire situation, two important points emerge: first, all of the bidders should have anticipated that some degree of offset would be required, since offset is common in military trade; second, they should have taken the offset program very seriously from the moment the requirement was announced. As it stands, none of the three bidders comes out looking very good from a management perspective, regardless of which one won the contract.

Finally, there are some unanswered questions about the Saudi side of the deal. In the first place, it is not common practice for governments to let independent intermediaries such as Lehman handle the offset programs. In the second place, Saudi Arabia could have hired an American economic development company for the industrial diversification program rather than trying to accomplish it through an offset; such a company would have done a better job for less money. Using this approach, the Saudis could have probably gotten a considerably lower price on the Peace Shield. In their guidelines, the Saudis stated that "each contractor should view its offset program as a means of earning additional profits from its participation in the PSP program, not as an additional cost to the contractor, nor as an incremental cost of the PSP." This is wishful thinking.

In general, there seems to have been a lack of knowledge concerning countertrade and offset on the part of Saudi Arabia. Lack of experience and the resulting lack of confidence in negotiating an offset may have led the Saudi committee to depend as heavily as it did on Lehman. As for the requirement for joint ventures, the Saudis seemed to believe that top American high-tech companies would automatically be experts in foreign industrial development; this is certainly not the case among military contractors, though it may be true for some of the older transnational corporations.

Both sides—the Saudi Offset Committee and Lehman Brothers, and the bidders Boeing, Litton and Hughes—seem to have stumbled through the offset proposal procedure, and in some respects, it is surprising that the contract ever materialized at all. Lack of communication, lack of preparation, and poor planning and crisis management characterize the experience.

BOEING'S PEACE SHIELD OFFSET ACTIVITIES

To organize the offset program, Boeing has set up a holding company, Boeing Industrial Technology Group (BITG) with its partners, ITT, Westinghouse, and Basil. (The Computer Sciences Corporation, originally a partner in BITG, is still involved in the project on its own.) Boeing's investment in the project will be $43 million. The offset commitment made by the Saudis is $300 million, according to the schedule of 35% of the technical component of the Peace Shield project. Fifty percent of the $300 million will be borrowed from the SIDF (Saudi Industrial Development Fund) and 25% from Saudi commercial banks. Total employment in the BITG project is expected to reach 5000 over the ten-year life of the program, with a staff of 30 persons in the BITG itself.

Offset Credits

According to the offset guidelines, Boeing will earn offset credits in the following four ways:

1. Equity contributions by the contractor (Boeing), which can include both cash and nonmonetary contributions.
2. Equity contributions by other parties (U.S., foreign, or Saudi Arabian).
3. Medium and long-term debt financing other than that provided by the Government, provided that the maturity of this debt approximates the anticipated implementation period of the offset program and that its average life is no less than three years. (Such debt may be refunded, provided the initial redemption schedule is not accelerated.)
4. Reinvested joint venture earnings. These may include the expansion of existing joint ventures in Saudi Arabia, or the creation of new ones. Equity investment is preferred, however.

The following are the first seven BITG projects to be completed; the list includes partner companies and values:

Aircraft modification center (Boeing, $180 million)
Advanced electronics center (Westinghouse, $263 million)
Aircraft accessories center (Dowty Group, $45 million)
Digital telecommunications center (ITT, $110 million)
Computer systems center (Boeing, $20 million)

Advanced biotechnology joint venture (Pioneer Overseas Group, $30 million)

Medical products joint venture (partner undetermined as of late 1986; $20 million)

Other projects scheduled (not necessarily BITG projects) are:

Jet propulsion center (General Electric, $168 million)

Helicopter production (Boeing, $311 million)

Applied technology center (Boeing, $45 million)

Power engineering center (Westinghouse, $450 million)

Large diameter steel pipes (Kaiser Steel, $20 million)

References

Asaro, Jerry. formerly of Litton Industries: interviews, 1984–1985.

"Boeing Peace Shield Report Clarified," *Countertrade Outlook*, Vol. 4, No. 45, November 24, 1986.

"Boeing Publicizes Its Saudi Peace Shield Offset Program," *Countertrade Outlook*, Vol. 3, No. 34, September 9, 1985.

Government of Saudi Arabia, Saudi Offset Committee. General Guidelines for the Peace Shield Offset Program, and *Peace Shield Investment Offset Program Supplement*, 1983.

"Saudi Official Cites Legitimacy of CT for National Development" and "Update on Peace Shield Offsets Given," *Countertrade Outlook*, Vol. 4, No. 44, November 17, 1986.

"Saudi Official Suggests General Offset Policy Is Serious Possibility" and "Report Given on Peace Shield Offset," *Countertrade Outlook*, Vol. 4, No. 13, March 31, 1986.

The authors worked as consultants for Litton Industries during the preparation of their Peace Shield offset proposal.

This part provides a representative sample of international countertrade practices. A mix of eleven countries was selected in order to demonstrate how countertrade practices vary in countries that are in different stages of economic development: five developing countries (Argentina, Brazil, Colombia, Egypt, and Malaysia), three industrial countries (Australia, Canada, and Greece), two socialist countries (China and the Soviet Union), and one OPEC country (Algeria). Companies can use this information not only to gain a general understanding of current countertrade practices, but to plan countertrade transactions with countries of interest.

Each country analysis includes information on countertrade regulations and practices, international trade patterns, and recent countertrade transactions. Countertrade regulations are described as presented by the governments, with any additional comments which might help the prospective countertrader. Lists of products each country has offered in countertrade are provided, along with names and addresses of state trading entities where available. Short descriptions of import and export trade controls are also provided. Such controls may affect a company's countertrade plans; for example, the company may wish to buy a counterpurchase product whose export is prohibited, sell a product whose import is prohibited, or dispose of counterpurchase products in a prohibited third country market (e.g., Israel and the Republic of South Africa).

The analyses of trade provide a good deal of insight into why these particular countries want countertrade (most of them have either poor export diversification, trade deficits, or both) and what products they would be most interested in buying and selling through countertrade. Areas covered in trade analysis include: aggregate import and export totals, import and export growth patterns, trade surpluses and deficits; top import and export products, and major trading partners by world area and country. Several sample countertrade transactions are listed for each country, in a standard format covering partner country/company, import items, export items, values of transaction, year, duration, type of transaction, and any necessary explanatory comments. The transactions cover nearly all types of countertrade. A total of 86 transactions is listed for the eleven countries.

Trade data were obtained from publications of the United Nations and the International Monetary Fund; all estimates were prepared by the International Market Information System. Trade controls information came from the U.S. Department of Commerce and the IMF. Information on countertrade regulations, practices and transactions was obtained from various sources, including USDOC, *Countertrade Outlook, Countertrade and Barter Quarterly, Journal of Commerce,* and *Financial Times.* Some trade or other data on particular countries may be missing due to unavailability of information.

The People's Republic of China is referred to as China. The abbreviation GDR is used for the German Democratic Republic (East Germany), while the name Germany represents the Federal Republic of Germany (West Germany), except in cases where the two names might be confused. The acronym LAIA is used for the Latin American Integration Association, rather than ALADI (Association Latino-Américaine d'Integration). The statistical areas discussed are Africa, the Americas (North, Central, and South America; North America includes Mexico), LAIA, CACM (Central American Common Market), the Caribbean, Asia, Europe, the EEC, EFTA, Eastern Europe, and Oceania. There are also references to the centrally planned economies.

All values are given in U.S. dollars unless otherwise specified. Values shown on the tables are in thousands of U.S. dollars. Import values are given c.i.f., unless flagged as f.o.b.; all export values are f.o.b.

Note that in the "products available for countertrade" lists, the statement "traditional exports are not available" usually does not apply to items traded under bilateral agreements.

12 Algeria

COUNTERTRADE

Countertrade Policy

Algeria does not have a formal countertrade law. However, countertrade is considered to be mandatory since all Algerian state enterprises now require counterpurchase for imports exceeding a "normal" value. Counterpurchase requirements also depend on the amount of foreign exchange allocated to each state enterprise. Algeria began to make countertrade demands in 1984 in an attempt to balance trade with its major suppliers, particularly France, Germany, Italy, Belgium and Spain. Some of these suppliers were required to accept large petroleum counterdeliveries. In the same year, the government announced that all bidders must include countertrade proposals in their responses to tender invitations, terming countertrade "an essential element" in the evaluation of their offers. This development indicates that countertrade is becoming institutionalized.

Aside from the need to balance trade, Algeria wants to use countertrade to ensure steady exports of petroleum at OPEC prices, conserve foreign exchange and promote the export of manufactured goods, hydrocarbons and agricultural products. Many of these products have proven hard to export because they are either noncompetitive as to quality or are in low demand on the world market.

The product most frequently countertraded by Algeria is petroleum. Oil barter is a little more complicated than usual in Algeria, however, since the state oil company SONATRACH requires that the formal offer to purchase the crude oil must come from the refinery that will actually process the oil. The normal oil industry arrangement, the nomination of a refinery by a broker, is unacceptable. The reason given for this requirement is to prevent the sale of Algerian oil to Israel, with whom all trade is prohibited. Observers believe that an additional motivation is to prevent Algerian oil from being sold in markets where Algeria already has exclusive barter arrangements.

In the counterpurchase of non-oil Algerian products, the procedure is for the foreign firm to first reach agreement on the terms of the sale to Algeria, then arrange the purchase of the Algerian products in a separate contract, to the extent agreed upon in the sales contract. Many state enterprises request 100% counterpurchase, though this can often be negotiated down to cover counterpurchase only for the hardware component of the import if the seller will agree to provide licenses and manufacturing know-how. One of the earliest such transactions was a buyback arrangement with the GDR, in which the East Germans built a factory to produce taps, screws, and bolts, and bought back a portion of the resultant products. All countertrade proposals are subject to approval by the Algerian Comite des Marches (Monetary Committee). Recent countertrade deals involved Germany, France, Brazil, Italy, and Japan. The value of Algerian countertrade is estimated to be at least $200 million per year.

Algeria has bilateral trade agreements with Albania, Brazil, China, Greece, Guinea, Guinea-Bissau, Morocco, Tunisia, the USSR and other CMEA countries, and Yugoslavia.

Products Available for Countertrade

The major products are crude petroleum (offered at non-negotiable OPEC prices) and gas. The Ministry of Commerce has prepared a list of 100 other products targeted for counterpurchase, which includes fish, olives, dates, wine, olive oil, iron ore, baryte, bentonite, zinc, asphalt, coke, petroleum derivatives, hydrocarbons, phosphates, mercury, paints, leather and artificial leather, textiles, cement bags, iron forgings, semifinished metal products, bolts, screws, taps, meters, lamps, electrical appliances, welding electrodes, sanitary ware, water valves, matchboxes and plastic consumer goods. The list is revised periodically. The most recent list includes: bulk and bottled wine; calcined phosphates; baryta, bentonite, mercury and various clays; cork boards; natural cork bottle stoppers; decorative cork sheets, blocks and floor tiles; rubberized cork; agglomerated cork bottle stoppers and discs; textiles; industrial fabrics and wool yarn; screws; washers; anchor bolts; mixing and single-line taps (faucets) for lavatory fixtures; pipe connectors; pipe traps; toilet flushing mechanisms; rail cars; wheelbarrows; garden rakes; and ceramic bathroom fixtures such as toilets, washbasins, bathtubs, bidets and showers.

In the following list some of the state enterprises responsible for handling these products are listed. Addresses and telexes are given where available.

Petroleum, petroleum products: SONATRACH (Société Nationale pour la Recherche, la Production, le Transport, la Transformation et la Commercialization des Hydrocarbures.)

Wine: ONCV, 122 Quai du Sud, Algiers; telex 52 072 or 52 964

Iron, phosphates: FERPHOS (Enterprise Nationale du Fer et Phosphates), Avenue des Jardins, B.P. 122, Tebessa; telex 81 765

Baryta, baryte, bentonite, clays, mercury: ENOF (Enterprise Nationale des Produits Miniers Non Ferreux), 31 Rue Hattab Mohammed, El-Harrach; telex 54 905

Zinc: SNS Service Export

Forgings, coke, asphalt: Enterprise Nationale de Siderurgie

Minerals: SONAREM

Bolts, screws, taps, meters, pipe connectors, pipe traps, toilet flushing mechanisms: En. B.C.R., Rue des Fréres, Meslem/Sétif; telex 86 966

Metal products: SN Metals

Cork products: ENL, Route des Maquissards, Jijel; telex 84 021 or 84 065

Textiles and yarn: Distritex, 4/6 Rue Patrice Lumumba, B.P. 478, Algiers; telex 59 929

Rail cars: Ferrovial, Route d'El-Hadjar, B.P. 63, Annaba; telex Metalik 81 814 or 81 998

Wheelbarrows: ENADQ, 5 Rue Amar Semaous, Hussein-Dey, Algiers; telex 53 847

Garden rakes: PNA, 2 Route Tenira, Sidi. Bel. Abbes.; telex 22 609

Electric appliances: EDIMEL

Welding electrodes: Enterprise Nationale de Transformation des Produits Longs

Sanitary wares: PROMETAL

Ceramic bathroom fixtures: Distrimac, Route de l'Arbas, El-Harrach; telex 54 910 or 54 060

Water valves: ENPMH

Key government and quasi-government organizations are the Institut Nationale Algerien du Commerce Exterieur (COMEX) and the Conseil Nationale du Commerce Exterieur (CNCE, Council for Foreign Trade). Both are located at Palais des Expositions, Pins Maritimes, Algiers. There are no foreign banks, foreign law firms, or foreign trading companies in Algeria.

TRADE CONTROLS

Algeria has a socialist state-trading economy. As of 1978, the government has had a monopoly over foreign trade; imports and exports may be handled only by state enterprises. (Waivers may be granted for a transitional period on a case-by-case basis.) The agency responsible for coordinating export trade under the Ministry of Commerce is the CNCE. Some exports are prohibited, notably used equipment and machinery, livestock, firearms, ammunition, explosives and certain radio equipment. All exports require licensing, except those of state enterprises having a monopoly right to export. Export proceeds must be repatriated immediately after collection.

All imports are permitted, in principle (there are some exceptions), in accordance with the annual import programs derived from five-year economic plans. Imports are implemented through five types of global import authorizations granted to state enterprises. Advance payment for imports may not exceed 15% of the import value, unless a waiver has been granted by the Ministry of Finance or the Central Bank. Trade with Israel and the Republic of South Africa is prohibited.

INTERNATIONAL TRADE

Imports

Algerian trade is fairly well balanced on an aggregate total basis, with imports running a little below exports and showing the same general downward trend. Imports have been $10.2–$10.7 billion per year since 1982 and have declined by an average 2.4% per year. There is usually a trade surplus of $1–$2 billion. Major imports are industrial and transport equipment, basic manufacturers, and food. The top food imports are wheat, milk, coffee and sugar, which together account for about half of total imports of food. In the services category, construction projects are the major import.

Most Algerian imports, 54.9%, come from the EEC, with an additional 11.0% originating in Asia and 9.8% in North America; other areas account for less than 5% each of imports. (Although Algeria has bilateral trade agreements with the USSR and other CMEA countries, only 4.5% of imports originate from this area.) Algeria's major import trading partner is France, which has a 23.6% share of the import total. Other important suppliers are Germany, 11.3% share; Italy, 8.2%; Spain, 7.0%; the United States, 6.0%; and Japan, 6.0%.

Exports

Algeria desperately needs to diversify exports. Over 90% of exports are in the mineral fuels product group; the Algerian export industry in other areas is virtually nonexistent. Crude petroleum accounts for about 50% of exports,

Import Total, Algeria (thousands)

	Value	Growth (%)
1980	10,543,955	—
1981	11,328,537	7.4
1982	10,738,150	−5.2
1983	10,395,142	−3.1
1984	10,285,548	−1.0
1985	10,244,406 (est.)	−0.4

Export Total and Petroleum Exports, Algeria (thousands)

	All Exports	Growth (%)	Exports, Crude Petroleum	Export Total (%)
1980	15,623,587	——	12,870,450	82.3
1981	13,296,163	−17.5	9,992,384	75.1
1982	11,475,900	−13.6	5,861,668	51.0
1983	11,158,364	−2.7	5,393,181	48.3
1984	12,795,280	14.6	6,377,172	49.8
1985	10,000,000 (est.)	−21.8	5,000,000 (est.)	50.0

refined petroleum products for 22%, and gas for 20%. Crude petroleum exports have been erratic over the past few years, at $5.8 billion in 1982, $5.3 billion in 1983, $6.3 billion in 1984, and about $5.0 billion in 1985. Exports of gas have also been uneven, varying from $2.5 billion to $1.7 billion per year between 1982 and 1985. Sales of petroleum products, however, have been going steadily downward, dropping by an average 14.7% per year; they were valued at $3.6 billion in 1982 and had dropped to $2.2 billion by 1985.

Some diversification has been achieved within the mineral fuels products group, with petroleum products and gas becoming more important relative to crude petroleum. Crude petroleum accounted for 82.3% of Algerian exports in 1980 and for much less, 50.0%, in 1985. Algeria is the 11th ranked world supplier of crude petroleum, with a 3.3% market share, and is the 13th ranked supplier of petroleum products with a 3.1% share. Within OPEC, Algeria is the fourth largest petroleum exporter.

Outside the mineral fuels group, some of Algeria's important export products are wine, which accounts for 0.3% of exports, or about $30 million per year; iron ore, about $20 million per year; and olive oil and zinc, each under $250,000 per year.

Over half of Algerian exports, 59.8% of the total, go to the EEC. North America is also an important market area, accounting for 23.7% of exports. Asia is the destination of 4.5% of exports. Exports to the CMEA countries account for only 0.3% of the total, indicating a trade deficit with them since they supply over 4% of Algerian imports. France is Algeria's major export partner, taking 34.0% of all Algerian exports, followed by the United States, 22.7%; the Netherlands, 9.6%; and Italy, 8.7%.

RECENT COUNTERTRADE TRANSACTIONS, ALGERIA

Partner Country:	France (Manufacture Francaise des Pneumatiques Michelin)
Import:	Truck tires
Export:	50% of payment in oil (about 1 million bbl.), other 50% to be paid in cash

Value: $28–$30 million (value of oil)
Year: 1985
Duration: Unspecified
Type: Oil barter

Partner country: Japan (Komatsu Ltd., with Algeria's SONATRACH
                            and SONACOME)
Import: Approximately 400 units of construction machinery—
                            72 bulldozers, 150 motor graders, dump trucks, etc.
Export: 1.4 million bbl crude oil
Value: Approximately $42 million
Year: 1985
Duration: Unspecified
Type: Oil barter

Partner country: Yugoslavia
Import: Tractors
Export: Zinc and phosphate rock
Value: Unspecified
Year: 1985
Duration: Unspecified
Type: Reciprocal trade

13 Argentina

COUNTERTRADE

Countertrade Policy

Argentina's countertrade regulations are listed in Decree 176/85, implemented in 1985. The decree establishes that Argentine goods and services can be traded for foreign goods and services, using various countertrade mechanisms. The decree does not make countertrade mandatory; however, the government has let it be known that bids containing countertrade proposals have a much greater chance of success than those that do not. The major provisions of the regulations are:

1. Anticipatory imports (seller buys Argentine products before contracting for exports) are specifically authorized.

2. Terms of financing for the Argentine exports must be similar to those of the imported goods. If the import traditionally has more favorable financing terms in international trade than the export, financing terms for the export must be adjusted to allow periodic amortizations to be written off against exports "for amounts equivalent to those of each quota until liquidation of the liability." Similarly, adjustments must be made for imports if it is the export product which has superior financing terms.

3. Imports taken in countertrade are exempt from the bank deposit requirement (prior bank deposit before issuance of import permit).

4. The authority responsible for countertrade is the Secretary of Foreign Trade, who regulates both private and bilateral transactions.

5. Countertrade transactions valued at less than U.S. $20 million require approval by only one agency (presumably the Secretary of Foreign Trade). Transactions of higher value must be reviewed by the National Council for Economic, Monetary, Commercial, and International Financial Matters.

6. Countertrade transactions with fellow LAIA members will be handled through the LAIA clearing account system. In the event that the LAIA system is not used, the Central Bank will specify an alternative settlement procedure.

7. Argentine exporters entering a countertrade transaction are not required to repatriate their proceeds, on the understanding that their earnings will be used to pay for imports.

Countertrade proposals must be filed with the Direccion Nacional de Promocion Comercial (National Export Promotion Board). The ideal proposal, according to Argentine countertrade legislation, would have the following elements: (1) the products to be exported will go to new markets or to markets where Argentina has lost share; (2) the products will be nontraditional exports; (3) international markets for these products have been difficult to penetrate; (4) the exports will be incremental sales to a preexisting market; (5) the countertrade operation will have a positive influence on a project of national interest. Some of these specifications seem contradictory—for example, item 1 specifies a new market, while item 4 specifies a preexisting market— but with a wide enough range of products and a sufficient time period, all of the objectives could conceivably be achieved within one large-scale countertrade operation. Buyback arrangements, turnkey projects, franchising, and subcontracting—all with payment in goods—are also projects which would be welcomed.

Some Argentine provinces have been making their own countertrade deals, exchanging local products for goods and services needed to carry out their particular economic development plans. The Province of Mendoza, for example, has conducted countertrade with the Soviet Union to get trolleys and with the GDR to get a turnkey plant for vegetable processing, in both cases giving wine as payment.

Argentina has countertraded with Eastern European countries since 1960, especially the Soviet Union and Czechoslovakia; lucrative supplier contracts have been awarded to these two countries without competition as a result of the countertrade activity. Agreements for the building of cargo ships are in force with Poland and Cuba. Argentina has bilateral agreements with LAIA (notably a large-scale compensation program with Mexico), the Dominican Republic, Peru, Bulgaria, Czechoslovakia, Hungary, Poland, the Soviet Union, and China. There is also a reciprocal credit agreement with Cuba. As of 1985, Argentina may pay all foreign oil companies for their production in crude oil, under Decree 1443/85 (the "hydrocarbons law").

Products Available for Countertrade

The products most frequently countertraded under bilateral trading agreements are wheat, corn, beef, soybeans, fruit juices, and wool. Since these products are hard currency earners, they may not be offered as counterpurchase items to private companies. Some of the nontraditional exports Argentina is interested in promoting through countertrade are fish, wine, chemicals (especially petrochemicals), textiles, iron and steel products, motor vehicles, and printing.

Key government organizations are the Ministry of Commerce, the Ministry of Finance, and the Banco de la Nacion Argentina.

TRADE CONTROLS

The import control system defines three commodity lists:

List 1. Prohibited imports which are luxury goods and items already produced domestically; they may not be imported without special authorization. They may not be imported through countertrade, except under government-to-government trade accords.

List 2. Various products, primarily capital goods, certain chemical products, and plastics. Special authorization is required for the import of these products.

List 3. Raw materials and feedstocks for the pharmaceutical industry, and some types of medical equipment. The approval of the Ministry of Public Health and Social Action is required for the import of these products.

A bank deposit is required prior to the issuance of an import license, except for countertrade items.

INTERNATIONAL TRADE

Imports

Argentine imports were booming in 1980, going up by 54.7% to $10.5 billion from $6.6 billion in 1979. Financing problems beset Argentina soon afterward, however; imports dropped by an average 23.1% annually from 1981 through 1983, falling to $4.50 billion in the final year. Imports began to pick up again in 1984, rising by 1.7% to $4.58 billion, and increased by 3.0% to $4.7 billion in 1985. This is a far cry from the spectacular 1980 growth, but it is at least an indication of general economic recovery. Also, though imports look rather dismal, it should be noted that the low import values give Argentina an impressive trade surplus: $932.5 million in 1982, $3.3 billion in 1983, $3.5 billion in 1984, and $3.7 billion in 1985. (Note: one third to one half of this surplus results from trade with the USSR.) Exports in 1984 and 1985 were nearly twice the value of imports.

Major import items are nonelectric machinery, gas, organic chemicals, telecommunications equipment, motor vehicles, electric machinery, switchgear, chemical plastic materials and crude petroleum, in order by annual import value. Imports that may be conditional upon counterpurchase of Argentine products include petroleum, petroleum-related equipment, coal, tur-

Import Total, Argentina (thousands)

	Value	Growth (%)
1979	6,692,396	——
1980	10,539,232	57.4
1981	9,430,213	− 10.5
1982	5,336,893	− 43.4
1983	4,504,200	− 15.6
1984	4,584,700	1.7
1985	4,722,241 (est.)	3.0

bines, transport equipment, aircraft, machine tools, radar systems, fertilizers, paper mills, engineering services and pharmaceuticals.

Argentina's major import trading partners by area and trade bloc are LAIA, 28.8% share of the Argentine market; North America, 23.1% share; and the EEC, 22.2% share. About 13% of imports come from Asia, 5.2% from EFTA and 1.5% from CMEA countries. Major trading partners by country are the United States, which supplies 22.1% of Argentine imports; Brazil, 12.9%; Germany, 9.0%; Japan, 8.0%, and Bolivia, 7.4%.

Exports

Argentine exports have historically been much more stable than imports, though they seldom show high growth. The only time exports have declined in recent years was in 1982, when value dropped by 16.6% from $9.1 billion to $7.6 billion. Exports have increased slightly each year since then, rising to $7.8 billion in 1983, $8.1 billion in 1984 and $8.4 billion in 1985. Annual growth rates range from 0.4% to 3.4%.

About 65% of Argentine exports are food products and crude animal products such as leather and wool. The major exports are wheat, 14.0% of the export total; corn, 10.0%; animal feed, 8.0%; cereal grains, 7.5%; and soft fixed vegetable oils, mostly sunflower seed and soybean oils, 5.0%. Wheat sales got a big boost in 1979, when the United States embargoed exports of wheat to the USSR; Argentina was able to get some of the U.S. market share, and has since established itself as one of the USSR's leading suppliers of wheat. Other important food and animal product exports are oilseeds (mostly soybeans and peanuts), leather, sugar, wool and canned meat.

Argentina is a major world supplier of several food products. It is the second ranked supplier of miscellaneous cereal grains (after the United States), with a 26.1% world market share; fourth ranked supplier of canned meat, with a 7.8% share; and sixth ranked supplier of animal feed and corn, with shares of 5.0% and 3.1%, respectively. In nonfood areas, Argentina is the world's fourth largest supplier of leather, with a 6.5% market share.

Argentina's major export markets by area and trade bloc are the Americas, 35.0% of exports (19.9% to LAIA markets, 14.0% to North America); the

Export Total, Argentina (thousands)

	Value	Growth (%)
1979	7,807,751	——
1980	8,021,402	2.7
1981	9,143,034	13.9
1982	7,624,936	− 16.6
1983	7,836,100	2.7
1984	8,107,400	3.4
1985	8,431,696 (est.)	0.4

CMEA countries, 21.9% of exports; the EEC, 21.3%; and Asia, 12.1%. The USSR, the most important trading partner country, is the destination of 20.8% of Argentine exports. Other major trading partners are the United States, which takes 13.4% of exports; the Netherlands, 7.9%; Brazil, 7.4%; and Germany, 4.4%.

RECENT COUNTERTRADE TRANSACTIONS, ARGENTINA

Partner country:	China (China North Industries Corp.)
Import:	Missile fuels, laser range finders for tanks
Export:	Speciality steel, copper, tin
Value:	Unspecified
Year:	1984–1985
Duration:	Unspecified
Type:	Reciprocal trade

Partner country:	China
Import:	Equipment, know-how for nonferrous mining industry; also chemicals and petroleum products
Export:	Equipment, know-how for nuclear power industry; also grain, beef, steel
Value:	Unspecified
Year:	1986
Duration:	Unspecified
Type:	Bilateral trade agreement
Comment:	This agreement has the special purpose of cooperation in development projects

Partner country:	Peru
Import:	Iron ore, industrial assistance

Export: Grain, industrial assistance
Value: $100 million
Year: 1986
Duration: Unspecified
Type: Bilateral trade agreement
Comment: This agreement gives special emphasis to joint projects
                         in shipbuilding, mining, nuclear technology, and fish
                         processing.

Partner country: Soviet Union
Import: Initially, road-building machinery and equipment for
                         hydroelectric power stations; turbines for a 1400 mega-
                         watts hydroelectric station under construction at Pied-
                         ra de Aguila; other industrial products
Export: Grain, wool, leather, meat, vegetable oils
Value: $500 million
Year: 1986
Duration: Five years
Type: Bilateral trade agreement
Comment: This agreement is intended to reduce Argentina's trade
                         surplus with the Soviet Union, which averages $1.5
                         billion per year

Partner country: Bulgaria
Import: Equipment and know-how for the leather processing,
                         nonferrous metal refining, and pharmaceutical (insulin)
                         industries
Export: Annual deliveries of: soybeans, 250,000 metric tons;
                         corn, 500,000 tons; wheat, 100,000 tons; beef, 10,000
                         tons
Value: Unspecified
Year: 1986
Duration: Five years
Type: Bilateral trade agreement

Partner country: Czechoslovakia (Czech FTO Skodaexport)
Import: Chemicals, raw materials, industrial products
Export: Annual deliveries, soybeans, 200,000 metric tons; un-
                         specified amounts of corn, beef
Value: Unspecified
Year: 1986

Duration:	Five years
Type:	Bilateral trade agreement
Partner country:	Poland
Import:	Chemical products, bearings, capital goods, optical equipment, pharmaceutical items, audio and photo equipment, technical services related to the capital goods provided
Export:	Tea, fish, rice, lemon and orange juice concentrate, pork, tobacco, wool tops, leather, pharmaceutical items, aluminum and alloys, machine tools, capital goods, paper, engineering services
Value:	$240 million
Year:	1985
Duration:	Three years
Type:	Bilateral trade agreement
Partner country:	United States (consortium of oil companies including Tesoro Petroleum, Mobil Corp., Zapata Corp.)
Import:	None; see comment
Export:	Petrochemicals, other unspecified products
Value:	$16 million
Year:	1986
Duration:	Unspecified
Type:	Debt liquidation countertrade
Comment:	The Argentine products are being given to pay debts to oil companies for previous imports of oil by the Argentine government

14 Australia

COUNTERTRADE

Countertrade Policy

Countertrade for civil and military procurements has been mandatory in Australia since the early 1970s. The policy was initiated primarily because of concern over defense spending; the government felt that some amount of compensation from foreign vendors of defense equipment was in order (particularly from U.S. vendors, who supplied most of the equipment). Other concerns were creation of new employment, technology transfer, and the development of export industries.

Virtually all Australian-mandated countertrade is of the coproduction offset type, though Australia often uses other countertrade methods when it is the seller rather than the buyer of a product. The Australian Ministry of Trade and Industry estimated in 1981 that the value of offset countertrade to Australia during the first ten years of the program was Aus. $400 million. According to a recent study by the government's Committee of Review on offsets, countertrade is now worth Aus. $50 million per year and provides 2,000 to 2,500 jobs annually. Most of the transactions are defense industry offsets. Offsets for 1986 are expected to reach Aus. $700 million.

Australia issued a revised countertrade policy in March 1986, after a lengthy study by the Committee on Review of Offsets. The major features of the new policy are:

1. Offset is required for all contracts valued at Aus. $2.5 million or above, with a foreign exchange component of Aus. $750,000 or more. (Previous minimum: $1 million contract value, $500,000 foreign exchange component.) This applies not only to single procurements, but to the aggregate value of all "similar products" purchased from a single foreign vendor by all federal government agencies during one fiscal year.

2. The minimum offset requirement is 30%. (No change.) This applies to the majority of contracts; however, in some cases a different figure may be specified.

3. Technology transfer is now the primary objective of the program, rather than creation of employment. The secondary objective is to create jobs through the development of new export industries. (Previous employment objective: adding jobs through development of existing export industries.)

4. Offset projects that qualify for credit now include the following:

    a. Research and development programs and training programs now qualify for offset credits. The maximum credit offered for such programs is 300%. The government stipulates that the programs must be both "separate from the contract for supplies" and "additional to the foreign supplier's usual customer services."

    b. Collaborative programs, those in which the foreign seller and the Australian partners cooperate throughout the entire process—concept, design, development, and production stages—qualify for offset credit.

5. Coproduction and technology transfer remain the major methods of earning offset credit. Counterpurchase of local products unrelated to the original contract may also earn credit, though to a comparatively limited extent. (No change.) These products must be roughly technologically equal to the imported items; for example, a computer system vendor could not accumulate offset credit by counterpurchasing Australian pencil sharpeners.

6. Direct offsets will not completely satisfy the offset requirement. They must be part of a comprehensive offset program. (No change.)

7. Alternative offset proposals to those originally agreed on may be offered by the foreign vendor during the course of the offset. (Previous: initial offset obligations were firm.)

8. Offset is required for sales above the specified threshold to all public entities and to one private company, Ansett. Offset is not required for sales to the following organizations: Australian Industry Development Corporation, Australian National, Australian National Line, Commonwealth Banking, Commonwealth Serum Laboratories, Export Finance and Insurance Corporation, Housing Loan and Insurance Corporation, Medibank, and Snowy Mountains Engineering. (No change.)

9. Dual tenders remain optional on the part of the Australian government. Some federal agencies (usually in the defense sector) request that bidders submit a "dual bid" with details of any price increments that were added to cover the costs of the offset. (Observers note that there is seldom any difference in value between the two bids.)

The official Australian position on the country's mandatory countertrade policy is that it does not violate any international obligations, and that it is necessary to ensure technology transfer and creation of employment. However, Australia resents being pressured to offer countertrade to other countries. The Ministry of Trade and Industry has stated in several publications that Australia is being "forced to accept countertrade by the aggressive reciprocal trade policies" of the CMEA countries and the developing countries, particularly in sales of such traditional Australian products as wheat, coal, iron ore, and beef. Furthermore, the government claims to have neither expertise nor mechanisms to handle countertrade, and says that private exporters should take the responsibility. This attitude of victimization is difficult to reconcile with Australia's own countertrade requirements, and the assertion of inability to handle countertrade is surprising considering Australia's extensive experience with countertrade and the sophistication of its countertrade program.

Products Available for Countertrade

Traditional food and crude materials exports such as wheat, beef, wool, alumina, iron ore, and so on are not available to industrial country countertraders, though they may be offered to CMEA and developing countries, as previously noted. Products available for industrial country counterpurchase are manufactured products with high added value and equivalent technological standards to the items imported. (See item 5 of countertrade policy.)

Countertrade and offset requirements are administered by the Ministry of Trade and Industry and by the Marketing Branch of the Defense Industry and Purchasing Division of the Department of Defense Support.

TRADE CONTROLS

Most items may be imported without import licenses. However, there are some import restrictions and quotas, particularly on raw food and processed food products. No restrictions are imposed on payments for imports. The Customs Tariff Act of 1975 provides for antidumping (countervailing) duties on imports that have injured or threaten to injure Australian industries.

The only exports that require licenses are specified raw or semiprocessed minerals, metals, fuels, petroleum products, and endangered wildlife species. Export proceeds must be remitted within six months unless otherwise authorized.

INTERNATIONAL TRADE

Imports

Although Australia usually has a trade surplus, imports have been growing considerably faster than exports—averaging 10.8% growth per year compared to 5.9% for exports—and in 1985, imports of $29.9 billion exceeded exports of $27.7 billion. Growth of imports has been erratic, with almost no increase

Import Total, Australia (thousands)

	Value	Growth (%)
1980	19,190,764	——
1981	23,516,787	22.5
1982	23,699,247	0.7
1983	19,144,807	− 19.2
1984	23,653,000	23.5
1985	29,921,045 (est.)	26.5

in 1982 and a drop of 19.2% to $19.1 billion in 1983. Since then, imports have been increasing by about 25% annually.

Imports are well diversified and are weighted toward transport equipment and high technology items, a typical pattern for an industrial country. The top 15 import products, in order by annual import value, are crude petroleum, petroleum products, trucks, passenger cars, data processing equipment, aircraft, paper and paperboard, telecommunications equipment, motor vehicle parts, measuring and controlling instruments, books, parts for nonelectric machinery and tools, sound recorders and phonographs, textile yarn, and household electrical equipment. These products each account for 1.2% to 5.7% of imports, and together account for 37% of the annual import total.

Asia is Australia's major supplier by area, providing 44.2% of imports, followed by North America, 23.6%, and the EEC, 20.7%. Imports from Oceania account for 4.6% of the total, EFTA countries for 3.4%, LAIA countries for 1.0% and CMEA countries for 0.5%. Japan and the United States are Australia's major import trading partners, supplying 22.1% and 21.7% of imports, respectively. Other leading suppliers are the United Kingdom, which has a 6.7% share of the Australian market; Germany, 5.8% share; Saudi Arabia, 3.7% share; New Zealand, 3.5% share; and Italy, 3.2% share.

Exports

Exports have shown more stable growth, or lack thereof, than imports. From 1980 through 1982, export value stayed at $21 billion annually. In 1983, exports fell by 8.3% to $19.4 billion. This was Australia's only bad sales period in recent years, and seemed also to signal the end of stagnant export growth. Exports went up by 17.4% in 1984, reaching $22.8 billion, and rose by 21.6% to $27.7 billion in 1985.

Australia needs export diversification and export upgrading. Despite years of mandated technology transfer and other high-added-value export product development programs, 88% of exports are still in four of the less sophisticated product groups: crude materials, 30%; food and live animals, 24%; mineral fuels, 23%; and basic manufactures, 11%. None of these groups includes high technology products. Machinery and transport equipment, the

Export Total, Australia (thousands)

	Value	Growth (%)
1980	21,407,616	——
1981	21,639,235	1.0
1982	21,214,834	− 1.9
1983	19,450,889	− 8.3
1984	22,839,000	17.4
1985	27,772,224 (est.)	21.6

major export area of most industrialized countries, accounts for only 4.0% of Australian exports. The top Australian export products are anthracite coal, 15.4% of the annual export total; wool, 8.4%; iron ore, 7.2%, beef, 7.0%; alumina, 5.4%; wheat, 5.4%; and petroleum products, 5.1%. Other important products, each accounting for 1.0% to 2.9% of the export total, are sugar, gas, aluminum, shellfish, lead, and iron and steel universals, plates and sheets. These thirteen products together account for 65% of Australian exports.

Australia is a major world supplier of many products. The country ranks first as supplier of wool, with a 43.3% world market share; uranium and thorium ores, 73.6% share; and alumina, 44.4% share. It is the second ranked supplier of anthracite coal, meat, unmilled cereals, raw hides and skins, pulpwood and iron ore, with world market shares in these products ranging from 3.6% (cereals) to 22.7% (pulpwood). Competitor countries in export of these items are the United States, the Netherlands, and Brazil. Australia ranks third as supplier of zinc ore, nickel ore, and shellfish, competing with Canada and Mexico, and ranks fourth in wheat, barley, and sugar; major competitors in the latter three products are the United States, France, and Cuba.

Most Australian exports, 50.5%, go to the Asian area. Other than that, the export market area pattern does not closely resemble the import pattern. Markets are fairly scattered, with 13.6% of exports going to the EEC, 8.0% to North America, 7.6% to Oceania, 3.4% to CMEA countries, 0.5% to EFTA, and 0.4% to LAIA countries. Japan and the United States are the major partners in export trade (as well as in import trade), however, the patterns are disproportionate. Whereas about an equal amount of Australian imports come from Japan and the United States, 26.1% of Australian exports go to Japan while only 6.9% go to the United States. Other major export markets are the United Kingdom, destination of 5.4% of Australian exports; the Republic of Korea, 3.8%; the USSR, 2.4%; and Malaysia, 2.4%.

It is probably true, bearing these statistics in mind, that the USSR and other CMEA countries are being "aggressive" in requesting reciprocal trade with Australia. The CMEA countries make it a practice to pressure other countries for countertrade when there is a trade imbalance; with 3.4% of Australian exports going to the CMEA and only 0.5% of imports originating there, Australia could reasonably expect some pressure for compensatory trade.

RECENT COUNTERTRADE TRANSACTIONS, AUSTRALIA

Partner country: Romania (with Australian firms Hancock Prospecting
                    Proprietary Ltd. and CRA Ltd.)

Import: Mining and handling equipment for a new iron ore
                    mine in Western Australia

Export: Iron ore, 48 million tons; initial shipments will be
                    about 1 million tons per year and will build up to about
                    5 million tons annually

Value: Total development cost of the mine, Aus. $350 million;
                    value of compensation, unspecified

Year: 1985

Duration: Fifteen years

Type: Compensation agreement

Comment: Shipments to Romania will account for about half of
                    the mine's production; the mine will have an estimated
                    five years of production left after the obligation to Ro-
                    mania is fulfilled

Partner country: United Kingdom (British Aerospace, with Australian
                    Hawker de Havilland Pty., Ltd.)

Import: None

Export: Construction of framework and landing gear compo-
                    nents for A-320 Airbus; provides 300,000 working
                    hours for Hawker de Havilland

Value: Aus. $24 million

Year: 1984

Duration: Unspecified

Type: Coproduction offset

Comment: This contract is part of a 1980 offset agreement be-
                    tween Trans Australian Airlines and British Aerospace
                    for the Airbus, value of the original contract is Aus.
                    $121 million

Partner country: United States (Sikorsky Aircraft Division of United
                    Technologies, with Royal Australian Navy)

Import: 16 helicopters, S-70 Seahawk

Export: Aircraft components

Value: Aus. $135 million

Year: 1984

Duration: Unspecified (long-term)

Type: Coproduction offset with technology transfer

Comment: The contract was apparently awarded to Sikorsky be-
                            cause the company made advance subcontracting com-
                            mitments to Australian firms as a good faith gesture;
                            this has since become known as *the Sikorsky approach*
                            and has been copied by other companies. Some of the
                            subcontracts given before the award were:
                                Hawker de Havilland Pty. Ltd., for manufacture of
                            the wing and upper and lower stabilizers for the Rotor
                            Systems Research Aircraft that will test Sikorsky's
                            new X-wing rotor system, Aus. $2 million.
                                Commonwealth Aircraft Corp. Ltd., three contracts:
                            (1) assistance in developing specifications and a pro-
                            posal to design and build helicopter maintenance train-
                            ers for the U.S. Navy, Aus. $10 million; (2) manufac-
                            ture of 250 sets of helicopter intermediate and tail rotor
                            transmissions, Aus. $3.5 million; and (3) manufacture
                            of various magnesium, steel, and aluminum helicopter
                            castings, Aus. $2.2 million.
                                Australian National Industries, manufacture of tita-
                            nium and steel forgings, Aus. $4.5 million.

Partner country: United States (General Electric Engine Business
                            Group)

Import: GE engines (in Boeing 737s and airbuses for Ansett
                            and Australian Airlines)

Export: Unspecified engine parts; also joint ventures such as
                            one with Shedden Pacific Co. in Melbourne to develop
                            an advanced technology power generation plant

Value: Aus. $101 million

Year: 1986

Duration: Unspecified (long-term)

Type: Direct/indirect offset and investment

15 Brazil

COUNTERTRADE

Countertrade Policy

Brazil does not have a formal countertrade policy. However, both the public and private sectors are heavily involved in countertrade; the private trading companies usually work in cooperation with the state trading companies, often assisting in the export of products under Brazil's numerous bilateral trading agreements, as well as straight counterpurchase deals and offsets. There are three known requirements concerning countertrade: (1) as of 1983 the government will no longer purchase oil from countries that do not import sufficient amounts of Brazilian products, (2) as of 1984 offset compensation is required for procurements of commercial aircraft, and (3) there are specific laws that permit import licenses for certain products only against export sales of equal or greater value. Additionally all private companies engaging in international trade are pressured to match or exceed the value of their imports with exports. For example, in order to take advantage of tax benefits under the BEFIX program, Brazilian companies are supposed to export goods worth three times the value of their imports.

The government channel for countertrade is CACEX (Carteira do Comercio Exterior). CACEX, the foreign trade department of the Banco do Brazil, implements the decisions of the National Council of Foreign Trade (CONCEX, a board headed by the Minister of Finance) within Brazil. The primary responsibility of CACEX is the issuance of import licenses and export certificates; in this capacity, it controls Brazilian foreign trade to a great extent. The countertrade unit of CACEX is the DEPM (Department of Promotion and Markets). This department screens all countertrade proposals and coordinates offset transactions for technology transfer, military procurements, and petroleum imports. Within the DEPM, there is an Export Promotion Division, CEPEX, which provides assistance in countertrade sourcing.

Petroleum imports are handled through the state-owned petroleum trading company, Petrobras (Petroleo Brasileiro S.A.). Petrobras has a trading subsidiary, Interbras (Petrobras Comercio Internacional S.A.), which handles various export products related to oil barter deals. Interbras is very influential, accounting for over 10% of Brazilian exports. The actual delivery of export merchandise under Interbras is handled by the Cotia Trading Company, a private firm. Although Petrobras and Interbras initiate and negotiate many of Brazil's countertrade deals, all transactions are subject to approval by CACEX.

Petrobras began to require countertrade for petroleum imports in 1981. By 1984 barter oil accounted for 31% of Brazilian oil imports; estimates are 70% for 1985 and 90% for 1986. Oil barter deals have been transacted with Angola, Iran, Iraq, Libya, Mexico, Nigeria, the Soviet Union, and Venezuela, among other countries. Through these deals and conventional purchases, Brazil has built up a supply of petroleum that far exceeds domestic demand, and is accordingly expected to become a more important supplier of petroleum products, such as gasoline.

The public sector accounts for most Brazilian countertrade. This sector is also the most important in Brazilian import trade, accounting for about 70% of the country's total imports (50% petroleum, 20% other products). Based on this figure, public sector imports were $9.5 billion in 1985. The percentage of public sector imports that are countertrade related is not known; though if all 1985 petroleum imports ($5.8 billion) had to be 50% offset with Brazilian exports, the value of counterpurchase exports for the year would be $2.9 billion. It is estimated that 5% of private sector trade is countertrade related, which would make the value of private sector counterpurchase exports $203.9 million for 1985 (total private sector imports for 1985 are estimated at $4.0 billion) on a 100% counterpurchase basis. The USDOC estimates that Brazilian countertrade, both public and private, is worth $2–$3 billion per year.

Brazil has a large number of bilateral trading agreements, having participated in this type of trade for many years. At the present time, Brazil has clearing agreements with Algeria, Bulgaria, Canada, China, Czechoslovakia, the Dominican Republic, the German Democratic Republic, Greece, Hungary, Nigeria, Poland, Romania, Saudia Arabia, and the LAIA countries. There are protocol agreements with Angola, Iran, and Iraq involving petroleum imports in exchange for Brazilian exports. These agreements account for about 30% of Brazilian external trade. Trade pacts with the CMEA countries have been so successful (on the Brazilian side) that there is a sizable business in Eastern European trade credits in Brazil. These credits are sold to private companies by the Central Bank (Banco do Brasil), and can be used either to sell the Eastern European products to a third party or to structure triangular and switch transactions. About two-thirds of the trade credit market in Brazil is held by Merban, the merchant banking subsidiary of Contitrade Services Corporation.

Products Available for Countertrade

Brazil offers a great variety of products in countertrade, traditional as well as nontraditional exports. Food products offered include sugar, poultry, beef, soybean oil, orange juice, coffee, and cocoa. Crude materials and semiprocessed items available include: iron ore, nickel ore, tin ore, leaf tobacco, cocoa butter, soybeans, soya oil cake, cotton, semiprocessed hides and leather, iron and steel semimanufactures, and grey iron alloys. Manufactured products available for countertrade include petrochemicals, oil drilling equipment, automobiles, armored cars, aircraft, aircraft components, ships, industrial machinery, electrical apparatus, and footwear. Services available include aerial photogrammetrical technology and steel technology. (Note: Many of Brazil's countertrading partners say that Brazilian products are noncompetitive. Quality does not seem to be the problem; the complaints are that the products, whether manufactured or nonmanufactured, are often valued above the world market price.)

TRADE CONTROLS

Import licenses and export certificates are issued by CACEX. All importers must be registered with CACEX. Importers must submit an annual import program to CACEX as the basis for an import license request; thereafter, imports conforming to the plan are automatically granted licenses.

The import of a few commodities is prohibited. CACEX has also suspended the issuance of licenses for a large number of "superfluous" items, which in effect, prohibits their import. There are limitations on the direct import of consumer goods. Import licenses may be temporarily suspended in cases where (1) imports are for speculative stock building purposes, (2) imports are causing or are threatening to cause serious damage to the national economy, and (3) imports originate in or are shipped from countries that "impede" Brazilian exports. Imports of specified minerals (including iron and steel alloys, copper, nickel, aluminum, lead, and zinc) are subject to control. Many domestic industries, such as the computer industry, are protected by import quotas or other restrictions. The import of commodities originating in or shipped from Cuba is prohibited.

Exports require certificates rather than licenses. Many exports are controlled or subject to prior approval by CACEX. Exports of specified commodities (certain primary products and raw materials required for domestic consumption) are often prohibited or suspended, and exports of some other commodities are conditional upon prior domestic sales. Exports of certain commodities are subject to an annual quota.

Coffee exports are subject to authorization by the IBC (Brazilian Coffee Institute). The sales contract must be based on a price that is at least equal to the minimum registration price (in U.S. dollars per pound, f.o.b.) fixed periodically by the IBC for the various types of coffee, though discounts are sometimes authorized. Exporters of coffee are required to surrender, without compensation, a portion of their foreign exchange proceeds in the form of a contribution quota which varies according to the type of coffee.

There are export taxes on a number of items. Tax rates vary from 9% to 20%; however, they are often phased down or eliminated. Products that have recently been subject to export taxes include textiles, leather items, footwear, certain steel products, livestock, forestry products, various agricultural products, cocoa, cocoa products, orange juice concentrate, manganese ore, and hematite.

The government provides various export incentives, primarily for exporters of manufactured products. These include tax credits, export financing, and export credit insurance.

INTERNATIONAL TRADE

Imports

Brazilian imports have dropped substantially in recent years, falling from $24.9 billion in 1980 to $13.5 billion in 1985. The average decline in value was 10.6% per year. Reasons for the decrease include pressure from the IMF to reduce imports, foreign exchange shortage, and a successful effort on Brazil's part to achieve a trade surplus. Brazil carried a trade deficit through 1982 ($888.2 million), and managed to get an $8.3 billion surplus in 1983 through a decline of 20.2% in imports and an increase of 24.5% in exports. The surplus rose to $11.7 billion in 1984 and was $15.3 billion in 1985.

The major cut in imports has been in petroleum; Brazilian imports of this product have dropped by an average of 8.7% per year since 1982. Other products that have shown relatively sharp import declines include live cattle, beef, nonelectric machinery, and semiprocessed iron, steel, and aluminum items.

Crude petroleum accounts for 40%–50% of Brazilian imports each year. Although the value of petroleum imports has been going down, the proportion of petroleum imports to total imports has remained roughly the same. After petroleum, the top import products are nonelectric machinery, wheat, organic chemicals, switchgear, electric power machinery, coal, copper, oilseeds, and manufactured fertilizers.

The majority of Brazilian imports, 40.2%, come from Asia (primarily the Middle East). The Americas supply 34.8% of imports, with 17.5% coming from North America and 16.7% from the LAIA countries. The EEC has a 12.6% market share in Brazil; EFTA has 3.4%, and the CMEA group has 2.6%. Brazil's major import trading partner by country is Saudi Arabia, which supplies 15.2% of imports; followed by the United States, 15.0%; and Iraq, 13.1%. Other important trading partners are Venezuela, which has a 5.0%

Import Total and Petroleum Imports, Brazil (thousands)

	Value	Growth (%)	Value, Petroleum	Petroleum Total (%)
1980	24,948,828	——	9,772,670	39.1
1981	24,072,516	− 0.3	11,289,109	46.8
1982	21,061,282	− 12.5	10,263,608	48.7
1983	16,800,992	− 20.2	8,888,000	52.9
1984	15,210,000	− 9.4	7,473,000	49.1
1985	13,597,740 (est.)	− 10.6	5,898,000	43.3

share of the Brazilian market; Japan, 4.6% share; Germany, 4.4% share; and Mexico, 4.0% share.

Exports

Exports have shown good growth, averaging 8.2% per year from 1980 through 1985. The only disappointing year was 1982 when sales fell by 13.3% to $20.1 billion. Value of exports jumped by 24.5% in 1983 ($25.1 billion), as Brazil made a tremendous effort to overcome its financial difficulties. Exports have continued to increase, though at much lower rates; they rose by 7.4% to $27.0 billion in 1984 and by 7.0% to $28.9 billion in 1985.

Food products are the most important Brazilian exports, usually accounting for about 40% of the export total. Products that have shown the strongest export growth are meat, dried fruit, preserved fruit, fruit juices, and coffee. Nonfood products with especially good export growth are cotton, petroleum products, chemical plastic materials, semiprocessed iron, steel, aluminum, and tin products (particularly iron and steel universals, plates, and sheets), and footwear.

Products with declining export values include agricultural machinery; office machines; nonelectric machinery; switchgear, and soybean, peanut, and castor oils. Since these are fairly important products, Brazil may wish to push them in countertrade as a method of getting sales back up to previous levels.

Top exports by value are animal feed (mostly vegetable oil residues), which accounts for 12.0% of the annual export total; soybeans and products, 9.5%; coffee, 9.4%; petroleum products (mostly gasoline), 7.0%; and iron ore, 5.9%. Sales of these products are $1.6–$3.7 billion annually. Other important exports, valued at $346 million to $1.0 billion per year (1%–4% of the export total) are passenger cars, trucks, footwear, fruit and vegetable juices, iron and steel semimanufactures (universals, plates, sheets), organic chemicals (mostly hydrocarbons and alcohol), cocoa, sugar, beef, poultry, tobacco, nonelectric power machinery (mostly piston engines), pig iron, canned meat, iron and steel shapes, wood pulp, and textile yarn, in order by value.

Brazil is a top world supplier of several food products. It is the leading

Export Total, Brazil (thousands)

	Value	Growth (%)
1980	20,132,064	——
1981	23,292,348	15.6
1982	20,173,041	− 13.3
1983	25,126,842	24.5
1984	27,005,000	7.4
1985	28,906,666 (est.)	7.0

supplier of coffee, with a world market share of 27.7%. Brazil ranks second as a supplier of animal feed, with a 24.7% share; cocoa, 16.8% share; and canned meat, 15.1%. (The major suppliers of these products are the United States, the Ivory Coast, and Denmark, respectively.) It is the third largest supplier of sugar, with a 4.9% world share. Outside the food products area, Brazil is the world's leading supplier of iron ore, 27.0% market share, and is the second ranked supplier of unmanufactured tobacco, 12.3% share, and soft fixed vegetable oils, 14.7% share. The United States is the top supplier of the latter two products.

By area, most Brazilian exports go to the Americas and Western Europe. Exports to the Americas account for 36.3% of the total; 27.2% of exports are destined for North America and 8.2% for the LAIA countries. Western Europe takes 32.1% of Brazilian exports, with 27.2% going to the EEC and 2.6% to EFTA. Asia is the third most important market area, accounting for 17.7% of the export total. Sales to the CMEA countries account for 6.5% of exports. (Only 2.6% of imports come from the CMEA area; this explains why Brazil has an abundance of Eastern European trade credits.)

Brazil's six most important export markets are industrial countries. The major market is the United States, which takes 25.9% of all Brazilian exports. Japan is the second most important export trading partner, buying 6.6% of exports, followed by the Netherlands, 5.9%; France, 5.8%; Germany, 5.2%; and Italy, 4.6%. The USSR, the United Kingdom, Argentina, and Spain are also important markets.

RECENT COUNTERTRADE TRANSACTIONS, BRAZIL

Partner country: United Kingdom (RAF with Brazilian EMBRAER)
Import: Unspecified
Export: 130 Tucano trainer aircraft; the aircraft will be manu-
                  factured in Northern Ireland by Shorts Brothers; the
                  first six aircraft will be shipped directly from Brazil
                  (the other 124 will be shipped to Ulster in ready-to-
                  assemble kits).

Value: $144 million
Year: 1985
Duration: Four years, ends 1990
Type: Coproduction offset
Comment: This is a very unusual transaction in that it is a devel-
                      oping country selling aircraft to a developed country,
                      instead of the other way around. The United Kingdom
                      apparently accepted this deal because it provides badly
                      needed employment; Brazil conducted a similar offset
                      in Egypt, selling 120 aircraft (many in kits) and training
                      Egyptian workers.

Partner country: United States (Shepard Oil, an alcohol producer, with
                      Brazilian Copesucar, a molasses producer)
Import: Alcohol
Export: Molasses
Value: Unspecified
Year: 1985
Duration: Unspecified
Type: Joint venture

Partner country: Malaysia (MITCO-Malaysian International Trading
                      Corp., with Brazilian Interbras)
Import: 90,000 bbl crude petroleum
Export: Various items, including chemicals, food, transporta-
                      tion equipment, machinery, iron ore, minerals
Value: $27 million
Year: 1985
Duration: Unspecified
Type: Oil barter

Partner country: Federal Republic of Germany (Ferrostahl)
Import: Two submarines, first to be built in Germany, second
                      in Brazil (includes technology transfer)
Export: Iron ore
Value: $200 million (value of iron ore)
Year: 1984
Duration: Unspecified
Type: Reciprocal trade/coproduction

Partner country: Malaysia (MITCO with Brazilian state-owned mining
                      corporation Comopanhia Vale do Rio Doce)

Import:	10,000 barrels of oil per day (about 1% of Brazilian consumption)
Export:	300,000 tons of iron ore per year
Value:	$40 million
Year:	1983
Duration:	Five years
Type:	Oil barter

Parnter country:	Iraq (with Volkswagen do Brazil)
Import:	Petroleum
Export:	Automobiles
Value:	$630 million
Year:	1984
Duration:	Unspecified
Type:	Oil barter

See also: Canada (countertrade deal with Spar Aerospace).

EXAMPLES OF RECENT BILATERAL CLEARING AGREEMENTS, BRAZIL

1983:	Mexico
Import:	Increase in oil imports from 60,000 to 80,000 bpd
Export:	Food, petrochemicals, oil products, oil drilling equipment
Value:	Unspecified
Duration:	Unspecified

1983:	Iran
Import:	Crude petroleum
Export:	Textiles, machine tools, compressors, agricultural machinery, iron, soybean oil
Value:	$1 billion
Duration:	Unspecified

1983:	Venezuela
Import:	63,000 bbl crude petroleum
Export:	25,000 tons sugar
Value:	Unspecified
Duration:	Three years

1983:	Soviet Union
Import:	20,000 bpd petroleum, turbines for hydroelectric equipment
Export:	Approximately 1 million tons of soybeans, soymeal, soybean oil, cocoa beans, liquer; 500,000 tons of corn per year
Value:	$300 million
Duration:	Five years

16 Canada

COUNTERTRADE

Countertrade Policy

Canada has required countertrade for major government procurements since 1975. Like Australia, Canada began its countertrade program because of heavy defense spending, and most of its offsets have been defense-related. Almost all are coproduction offsets, though most arrangements involve some amount of indirect offset. The United States has been the country most affected by Canadian offset practices, since it is the major supplier of Canada's defense equipment.

In Canada, the offset requirement is called the *industrial benefits program*. Technology transfer, industrial development, export diversification, and the development of new export markets are the major objectives of the Canadian program. Exports are of special concern in Canada because of their composition and destination; most exports are raw materials, and about 75% of all exports go to the United States. Canada would like to develop exports of manufactures, and at the same time lessen its dependence on the U.S. market by building up diverse international markets.

Employment and regional economic development are also important considerations in Canada's attitude toward countertrade. During the early 1980s, 50% of the employment in the aircraft industry in Ontario and 40% in Manitoba could be attributed to offset, according to a report issued by the Canadian Institute for Strategic Studies. To date, however, not all provinces have benefited equally from offset trade. For example, Ontario and Quebec got 92% of the offset contracts associated with the CP-140 and CF-18 fighter aircraft procurements (67 and 25%, respectively), while the Maritime provinces of Nova Scotia, New Brunswick, and Newfoundland received nearly nothing.

The major features of Canada's countertrade regulations are:

1. Offset is required for all government procurements over C$100 million.
2. Offset percentages range from 50% to 100%.

3. The maximum penalty for nonperformance is 25%.

4. The RFP will define the type of compensation required for a particular project and will specify eligibility criteria. A typical RFP for military offset will cover the following areas: lowest possible cost, establishment of maintenance facilities, technology transfer, coproduction, export development, penetration of new export markets, employment, regional economic development, and import substitution. The RFP may also include a list of 100 or more products targeted for industrial and export development.

5. The government does not direct subcontracts to specific Canadian suppliers. The bidder may select his own subcontractors from the pool of qualified Canadian companies.

6. There is some flexibility in offset requirements. Contracts may be renegotiated during the period of the agreement if the original obligations cannot be met.

7. Offset credits: Credits are earned primarily by R&D investment, coproduction, and technology transfer. Counterpurchase can earn credit, provided that the items are fully manufactured products, preferably those with high added value; raw and semiprocessed materials or semimanufactures do not qualify. Export of the products should result in additionality. Tourism development can also earn credit, to a limited extent.

Canada, like other developed countries that require offset trade, does not approve of mandated countertrade in other countries, although the government does acknowledge that countertrade is necessary to make sales to some countries. (Since Canada has trade surpluses with most countries, the government may also feel that an open endorsement of countertrade might cause the countries to demand more countertrade in order to balance trade.) The Canadian government's policy on countertrade is:

> From a multilateral policy perspective, Canada has traditionally adopted the view, in international forums and in concert with our major trading partners, that countertrade:
>
>> is a regressive trade practice which distorts the multilateral flow of goods and services;
>>
>> prejudices the export opportunities of small- and medium-size firms;
>>
>> deals inefficiently with the economic and financial constraints it attempts to resolve;
>>
>> manifests a regrettable trend to bilateralism; and
>>
>> tends to remove trade from the purview of normal GATT disciplines through its lack of transparency.
>
> From a bilateral relations viewpoint, Canada has always made it clear to its trading partners that the Government of Canada will not become directly involved in countertrade deals. It has been the government's position that the

initiative and responsibility for entering into countertrade rests with the exporters alone.*

There is increasing participation in countertrade by the Canadian private sector. A private sector task force appointed by the government estimated that 5% of recent Canadian exports resulted from countertrade (excluding trade with the United States), although the *Countertrade Primer for Canadian Exporters* gives this figure as 0.5%. The Canadian industrial sectors most often involved in countertrade are air, rail and urban transportation; telecommunications; defense products; high-technology products; resource and energy extraction, processing and generation equipment; agricultural and forestry equipment; and engineering and consulting services. Most of the products that Canadian companies take as counterpurchases end up in third countries, as the quality of the manufactured goods offered by developing countries is usually not acceptable in the Canadian market. A quasi-government group, the Canadian Industrial Benefits Association (CIBA), has recently been formed to provide a forum for both foreign vendors and Canadian exporters involved in offset and countertrade. The group operates informally and is open to all parties involved in Canadian offsets as well as service providers such as consultants. CIBA's address is: R.C. Brown, Coordinator, Litton Systems Canada Ltd., 220 Laurier Avenue West, Ottawa, Ontario, KIP 5Z9. (Telephone: 613-236-2358; telex 053 4233.)

Products Available for Countertrade

Manufactured products as noted previously in item 7.

Offset programs are administered by the Office of Industrial and Regional Benefits, Major Public Procurements Section.

TRADE CONTROLS

Import licenses are required for the following items: certain drugs; certain agricultural items; certain textile products, clothing, and footwear; endangered species of flora and fauna; natural gas; and materials and equipment for the production or use of atomic energy. Licenses are not issued for some agricultural products, such as certain dairy products. Imports of oleomargarine, used automobiles, and a few other products are either tightly controlled or prohibited. Imports of nonrubber footwear are subject to a global quota.

Export of some commodities is controlled for supply reasons; these include

---

*Department of External Affairs, *Countertrade Primer for Canadian Exporters*, 1985, p. 3.

petroleum, some petroleum products, and natural gas. Export of strategic materials is controlled to all destinations except the United States. All exports to Albania, Bulgaria, China, Czechoslovakia, the GDR, Hungary, North Korea, Mongolia, Poland, Romania, the Soviet Union, and Vietnam are subject to control, although export of some goods is permitted with special authorization. Repatriation of export proceeds is not required.

INTERNATIONAL TRADE

Imports

Canada usually carries a sizable trade surplus, ranging from $4 billion (1981) to $18 billion (1984). Imports seem to be on an wpward trend, after having fallen for two consecutive years; they went down by 12.4% in 1981, decreasing to $64.8 billion, and fell by a further 16.3% in 1982 to $54.2 billion. In 1983 imports rose by 11.4% to $60.4 billion. They continued to rise in 1984, to $72.3 billion, and 1985, to $79.4 billion, with respective growth rates in those years of 19.6% and 9.7%. The import growth rate averages 2.4% per year, though this is not a very representative figure considering the growth pattern. Exports have remained well ahead of imports, though the trade surplus in 1985, $9 billion, was only half what it was in 1984.

Canada's top 19 import products (excluding motor vehicles and parts, most of which are intercompany shipments from U.S.-based companies), in order by import value, are crude petroleum, data processing equipment, aircraft, books, telecommunications equipment, electrical machinery, measuring and controlling instruments, parts and accessories for data processing and office machines, fresh and dried fruits and nuts, transistors and valves, coal, civil engineering equipment, miscellaneous base metal manufactures, special industry machinery, parts and accessories for nonelectric machinery, petroleum products, agricultural machinery, precious metal ores, and nonroad tractors. These products account for 0.8% to 4.3% ($500 million to $2.6 billion) of the annual import total. Other important products, each valued annually at 0.6% of the total (about $400 million) are toys and sporting goods, chemical polymerization products, paper and paperboard, medicinal products, ships and boats, miscellaneous articles of plastic, chemical condensation products, miscellaneous chemical products, household electrical equipment, and fresh vegetables.

By area, 72% of Canadian imports come from North America, 11.5% from Asia, 7.9% from the EEC, 4.1% from LAIA countries, and 1.8% from EFTA. Imports from the Caribbean, CMEA countries, Africa and Oceania account for less than 1% each of the total. The United States dominates the Canadian market, providing 72% of all imports. Other important trading partners are Japan, which has a 5.9% market share; the United Kingdom, 2.4%; Germany, 2.1%; Mexico, 1.4%; and Venezuela, 1.3%.

Import Total, Canada (thousands)

	Value	Growth (%)
1980	57,707,191	——
1981	64,897,219	− 12.4
1982	54,259,133	− 16.3
1983	60,477,193	11.4
1984	72,369,000	19.6
1985	79,434,805 (est.)	9.7

Exports

Exports have shown higher growth than imports, averaging 7.2% per year, but they have been erratic. In 1981, exports increased by 8.2% to $68.2 billion, though in 1982 they fell by 1.9% to $66.9 billion. Two years of good growth followed, with value rising by 8.1% to $72.4 billion in 1983 and by 22.8% to $88.9 billion in 1984. There was a slight decline in exports in 1985; they fell by 1.1% to $87.9 billion. This export pattern reflects demand in the U.S. market to a large extent, since most Canadian exports go there.

Canada's top export is passenger motor vehicles; however, most of these are intercompany shipments to the United States. Exports of cars, trucks, engines, and motor vehicles parts account for 24% of the annual export total. Intercompany shipments of motor vehicles and parts enter the U.S. duty-free, under the Auto Pact of 1965.

Other than these products, the four major exports are paper (primarily newsprint), which accounts for about 5.5% of the export total; natural gas, 5.5%; wheat, 5.1%; and shaped wood, 4.5%. Annual value of these items is $3–$4 billion. Exports valued at $1–$2 billion per year (1.3% to 3.8% of the total) are crude petroleum, wood pulp, aluminum, railway vehicles, coal petroleum products, data processing equipment, telecommunications equipment, electric current, aircraft, and nickel and zinc ores. Other important export products are manufactured fertilzers, iron ore, barley, fresh fish, copper, miscellaneous engines, civil engineering, hydrocarbons, fresh meat, and asbestos. These products are each worth $500–$900 million per year, or about 1% of the export total. These 6 products account for 43% of Canadian exports; combined with motor vehicles and parts, they account for 70% of the total.

Canada is the top world supplier of a number of products. Among these are asbestos, in which Canada has a 71.7% world market share; sulphur, 48.9% share; miscellaneous cereal meals and flour, 37.4% share; shaped wood, 35.5% share; wood pulp, 31.7% share; nickel ore, 26.1% share; zinc ore, 22.7% share; paper and paperboard, 21.7% share; and fresh fish, 13.0% share. Products in which Canada ranks second include natural gas, wheat, manufactured fertilizers, barley, and prepared fish. Canada would like to

Export Total, Canada (thousands)

	Value	Growth (%)
1980	63,105,060	——
1981	68,281,203	8.2
1982	66,977,001	− 1.9
1983	72,419,988	8.1
1984	88,954,000	22.8
1985	87,908,784 (est.)	− 1.1

add some advanced manufactures and high technology products to this list, and hopes that countertrade will help achieve this objective.

Most Canadian exports, 73%, go to North America. Of the remainder, 10.9% go to Asia, 7.4% to the EEC, 2.1% to LAIA, and 2.0% to the CMEA area. Exports to other areas are very small. The United States market accounts for exports to North America. Other important export markets are Japan, 5.0% of the export total; United Kingdom, 2.7%; USSR, 2.0%; China, 1.6%; and Germany, 1.3%.

RECENT COUNTERTRADE TRANSACTIONS, CANADA

Partner country:	United States (McDonnell Douglas)
Import:	CF-18 fighter aircraft
Export:	Unspecified
Value:	$5 billion; value of offset, $2.9 billion (58% offset)
Year:	1980
Duration:	Unspecified; long-term
Type:	Coproduction offset
Comment:	The Canadian aerospace and electronics sectors are to receive at least 60% of total benefits, of which a minimum of 10% must be technology transfer. Tourism development can qualify for a maximum of 10% of the offset obligation.

Partner country:	Belgium (with Canadian firm Bombardier)
Import:	Unspecified
Export:	2500 Iltis military vehicles
Value:	Value of vehicles, $50 million; total value, $200 million, including offset spending
Year:	1984
Duration:	Unspecified

Type:	Coproduction offset; the offset percentage is 300%
Comment:	This is an unusually high offset percentage, and it is also the highest offer that Belgium has ever received on a defense contract. Belgium usually asks for about 70% offset.

Partner country:	Brazil (Brazilian state telecommunications company, Embratel, with Canada's Spar Aerospace, Ltd.)
Import:	Initially, processed and fresh foods to be sold in Canadian supermarket chains; other products later for Canadian and other markets
Export:	Two satellites and related ground control system
Value:	Satellites and control systems, $160 million; counterpurchase of Brazilian products, $60 million; additional development of $105 million in Brazilian exports on a best efforts basis (no penalty for nonperformance)
Year:	1983
Duration:	Four years
Type:	Counterpurchase
Comment:	After the first year, in which it was unable to handle the Brazilian products, Spar established an in-house trading company so that it could fulfill the offset obligation. This experience shows the importance of advance planning in countertrade.

Partner country:	Pakistan (Pakistan International Airlines (PIA), with Canada's CP Air; Page Avjet of Orlando, Florida acted as principal for CP Air)
Import:	Aircraft, four PIA Douglas DC-10-30's
Export:	Aircraft, four CP (CP Air) Boeing 747-200s
Value:	Unspecified
Year:	1985
Duration:	11 months (December 1985–December 1986)
Type:	Aircraft barter
Comment:	The planes were swapped (actually each set of planes was first sold to the intermediary, Page Avjet) because CP Air wanted to get rid of its Boeing fleet and PIA wanted to get rid of its Douglas fleet, with facilitation of efficient maintenance and repair being the motivation on both sides. The deal became possible on the Pakistani side because of an offset arrangement with the Boeing Company. Boeing sold six 737-300 aircraft

to PIA, and accepted an offset obligation to build a spare-parts factory for Boeing aircraft in Pakistan. There was no such arrangement with Douglas; PIA had been having to send the Douglas aircraft overseas for maintenance, and now that it had a Boeing repair facility it did not want to keep the Douglas planes. CP Air did not want the continued expense of dual repair facilities for its mixed Boeing-Douglas fleet, preferring to have all Douglas aircraft. The two companies did not deal directly with each other because CP Air wished to have Page Avjet act as principal.

Partner country:	Republic of Korea (Hyundai)
Import:	Automobiles, steel and electronics products
Export:	None; the Hyundai Automobile Division will build an automobile parts plant in Newmarket, Ontario (value: C$25 million) and an automobile assembly plant in Quebec (value: C$300 million).
Value:	C$600 million, value of imports from Hyundai
Year:	1985
Duration:	Unspecified
Type:	Reciprocal trade/investment
Comment:	The original agreement, signed in 1984, provided for counterpurchase by Hyundai of C$60 million in Canadian manufactured goods and C$240 million in commodities such as coal, wheat, and timber. This was arranged by Canada's Foreign Investment Review Board (FIRA). When Hyundai offered to build the auto plants, it was released from the counterpurchase requirement.

Partner country:	India (MMTC, the Minerals and Metals Trading Corp., with Canpotex, a Saskatchewan potash export consortium)
Import:	Wedge wire particle screens for use in the Saskatchewan mining industry
Export:	Potash, 260,000 metric tons
Value:	Unspecified
Year:	1986
Duration:	Unspecified
Type:	Counterpurchase; terms (payment by India): 77% cash, 23% goods

Comment:	Canpotex received a concession from India on the percentage of the counterpurchase; 23% instead of the Indian requirement of 50% for fertilizer suppliers in 1986; the levels for these suppliers are scheduled to rise to 75% in 1987 and 100% in 1988. Canpotex apparently accomplished this by convincing MMTC that Saskatchewan was a new market for Indian mining equipment (thus exports would be 100% incremental), and that the province was a good growth market; however, Canpotex's counterpurchase obligations are expected to increase in the future.
Partner country:	India (India, MMTC With Canamax Resources in Manitoba)
Import:	Equity investment by MMTC of 15%–30% in potash mine; hydroelectric generating equipment
Export:	Potash; MMTC will purchase up to 500,000 metric tons of the mine's annual output.
Value:	Unspecified
Year:	1986
Duration:	Unspecified
Type:	Joint venture/buyback

17 China

COUNTERTRADE

Countertrade Policy

China does not formally require countertrade at this time; however, officials of the Ministry of Foreign Economic Relations and Trade (MOFERT) and the State Economic Committee (SEC) have stated that foreign corporations wishing to sell to China must be willing to offer countertrade. In practice, countertrade is a necessity for all but the highest priority imports, and even for these imports the seller may be pressured to make some sort of reciprocal arrangement. This is not strictly a matter of foreign exchange shortage. China is just as interested in modernization as in saving foreign exchange, and feels that foreign companies can help in the modernization process by transferring technology and skills. Export development is also a high priority in countertrade arrangements. The need for technology is important in export development-related countertrade, too; the Chinese would like to produce better products for export, as many of their manufactures are technologically years out of date.

The countertrade process is not very organized in China yet. Buyback deals run fairly smoothly since China has been making this sort of arrangement with foreign companies since 1978, but other types of countertrade may be a little difficult to work out. There is no linkage between ministries for counterpurchases; this means that products purchased in a province other than that in which the joint venture is located (or the province which bought the foreign import) do not qualify as counterpurchases. A very determined company can go through the elaborate process of lining up separate agreements with state corporations and their various ministries in order to select products elsewhere, but even this approach is often unsuccessful.

MOFERT established a countertrade unit that was supposed to consolidate the countertrade requirements, paperwork and approval procedures of different ministries. However, the countertrade unit's objective of centralizing the negotiation of countertrade is in conflict with the current government policy of decentralization, so it has not been able to function effectively. As a result, most countertrade deals are still conducted on an ad hoc basis.

The value of Chinese countertrade transactions was about $800 million in 1985. Chinese enterprises were involved in countertrade with 20 countries that year, including Algeria, Argentina, Brazil, France, the Federal Republic of Germany, Greece, Indonesia, Japan, Singapore, Sweden, Tunisia, the United States, and Zimbabwe. Major products imported into China through the countertrade arrangements are timber, steel, cement, plywood, pig iron, chemical fibers, motor vehicles, and sugar.

The Seventh Five-Year Plan

Companies wishing to export to China should familiarize themselves with the current economic plan; the level of countertrade, if it is required, will depend on the priority of the import in the economic plan. China's Seventh Five-Year Plan, which covers the years 1986 through 1990, is designed to facilitate stable, moderate development. The major general objective of the plan is to continue the changeover from a rigid socialist economic system to one which is still socialist, but tailored to China's needs. Other broad objectives are to maintain economic growth, raise standards of living, decentralize decision-making, and remove the provincial governments from production unit control.

Specific objectives of the plan are to expand the energy, telecommunications, and transportation sectors; renovate existing enterprises; and to develop science, education, and technology. Emphasis will also be placed on the production of food, durable consumer goods, building materials, machinery, and electronics, as well as further development of service industries. There will be heavy emphasis on export promotion and the generation of foreign exchange. The Chinese are expected to insist that new joint venture proposals include plans for generating foreign exchange.

The total volume of foreign trade is planned to increase by 40% over the five-year period, with imports projected to grow at an average annual rate of 6.1% and exports at 8%; however, Chinese officials indicate that they expect a trade deficit for the next few years. GNP is projected to grow by an average 7.5% annually, a drop from 11.7% in 1984 and 12.5% in 1985. Industrial output growth is also projected to grow at an average rate of 7.5% Agricultural output is projected to increase by 4% per year, or by 6% if rural industries are included.

The plan covers the development of 925 large- and medium-scale projects, about half of which are scheduled for completion by 1990. A total of $62.5 billion will be allocated for these projects. Total state investment in technical transformation and equipment renewal will be $86 billion.

The budget for capital investment in the energy sector has been increased by 57% over the 1981–1985 period (the Sixth Five-Year Plan). New coal mines are to be developed, with a projected total output of 167 million tons per year, as well as new oil fields with a projected annual output of 60 million tons. Most new electricity generation will come from coal-fired plants, although there are also plans for the construction of large hydroelectric plants on the Yellow, Yangtze, and Pearl Rivers.

In the transport sector, the budget allocation has been increased by 46% over the previous five-year plan. The emphasis will be on port handling capacity. Automobile production will receive much less emphasis, projected to grow by only 5% annually compared to 14% under the previous plan.

In manufacturing, the Plan calls for substantial investments in chemicals, synthetic materials, aluminum, petrochemicals, open pit mining, equipment, energy-saving electrical machinery, microcomputers and peripherals, and fiberoptics R&D.

The highest import priorities under the new plan will be advanced technologies, key equipment and computer software. Foreign exchange will also be allocated for import-related projects in the areas of energy, transport, telecommunications, raw and semifinished materials (especially for electric power plants, port facilities and petroleum development), and the upgrading of machine-building and electronics industries. Prospects are not good for the import of consumer durables, on the other hand, since the Plan's emphasis is on import substitution in these product areas.

Some General Considerations for Beginning Business Operations in China

Identification of potential Chinese business partners should be left to the government; working backward by finding the plant first and then seeking government approval is not advised, as this can result in many delays and unacceptable changes. The first place to go is the relevant ministry; then to the appropriate commission for trade or investment; next to the corporation; and finally to the plant. It is always helpful, of course, to know the top people in the various agencies (such as the vice mayor of a city in a free economic zone); these people can often bypass a lot of red tape.

In structuring the business transaction, the foreign company should make sure that the transaction or enterprise conforms to the existing government requirements. Requesting something new will involve a lengthy approval process.

Timing is also an important consideration in planning the size of the project. A small simple project will take far less time to approve than a large complex project, since the latter may require approval from a number of government agencies. Most large projects are done in phases, to minimize red tape.

There are four major parties involved in the decision to sign a contract: the appropriate ministry, the Bank of China, the Chinese corporation, and the shipping company. Decision-making in an existing enterprise is shared with the Bank of China in foreign exchange matters, and with the shipping company in transport considerations. The foreign partner should obtain a clear description of the authority given by the government to the joint venture.

Joint venture agreements should also be interpreted as to whether there is recourse to arbitration in case of conflict.

Although there are now 126 wholly foreign-owned corporations in China, these make up only a small percentage of the total of 6,664 enterprises using foreign investment. Wholly foreign-owned enterprises are not especially popular with the Chinese, though the foreign companies naturally prefer full ownership because it gives them flexibility and control over profits. The Chinese are not against high profits; however, they want to share in the profits, and full foreign ownership of an enterprise obstructs this goal.

Products Available for Countertrade

Products that China has offered for countertrade include rice, corn, tea, cotton, jute, coal, crude petroleum, cotton textiles, bicycles, farm machinery, and cashmere sweaters.

Coal is a special target for compensation trade. China wants to expand coal production to 1.2 billion tons annually by 2000, an increase from 770 million tons in 1984. Surface mine output is planned to increase by 10% annually and underground production by 8% to 9%. This will require mechanization of China's numerous small family-owned mines (which account for 26% of national coal output), so that these mines can supply local energy needs. It will free railway capacity for the shipment of coal from the large state-owned coal mines to the ports for export.

China has bilateral trade agreements with 34 countries: Afghanistan, Albania, Algeria, Argentina, Bangladesh, Brazil, Bulgaria, Burkina Faso, Cuba, Czechoslovakia, Ecuador, Egypt, the GDR, Ghana, Greece, Guinea, Hungary, Indonesia, Iran, North Korea, Malaysia, Mali, Mexico, Mongolia, Nigeria, Pakistan, the Philippines, Poland, Romania, Sierra Leone, Turkey, the Soviet Union, Vietnam, and Zambia.

TRADE CONTROLS

Licenses from MOFERT are required for all import and export transactions. Minimum import tariffs apply to items originating in countries with which China has reciprocal trade agreements, while the general rate applies to all other countries. Import duties are levied on the c.i.f. value of goods. There is a schedule of 20 rates on the minimum tariff (ranging from 5% to 150%) and a schedule of 24 rates on the general tariff (7.5% to 250%). There is also a commercial turnover tax on imports. Raw materials imported for further processing are exempt from both customs duties and taxes, provided that the end products are exported within a specified period.

The import and export of weapons, ammunition and explosives, and radio receivers and transmitters is prohibited, in principle; actually, China exports some weapons. Trade in items such as manuscripts, printed and recorded materials, and films that are considered politically, culturally, or morally detrimental is also prohibited. Additionally, there are prohibitions against the export of valuable cultural relics; rare books, rare animals, and plants; precious metals; and artifacts made of precious metals. China has a "quality control" inspection license requirement for the export of specified machine tools. There is a tariff on all exports. Foreign exchange proceeds from exports must be repatriated to the Bank of China unless other arrangements have been made with the bank.

All trade (including indirect trade) with Israel, the Republic of Korea, and the Republic of South Africa is prohibited.

INTERNATIONAL TRADE

Imports

Chinese imports remained fairly stable from 1980 through 1983, at $19.5 billion in 1980, $21.5 billion in 1981, $18.9 billion in 1982, and $21.3 billion in 1983. In 1984, imports went up by 22.7% to $26.1 billion, and in 1985 they jumped by 54.1% to $440.3 billion. The average annual import growth rate for the six-year period is 17.4%.

Until 1985, China did not have very large trade deficits—$1.3 billion in 1980 and 1984, and a few million in 1981—and had small surpluses in some years. In 1985, the deficit swelled to $13.8 billion. This is probably one of the reasons for increased Chinese interest in countertrade.

About 70% of Chinese imports come from 12 countries: Japan, the United States, the Federal Republic of Germany, Canada, Australia, Romania, the United Kingdom, France, the USSR, Italy, North Korea, and Argentina, in that order. Japan and the United States together supply about half the market, accounting for 45% of Chinese imports for the five-year period 1980–1984.

In 1984, the shares of the top five suppliers were: Japan, 31.2%; United States, 14.7%; Germany, 4.7%; Canada, 4.0%; and Australia, 3.9%. China had trade deficits in 1984 with all of these suppliers. The largest deficits were with Japan, $3.0 billion, and the United States, $1.5 billion. Deficits ranged from $484 million to $798 million with Germany, Canada, and Australia.

Import Total, China (thousands)

	Value*	Growth (%)
1980	19,577,000	——
1981	21,564,000	10.1
1982	18,939,000	− 12.1
1983	21,324,000	12.5
1984	26,185,000	22.7
1985	40,354,000	54.1

*f.o.b. country of origin

Export Total, China (thousands)

	Value	Growth (%)
1980	18,268,000	——
1981	21,561,000	18.0
1982	21,913,000	1.6
1983	22,151,000	1.0
1984	24,871,000	12.2
1985	26,478,000	6.4

Exports

Chinese exports have been slightly less erratic than imports, considering that export value has increased each year. Growth is slow, though, averaging 7.8% per year for the 1980–1985 period. Export value gradually went up from $18.2 billion in 1980 to $26.4 billion in 1985.

About half of total Chinese exports, 48%, go to 13 countries: Japan, the United States, the Federal Republic of Germany, Singapore, the United Kingdom, Romania, Brazil, the Netherlands, North Korea, the USSR, Italy, France, and Thailand. These countries accounted for 1% or more of the Chinese export total for the 1980–1984 period.

Japan is China's best market, accounting for about 22% per year ($4–$5 billion) of total Chinese exports. The United States is the second largest market, accounting for 7% of Chinese exports. The other eleven countries account for less than 4% of exports: Germany and Singapore, 3–4%; and the United Kingdom, Romania, Brazil, the Netherlands, North Korea, the USSR, Italy, France, and Thailand, 1%–2%. Chinese export growth is very erratic in all of the top markets.

RECENT COUNTERTRADE TRANSACTIONS, CHINA

Partner country: United States (McDonnell-Douglas, with Shanghai Aviation International Corporation)

Import: Technology, know-how, training, and equipment for the construction of 30 to 45 twin-engine MD-82 commercial aircraft

Export: Aircraft

Value: Total transaction value, $1 billion; offset value, $300 million

Year: 1986

Duration: Twelve years

Type: Commercial aviation offset. Offset is 30%.

Comment:	Aircraft valued at $300 million are to be exported from China on a best-efforts basis. Chinese engineers will participate in designing new generation MD aircraft. As part of its training commitment, McDonnell-Douglas sent 42 of its managers to China and brought 1,200 Chinese technicians to Long Beach, California.

Partner country:	USSR
Import:	Ten 210-mw electric power generating stations
Export:	Textiles and light industrial products
Value:	$400 million (est.)
Year:	1986
Duration:	Unspecified
Type:	Bilateral trade agreement
Comment:	This is part of a larger agreement under which the Soviet Union will supply China with generating capacity totaling 6,800 mw through 1991.

Partner country:	Indonesia
Import:	Cement
Export:	Coal
Value:	$13 million
Year:	Unspecified
Duration:	Unspecified
Type:	Bilateral trade agreement

Partner country:	United States (Occidental Petroleum Company, with the following Chinese entities: Chinese National Coal Development Corp., China International Trust and Investment Corp., and the Bank of China)
Import:	Development of a large surface mine in Shanxi Province
Export:	Coal
Value:	$650 million
Year:	Unspecified
Duration:	Unspecified
Type:	Joint venture, buyback of production

Partner country:	Federal Republic of Germany (Volkswagen A.G.)
Import:	Automobile engine factory in Shanghai, automobile assembly plant in Beijing

Export: Automobile engines
Value: Unspecified
Year: 1985
Duration: Unspecified
Type: Joint venture, buyback of portion of production (the
                     fully assembled cars will be sold in China rather than
                     exported)

Partner country: United States (Phillip Morris Inc. with Guangzhou No.
                     2 Cigarette Factory)
Import: Machinery, know-how and training for the manufacture
                     of cigarettes; all raw materials for cigarettes
Export: Cigarettes
Value: $500,000 (value of equipment)
Year: 1980
Duration: Initially, approximately five years (time required to
                     produce enough cigarettes to pay for the equipment)
Type: Buyback
Comment: Phillip Morris buys back all output; the Chinese pay-
                     ment is 100% in products, no cash

Partner country: Japan (Mitsui Trading Company, selling textile machin-
                     ery manufactured by the Japanese firm Unitika to the
                     Dongsheng Cashmere Sweater Mill)
Import: Equipment and know-how for the manufacture of cash-
                     mere sweaters
Export: Cashmere sweaters
Value: Unspecified
Year: 1979
Duration: Unspecified; long-term
Type: Buyback
Comment: Mitsui will buy back 100 tons annually of the mill's
                     output of cashmere (total production is estimated at
                     510 tons per year) and sweaters

Partner country: United States (AMF Company)
Import: Know-how, technology, and equipment for the manu-
                     facture of athletic balls (sporting goods) by using an
                     existing factory
Export: Athletic balls

Value:	Unspecified
Year:	1980
Duration:	Unspecified; long-term
Type:	Buyback
Comment:	AMF buys back the entire output of the ball factory. The balls are then exported worldwide.
Partner country:	United States (AMF Company, with China's China National Machinery Import–Export Corp., the Electronic Components Industrial Corp., and the Shanghai Radio Factory)
Import:	Know-how, technology and equipment for the manufacture of small electrical relays in an existing factory; training in the use and maintenance of the relays
Export:	Electrical relays
Value:	Unspecified
Year:	1982
Duration:	Unspecified; long-term
Type:	Buyback
Comment:	The Chinese will be the sole producers of the relay; AMF buys back the entire output of the factory and exports the relays, with particular emphasis on Southeast Asian markets.
Partner country:	Japan (Mitsui Trading Company, selling textile machinery manufactured by the Japanese firm Unitika to the Inner Mongolian Regional Textile Industrial Company)
Import:	Equipment and know-how for the manufacture of cotton underwear
Export:	Cotton underwear
Value:	$13 million
Year:	1982
Duration:	Unspecified; long-term
Type:	Buyback
Partner country:	France (Brissonneau and Lotz, with the China Corporation Shipbuilding Industry)
Import:	Components for the manufacture of ship deck equipment (electric machines, control devices, cog wheels, and brakes); manufacturing know-how

Export: Parts for deck cranes
Value: FFR 1 million
Year: 1980
Duration: Unspecified
Type: Buyback

See also: ''Recent countertrade transactions'' for Argentina and Greece.

18 Colombia

COUNTERTRADE

Countertrade Policy

Countertrade is not mandatory in Colombia; however, the government has a formal countertrade policy and has passed legislation. The Colombian law covering countertrade is Decree No. 3707 of January 1986, which supercedes Decree No. 370 of 1984. Among other things, the law permits imports of prohibited or otherwise restricted (low priority) items on the condition that Colombian exports are purchased, and also facilitates imports of needed items for which foreign exchange is not available. The apparent objective of the policy is simply to promote exports through counterpurchase rather than to encourage coproduction and technology transfer. However, as countertrade appears to have become institutionalized in Colombia, there will probably be requirements for the offset of public procurements and interest in the more sophisticated forms of countertrade in the near future.

The major features of the new countertrade law are:

1. Applications for countertrade transactions must be submitted to the Ministry of Development for manufactured products, and to the Ministry of Agriculture for agricultural and other products under that ministry's jurisdiction. The relevant ministry will make a recommendation on the proposal to INCOMEX (Instituto Colombiano de Comercio Exterior Colombian Institute of Foreign Trade), which will then make its own recommendation and pass the proposal on to the Foreign Trade Council. The FTC makes the final decision. (Previously, applications were submitted directly to INCOMEX.)

2. There are, in theory, no restrictions on the types of products imported and exported under countertrade arrangements. Prohibited imports (those considered unnecessary), such as computers for the private sector and jeeps, may be purchased through countertrade, and traditional cash-earning exports may be offered as counterpurchases. The FTC will decide on a case-by-case basis whether countertrade is necessary to promote a nontraditional export

or maintain foreign markets for a traditional export. (Previously, there were numerous product restrictions.)

3. The Colombian exporter must post a bank guarantee ensuring that the foreign exchange earned from the counterpurchase will be remitted to the Banco de la Republica. (Previously, there were numerous special guarantee requirements for both importer and exporter.)

4. Offset is 200%; that is, there is a 2-to-1 counterpurchase requirement. Sellers to Colombia must buy $2 worth of Colombian exports for every $1 of imports sold. (No change.)

5. The counterpurchase of the Colombian export must be made before the import is sold. (No change.)

6. The transaction must result in incremental exports (additionality requirement). (No change.)

7. Prices of both imports and exports must be referenced to prevailing international market prices, meaning that foreign vendors are not supposed to factor in disagios or other countertrade costs. (No change.)

8. The Colombian importer must pay for the purchase in hard currency over a specified period of time. (No change.)

9. The import or export transaction could not have taken place using conventional trade mechanisms. (There are many exceptions to this rule.) (No change.)

10. Counterdelivered exports are not eligible for the export promotion tax rebate. (The rebate for countertrade exports was abolished by Decree No. 187 of January 1985.) Additionally, the SEIC or Systemas Especiales de Intercambio Commercial, an export promotion mechanism which allowed foreign exporters to get credit on counterdeliveries from Colombian exporters in private transactions, was abolished in late 1986 by Decree 1459.

11. Contracts must be registered within three months of government approval of the countertrade proposal.

12. The general foreign trade rules that apply to conventional transactions also apply to countertrade transactions.

There is a great deal of countertrade activity in Colombia; at least 300 countertrade deals have been approved since 1984, about 200 of which were bilateral or triangular arrangements. The aggregate value of Colombian countertrade is still small, though, estimated at roughly $150 million in exports per year.

Private sector practitioners have reported considerable difficulty in countertrade with Colombia. It is not clear how high the success rate is; some companies say that only 30% of the proposals are approved, while other sources indicate that 80% of all proposals are accepted. The two major problems are slow processing of proposals and difficulty in locating Colombian products that can be exported in quantities large enough to fulfill the counterpurchase requirement.

Colombia has bilateral clearing agreements with LAIA, CACM, Bulgaria, the GDR, Hungary, Poland, Romania, and Yugoslavia, and has reciprocal credit agreements with Cuba, the Dominican Republic, and Spain.

Products Available for Countertrade

Products which Colombia has countertraded include rice, bananas, shrimp, meat, coffee, fruit, fish, cane brandy (aguardiente), cotton, cotton yarn, medicinal herbs, coal, loofah body scrubbers, chemical products, textiles, gas cylinders, leather goods, footwear, clothing, pantyhose, furniture, and printed matter (magazines, books).

TRADE CONTROLS

All imports must be registered, and many require an import license; the government maintains two import product lists, the "free list" and the list of products that require licenses, which is revised periodically. Some imports may be temporarily prohibited, and licenses are usually not issued for firearms, habit-forming drugs, certain food items, certain textiles and clothing, and jewelry. Additionally, licenses may not be issued for the import of products that are available locally. There is a high fee for import registration. Advance import payment deposits must be made for most products. Other charges connected with imports are advance license deposits, ad valorem taxes, and a stamp tax, in addition to regular customs duties.

Exports of some commodities are prohibited, and exports of some items, such as beef, are reserved for state enterprises. No licenses are required, but all exports must be registered. Some exports are taxed (such as coffee), but exporters of 237 specified commodities are eligible to receive tax reimbursement certificates (CERT) for 15%, 20% or 25% of the f.o.b. export value as an export promotion incentive. As previously noted, countertrade-related exports are not eligible for the CERT program.

INTERNATIONAL TRADE

Imports

Colombian imports increased steadily until 1983, when they fell to $4.9 billion from $5.4 billion in the previous year. Since then, imports have declined by about 9% per year, dropping to $4.4 billion in 1984 and to $4.0 billion in

Import Total, Colombia (thousands)

	Value	Growth (%)
1980	4,662,604	——
1981	5,199,149	11.5
1982	5,463,078	5.0
1983	4,966,910	−9.0
1984	4,497,500	−9.4
1985	4,070,238 (est.)	−9.5

1985. Colombia usually carries a trade deficit of about a billion dollars a year; by 1985, it had been reduced to $555 million.

The major import product is crude petroleum, which accounts for about 8% of the annual import total, followed by petroleum products, 5%; passenger cars, 4%; and telecommunications equipment, 3%. Other important products are wheat, iron and steel semimanufactures (universals, plates, sheets), motor vehicle parts, paper and paperboard, civil engineering equipment, parts for nonelectric machinery, special industry machinery, and ships.

Most Colombian imports, 65%, come from the Americas: primarily from North America, 39.2%; and LAIA, 20.1%. The EEC provides 13.9% of imports, Asia, 11.9%, EFTA, 4.0%, and the CMEA countries, 2.4%. The United States is Colombia's major import trading partner, with a 35.6% market share, followed by Japan with an 11.1% share, Venezuela with 7.9% and Germany with 4.9%. Other important trading partners in imports are Brazil, Canada, France, Spain, the Netherlands Antilles, and the United Kingdom.

Exports

Export performance has been fairly good in recent years. Sales fell by 25% in 1981, dropping to $2.9 billion, but have increased by an average 4.5% per year since then. Exports totaled $3.0 billion in 1982 and 1983, rising to $3.4 billion in 1984 and to $3.5 billion in 1985.

Export diversification is badly needed, as Colombia depends on coffee for half its export sales. There are not many other products exported in large volume; petroleum products, bananas, and cut flowers, together with coffee, account for 75% of exports each year. Other important products (1–2% of exports) are sugar, pig iron, emeralds, and books and magazines.

Colombia is the second largest supplier of coffee, with a 13.4% world market share; second ranked supplier of cut flowers, 10.9% share; and fifth ranked supplier of bananas, 7.7% share. Brazil, the Netherlands, and Costa Rica are the respective top suppliers of these products.

About half of Colombian exports go to Europe. The EEC is Colombia's major export market by area, taking 36.5% of all exports; EFTA takes 5.5%, and the CMEA countries, 3.6%. The other large market is North America,

Export Total and Coffee Exports, Colombia (thousands)

	Value	Growth (%)	Exports, Coffee	Coffee, Total (%)
1980	3,945,048	——	2,371,838	60.1
1981	2,955,476	−25.0	1,462,188	49.4
1982	3,073,863	4.0	1,579,527	51.3
1983	3,080,893	0.2	1,541,445	50.0
1984	3,461,600	12.3	1,798,800	51.9
1985	3,514,400 (est.)	1.5	1,827,800 (est.)	52.0

destination of 29.2% of exports. Although 20% of imports come from the LAIA countries, only 8.5% of exports go there; the trade pattern with Asia is similar, with 11.9% of imports originating there but just 5.3% of exports sold in the region. Colombia's major markets by country are the United States and Germany, which take 28.3% and 18.4% of exports, respectively. Other important export trading partners are the Netherlands, Italy, Japan, Venezuela, and Spain.

RECENT COUNTERTRADE TRANSACTIONS, COLOMBIA

Partner country: Romania (with private Colombian mining company Intermin)

Import: Capital equipment for coal mine. Also, operating capital for the mine will be provided by shipping manufactured products to Colombia, where they will be sold and the resulting pesos (soft currency) used to cover the mine's in-country expenses. The products include jeeps, tractors, and pipeline systems. These items are in high demand in Colombia because import license requirements make it difficult to get them for cash.

Export: Coal

Value: $6 million each side

Year: 1985.

Duration: Five years

Type: Bilateral clearing agreement

Partner country: United States (Otis Elevator Co.)

Import: Elevators

Export: Weekly periodical, *Magazine al Dia*

Value: Elevators, $291,000; periodical, $364,000

Year: 1985
Duration: Unspecified
Type: Reciprocal trade

Partner country: United States (with Colombian firm Comlasa de Col-
                       ombia SA)
Import: Computers
Export: "Aguardiente Antioqueno" (cane brandy)
Value: Computers, $493,446; brandy, $500,000
Year: 1985
Duration: Unspecified
Type: Reciprocal trade

Partner country: Mexico
Import: Benzoic acid
Export: Benzoate of methyl, salicylic acid
Value: $58,000, each side
Year: 1985
Duration: Unspecified
Type: Barter/reciprocal trade

Partner country: Peru (with Colombia's Ingral SA)
Import: Fish
Export: Meat
Value: $1.2 million
Year: 1984
Duration: Unspecified
Type: Barter/reciprocal trade

Partner country: Japan (with Colombia's Automoviliaria Andina Ltd.)
Import: Jeeps
Export: Cotton fiber from Associacion Colombiana de Algodo-
                       neros
Value: $2.1 million
Year: 1984
Duration: Unspecified
Type: Reciprocal trade

Partner country: Israel
Import: Unspecified goods and services
Export: Coal, 5 million tons
Value: $200 million
Year: 1985
Duration: Unspecified
Type: Barter/reciprocal trade

19 Egypt

COUNTERTRADE

Countertrade Policy

Egypt has engaged in bilateral trade for many years. Most countertrade is conducted in the public sector, and there are no special incentives for private sector countertrade. The Ministry of Economy and Foreign Trade has issued formal countertrade guidelines covering the two types of transactions permitted:

1. *Transactions Involving Foreign Exchange.* An escrow account must be set up in a Western European bank (usually a Swiss bank). Hard currency payments are deposited by the foreign buyer; the foreign exchange is then sold to the Egyptian importer at fixed exchange rates plus a high premium. This hard currency can be used only for the purchase of products authorized by the Ministry. Under this type of arrangement, the Egyptian counterpurchase products are delineated in the contract, and they are traded at official minimum prices.

2. *Straight Barter Transactions.* This type of arrangement is used to obtain raw materials, and is restricted on the Egyptian side to manufacturers engaged in direct export. The foreign products must be used in-house (with some exceptions) and cannot be sold on the open market. In a straight barter deal, the Egyptian products must be traded at prices above the official minimum.

Egypt has bilateral clearing agreements with China, the GDR, Greece, Hungary, Jordan, North Korea, Romania, the Sudan, the USSR and Zambia.

Products Available for Countertrade

Unlike most other developing countries, Egypt offers traditional exports for counterpurchase. The product list prepared by the Ministry includes citrus, potatoes, onions, garlic, cotton, phosphates, crude petroleum, petroleum products, cotton and linen textiles, cement, and semifinished aluminum products.

TRADE CONTROLS

Import licenses are required for many private sector imports; no export licenses are required. Imports are regulated by exchange allocations to the foreign trade committees of the economic sectors. This has the effect of restricting imports of nonessential or domestically produced goods, though in principle almost anything can be imported as long as the foreign exchange is acquired outside the official and commercial bank markets. Exports of cotton, rice, and petroleum are handled by the public sector, and the export of many other products is supervised by the appropriate foreign trade committees. Foreign exchange proceeds must be surrendered within 90 days of shipment. All trade with South Africa is prohibited.

INTERNATIONAL TRADE

Imports

Egyptian imports have been very erratic. They plummeted by 42.9% in 1979, but increased by 26.6% in 1980 and by 81.8% in 1981. Since then, growth has been much slower: at 2.6% in 1982, 13.1% in 1983, and 9.9% in 1984, (data not available for 1985). The average annual growth rate, 15.1%, is not very representative of the actual growth pattern.

Egypt has carried an extremely large trade deficit for many years; it was about $6 billion in 1981 and 1982, $7 billion in 1983, and $5.3 billion in 1984. Exports in 1984 were only $3.8 billion, while imports were $9.2 billion. Egypt has been able to finance its imports so far through grants and loans from the United States, Western European countries, Japan and the United Nations. Although this assistance has apparently made it less urgent for Egypt

Import Total, Egypt (thousands)

	Value	Growth (%)
1978	6,726,640	——
1979	3,837,387	−42.9
1980	4,859,982	26.6
1981	8,839,464	81.8
1982	9,077,949	2.6
1983	10,274,000	13.1
1984	9,250,000	9.9
1985	Not available	——

than for some other developing countries to follow the IMF directive to cut imports and increase exports, export development is still a very high priority of the Egyptian government.

The major Egyptian import areas are machinery and transport equipment, food and live animals, and basic manufactures; these aggregate categories account for 29.3%, 26.1%, and 20.0% respectively of total imports. Most categories are dominated by a single product; for example tobacco accounts for 99% of beverages and tobacco imports, shaped wood for 58.8% of crude materials imports and wheat for 29.6% of food imports.

The top import products are road motor vehicles, which account for about 9% of annual imports; wheat, 8%; miscellaneous nonelectric machinery, 5%; and cement, 4%. Some of the other major import items are corn, special industry machinery, wheat flour, shaped wood, and iron and steel shapes.

Egypt's major supplier by area is Europe, which supplies 55% of the country's imports (EEC, 39.8%; CMEA, 7.5%; EFTA, 5.6%; other, 3.8%). The Americas is the second ranked supplier area, providing 24% of imports (North America, 20%). Asia supplies 12% of imports, Oceania supplies 2%, and Africa supplies 1%. Top import trading partners by country are the United States, which has a 19% share of the Egyptian market; Germany, 10%; Italy, 7.6%; and France, 7.5%. Other important suppliers are the United Kingdom, Japan, the Netherlands, Romania, Greece, and the USSR.

Exports

Egyptian exports have been about as erratic as imports. Annual growth rates (not shown on the accompanying table) were 5.9% in 1979, 65.5% in 1980, 6.1% in 1981, minus 3.4% in 1982, 18.3% in 1983, and 4.6% in 1984 (data for 1985 not available). The average growth rate is 16.1%. Exports were valued at $3.8 billion in 1984 and are estimated at $4.1 billion for 1985.

Egypt is dependent on three products for 80% of exports: crude petroleum, petroleum products, and cotton. Petroleum has displaced cotton as the major export. In 1978, petroleum exports were only slightly higher than cotton, accounting for 20.6% of the total compared to 20.4% for cotton, but by 1984 petroleum represented 55.0% of exports and cotton only 15.4%. (Egypt is still the world's second ranked cotton supplier after the United States, though, with a world market share of 6.6%.) Petroleum products appear to be a less stable export item, though they have recently accounted for an increasingly large share of the export total. Other important export products are textile yarn, aluminum, potatoes, oranges and other citrus fruits, and perfume oils.

By area, most Egyptian exports go to Europe, 58% (44% to the EEC, 13% to the CMEA countries). Asia is the other big market, taking 24% of Egyptian exports. Only 5% of exports go to the Americas (mostly to North America) and 4% to Africa. Less than 1% of exports go to Oceania. Italy is Egypt's major export trading partner, taking 22% of exports, followed by Israel, 14%; and France, 7%. Other important export markets are the USSR, the Netherlands, the United States, Japan, Romania, Germany, and Greece.

Export Total and Major Exports, Egypt (thousands)

	Export Total	Petroleum, Petroleum Products, Cotton, Total (%)	Petroleum	Total (%)
1978	1,737,150	48.0	359,493	20.6
1979	1,839,729	62.9	566,413	30.7
1980	3,045,959	78.6	1,761,823	57.8
1981	3,232,182	78.8	1,757,896	54.3
1982	3,120,195	79.4	1,730,354	55.4
1983	3,693,000	79.4	2,031,150 (est.)	55.0
1984	3,864,000	81.0	2,125,000 (est.)	55.0

	Petroleum Products	Total (%)	Cotton	Total (%)
1978	122,202	7.0	354,867	20.4
1979	196,855	10.7	396,856	21.5
1980	194,208	6.3	443,451	14.5
1981	319,692	9.8	477,392	14.7
1982	335,234	10.7	419,456	13.4
1983	395,151 (est.)	10.7	505,941	13.7
1984	413,448 (est.)	10.7	595,056	15.4

RECENT COUNTERTRADE TRANSACTIONS, EGYPT

Partner country: United States (General Motors with Egypt's GOFI, General Organization for Industrialization)

Import: Joint venture manufacture of two small General Motors cars, the Corsa and the Ascona, and components for the cars

Export: Components noted above; of the components produced in Egypt, 50% to 90% must be exported.

Value: $1 billion

Year: 1986

Duration: Unspecified (exceeds five years)

Type: Direct offset, buyback type

Comment: GOFI's objective in this project was to assist Egypt's nationalized firm NASCO (Nasr Automotive Manufacturing Co.) in the development of integrated car production. General Motors, in addition to helping achieve this general goal, will develop a local components manufacturing industry. While the cars will be produced for import substitution, the components are to be produced on a large scale for export. General Motors agreed to a 50% local content requirement for the first five years and to a higher percentage thereafter. Under the present production schedule, 90,000 cars will be produced annually five years from startup.

General Motors' offset plans involve 15 of its associated U.S. and European suppliers. These suppliers include:

Bendix: Brake/clutch linings

B.F. Goodrich: Radial tires

Diavia: Air conditioning equipment

Kelsey-Hayes: Wheels and brakes

ITT: Electrical components

Lucas: Lighting systems and parts

Pittsburgh Plate Glass: Paints

Roth-Technik: Exhaust systems

TRW: Steering system components

Sheller Globe: Interior plastic moldings

United Technologies: Electrical components

Valeo: Radiators

Partner country:	Romania
Import:	Construction steel, wood, newsprint, tractor spare parts, cement
Export:	Cotton, finished textiles, citrus, pharmaceuticals
Value:	$84 million annually
Year:	1985
Duration:	Unspecified
Type:	Bilateral clearing agreement

Partner country:	Hungary
Import:	Unspecified
Export:	Cotton, finished textiles, citrus, pharmaceuticals
Value:	$66 million annually
Year:	1985
Duration:	Unspecified
Type:	Bilateral clearing agreement

Partner country:	Greece (Greek ITCO, with Egyptian state-owned Misr Trading Co.)
Import:	Bauxite, olives, paper, refractory bricks, window glass, other products

Export: Cement, cotton, groundnuts, herbs, mineral salts,
                            naphtha, phosphates, urea, other products
Value: $15 million annually
Year: 1985
Duration: Unspecified
Type: Bilateral clearing agreement

Partner country: Australia (Australian Wheat Board)
Import: Wheat, 10 million tons
Export: None; Egypt received low-interest credits through
                            Australia for the construction of wheat storage facili-
                            ties (silos)
Year: 1986
Duration: Five years
Type: Concessionary financing countertrade

Partner country: Jordan
Import: Cement, 1.5 million tons
Export: Rice, 10,000–15,000 tons
Value: Unspecified
Year: 1986
Duration: Unspecified
Type: Bilateral clearing agreement

See also: Brazil, "comment" section on Brazilian aircraft deal with the
United Kingdom.

20 Greece

COUNTERTRADE

Countertrade Policy

As a member of the European Economic Community, Greece is theoretically not supposed to promote or practice countertrade on a government level (other than military offsets), or participate in bilateral trade agreements. However, the Greek government has a formal countertrade policy concerning defense procurements and large civil procurements. This policy stops just short of stating that countertrade is mandatory, though all state enterprises have been directed to obtain offset concessions from foreign vendors. Greece has numerous bilateral clearing agreements, mostly with socialist countries, and is in the process of expanding these agreements and negotiating new ones. The force behind this activity appears to be aggressive export promotion. Greece has a large merchandise trade deficit; to date the country has gotten by on income from tourism and shipping (in fact, it is classified by the IMF as a "service and remittance country"), but the current government seems determined to balance trade, and has seized upon countertrade as a mechanism. The stated objectives of the Greek countertrade policy are export development and technology transfer. Unlike Canada and Australia, two other developed countries that practice countertrade, Greece does not consider employment to be a major objective of its countertrade program.

Main features of the Greek countertrade policy are:

1. *Offsets.* Foreign suppliers offering direct offsets will be favored over those offering indirect offsets, who will in turn be favored over those who do not offer reciprocity. Direct offsets involving technology transfer are the most desirable.

2. *Offset Percentages.* The Greek goal appears to be 100%, although many important deals have involved offset percentages as low as 40%; this seems to be the minimum acceptable offset.

3. *Offset Credits.* Credits may be earned by the usual methods, including coproduction, licensed production, joint ventures, technology transfer, counterpurchase, and tourism.

4. *Greek Private Sector Involvement.* Offset credit is not limited to arrangements with state enterprises and cooperatives. Foreign vendors may earn credit with a state enterprise by transferring technology to a private firm or by obtaining counterpurchases from a private firm.

5. *Counterpurchases.* The government requires the foreign vendor to select counterpurchase products from a prepared list. Most of the items on the list are traditional exports. Bids that contain a counterpurchase proposal should include the following information:

    a. Identification of the counterpurchase products

    b. Total value of the products proposed for counterpurchase

    c. Identification of the countries in which the counterpurchases will be liquidated

    d. Period of time over which the Greek products will be taken

6. *Third Countries.* In some cases, foreign vendors to Greece can take payment in counterpurchases from an Eastern European country that is indebted to Greece. Greece will then credit the import from the foreign vendor as a payment on the debt.

Greek countertrade is under the jurisdictions of the Ministry of National Economy (military offsets) and the Ministry of Commerce (civilian offsets and other nonmilitary countertrade). Exports under offset and countertrade are handled by the state International Trading Company (ITCO). ITCO is also responsible for all countertrade contracts with socialist countries. A new unit within the Ministry of Commerce, the Department for Promotion of Exports of Products and Services (DPEPS), has the responsibility of overseeing and enforcing offsets.

ITCO was established in 1984 to coordinate and promote exports by using the purchasing power of state and quasi-state enterprises. The shareholders are four state-controlled banks: the Hellenic Industrial Development Bank, the National Investment Bank for Industrial Development, the Agricultural Bank, and the Investment Bank. In early 1986 ITCO released a report on its business from May 1984 through December 1985. Major findings of this report were: (1) ITCO generated US $41 million in exports; (2) 73% of the organizations that exported under ITCO's countertrade arrangements were private companies (of 51 companies, 37 were private, 8 were cooperatives and 6 were state enterprises); (3) the major products exported were agricultural commodities, light industrial products, processed food products, chemicals, footwear, and textiles, in order by value; (4) the major export markets were Arab countries, EFTA countries (especially Switzerland), Eastern European countries, African countries and Asian countries, in that order; and (5) 45% of the exports resulted from offsets and 30% from bilateral clearing agreements, with the remaining 25% unspecified.

DPEPS, established in 1986 within the Ministry of Commerce, is part of the Special Secretariat of Foreign Trade. It will deal not only with foreign vendors but with Greek enterprises, to ensure that the enterprises obtain offset commitments. The responsibilities of DPEPS are to:

1. Prepare offset agreements in cooperation with the General Secretariat of Public Procurement and other government units.

2. Enforce compliance of the trading partner with the terms of the offset agreement as well as the actual fulfillment of the obligation. For example, if the offset obligation requires a bank guarantee of fulfillment, DPEPS will be responsible for assuring that the trading partner actually provides the guarantee.

3. Monitor the functioning of the Greek offset system and recommend desirable changes to the appropriate officials of the ministries.

4. Conduct research on possible methods of linking Greece's export promotion policy with its offset policy. For example, DPEPS will study ways to ensure that exports in fulfillment of offset obligations are incremental.

Greek state enterprises are required to: advise DPEPS whenever they issue tender documents; after bids are received, advise DPEPS of the low bidder or the bidders that were short listed; and appoint a liason officer to maintain contact with DPEPS.

Greece has bilateral clearing agreements with Albania, Algeria, Bulgaria, China, Czechoslovakia, Egypt, the GDR, Hungary, India, Iran, Libya, Mexico, Poland, Romania, and the Soviet Union. Greece buys 75% of its oil from Arab countries on the basis of long-term bilateral agreements; some of the more recent deals have been with Algeria, Iran, and Iraq, in which Greece has traded construction work, agricultural products, and manufactured goods for oil. In new agreements with Eastern European countries, Greece is interested in settling debts owed by the countries from previous bilateral agreements and in settling social insurance claims of Greek nationals.

Products Available for Countertrade

Products Greece has offered for countertrade include dried figs, peeled tomatoes, tomato paste, raisins and currants, canned fruits and vegetables, olives, olive oil, flour, chicken, eggs, wines, cigarettes, unmanufactured tobacco, emery, magnesite, sulphur, asbestos, cement, clinker (cement pellets), finished marble, construction materials, fertilizers, chemicals, aluminum profiles, iron and steel plates and sheets, steel tubes and pipes, pipe fittings, paper, ceramic tile, cotton yarn, wool and cotton textiles, cables, agricultural machinery, electrical appliances, furniture, fur apparel, textile apparel, footwear, and toys. Services countertraded include construction work and ship repair.

ITCO handles countertrade export products. Its address is:

ITCO S.A.
44, B. Konstantinou Avenue
116–35 Athens, Greece
Telephone: 7229046-7-8
Telex: 225020 ITCO GR

TRADE CONTROLS

There are a number of restrictions on imports. All imports require approval
(except those valued at c.i.f. of the equivalent of U.S. $1000 or less) and
some require licenses, according to which list they are on. Some items on
Lists A and B can be imported without licenses if they come from EEC
countries. There are special regulations for certain imports, such as goods
under monopoly control, medicines, narcotics, sulphur, and motion picture
films. Private sector imports are subject to restrictions on the method of
payment; controls over the time period required to make final settlement
and the time of shipments; and various advance deposit requirements. The
deposits do not bear interest. Certain companies, public agencies, and organizations that have been designated public service institutions are exempt
from advance deposit requirements, however. Also exempt are duty-free
imports and imports of raw materials and semifinished products for re-export,
as well as imports of finished products for re-export. Most imports are subject
to a stamp tax based on the c.i.f. duty-paid and the tax-paid value. Nearly
all exports require individual licenses. Most are free of quantitative limitations. As of 1981, all transactions for exports are undertaken by commercial
banks. Export proceeds must be repatriated within 90 days of shipment,
though extensions can be granted. Industrial exporters can obtain subsidies
in the form of interest rebates on loans or income tax deductions.

INTERNATIONAL TRADE

Imports

Greek imports, though slow-growing, are still far higher than exports; the
trade deficit in 1985 was $5.3 billion, based on imports of $9.8 billion and
exports of $4.4 billion. Import growth was erratic through 1983, with value
increasing by 9.7% in 1980, falling by 16.6% in 1981, going back up by 14.0%
in 1982 and back down by 5.1% in 1983. Since then growth has been very
sluggish, as 1.2% in 1984 and 2.3% in 1985.

Slightly over half of Greek imports consist of mineral fuels and machinery
and transport equipment, with the former accounting for 28% of annual imports and the latter for 25%. Basic manufactures account for 17% of imports,

food for 12%, and chemicals for 8%. The other product groups account for less than 7% each of imports.

The top import product is crude petroleum, which accounts for about 25% of imports each year. There are no other dominant imports; the next most valuable product, ships, accounts for only 6% of imports. Other important products, in order by value, are meat, furskins, iron and steel primary forms, passenger motor vehicles, trucks, chemical polymerization products, milk and cream, paper and paperboard, medicinal products, motor vehicle parts, heavy iron and steel products (universals, plates, sheets) and petroleum products. These 14 products account for 52% of annual Greek imports.

Most Greek imports come from Europe, 60%, and Asia, 28%. Since Greece is in the EEC, the bulk of European imports (48% of total imports) comes from the trade bloc. About 5% come from EFTA and 5% from the CMEA countries. Roughly 7% of imports come from Africa, and 6% from the Americas, primarily North America. Greece's major import trading partner is Germany, which has a 17.3% share of the Greek market. Saudi Arabia has a 12.4% share and Italy has an 8.9% share. Other important trading partners are Japan, France, the Netherlands, the United Kingdom, the United States, Libya, and Egypt.

Exports

Export performance is not very encouraging. The highest that exports have been in recent years is $5.1 billion, in 1980; since then, exports have stayed around $4.5 billion per year. They were $4.4 billion in 1985. The average growth rate of exports is 3.4%; they increased by 32.6% in 1980, fell by 17.3% in 1981, went up by 1.1%, 2.6% and 9.1%, respectively in 1982, 1983, and 1984, and back down by 7.5% in 1985. It is easy to see why Greece is so anxious to use countertrade to increase exports.

Greece has the export structure of a developing country: 30% of exports are basic manufactures and 22% are food products. Only 4% of annual exports are machinery and transport equipment, in striking contrast to the other EEC countries. In other product groups, 14% of exports are miscellaneous manufactures, 7% are mineral fuels, 7% are crude materials, 6% are animal and

Import Total, Greece (thousands)

	Value	Growth (%)
1979	9,593,834	——
1980	10,531,301	9.7
1981	8,780,644	− 16.6
1982	10,012,196	14.0
1983	9,499,594	− 5.1
1984	9,616,217	1.2
1985	9,839,780	2.3

Export Total, Greece (thousands)

	Value	Growth (%)
1979	3,877,426	——
1980	5,141,664	32.6
1981	4,249,461	− 17.3
1982	4,296,669	1.1
1983	4,412,232	2.6
1984	4,814,318	9.1
1985	4,453,038	− 7.5

vegetable oils and fats, 5% are beverages and tobacco, and 4% are chemicals. It does not appear that Greece's countertrade program has helped increase exports of machinery and transport equipment yet. As noted earlier, ITCO reported that its highest value export category in the first 20 months of operation was agricultural commodities.

There is no single product which dominates exports; the highest value product category, fresh and dried fruit and nuts (primarily grapes, raisins, olives, and oranges) accounts for only 7% of annual exports. The next most valuable exports are petroleum products, textile yarn, cement, olive oil, unmanufactured tobacco, preserved vegetables, aluminum, wheat, women's nonknit outerwear, headwear, preserved fruit, knit undergarments and base metal ores and concentrates (primarily alumina). These 14 products account for 58% of annual Greek exports.

Most Greek exports, 65%, go to Europe; 53% to the EEC, 8% to the CMEA countries, 2% to EFTA, and 2% to other European countries. Asia takes 18% of exports, Africa 10%, and the Americas 7% (almost all North America). Germany is Greece's top export market, taking 20% of exports. Italy is the second most important export trading partner, taking 13.5% of exports, followed by France, 7.4%; Saudi Arabia, 7.3%; and the United States, 6.3%. Other important export markets are the United Kingdom, the Netherlands, Egypt, the USSR, and Libya.

RECENT COUNTERTRADE TRANSACTIONS, GREECE

Partner country: France (Government of France and Dassault Co., with Greek Air Force and Hellenic Aerospace Industry Co.)

Import: Coproduction of aircraft and technology transfer: 40 Mirage-2000 jet fighters, including spare parts, technical support, and training; investment and technological assistance from Dassault to Hellenic Aerospace for manufacturing of parts and assembly of integrated components for aircraft

Export: The direct offset portion includes: (1) manufacture of
                   doors, landing gear, parts of the wings, large parts of
                   the fuselages, and the power supply and symbol gener-
                   ators (among other electrical components) for the radar
                   and (2) assembly and testing of 50 SNECMA engines.
                   The indirect offset portion includes incremental ex-
                   ports of agricultural products and ores; exports of oth-
                   er products

Value: Approximately $900 million

Year: 1985

Duration: Fifteen years

Type: Military offset, mixture of direct and indirect offset;
                   the offset is minimum 100%, maximum 200%; 150% of
                   the obligation will be fulfilled by Dassault and 50% by
                   the French government

Comment: The major provisions of the deal are:

1. The time period for the offset is broken down into
   three-year periods. In the fourth year after each
   period, Dassault must pay a penalty if the prior
   period's offset obligations were not fulfilled.

2. There is a credit weighting system for eligible offset projects, with a minimum weight of 40% and a
   maximum weight of 80%, depending on Greek
   value added and other factors. If all projects selected by the French are weighted at 80%, the total offset will be 200%; if all projects are weighted
   at 40%, the offset will be 100%.

3. The French must fulfill a minimum of 30% of the
   total offset commitment through investment and
   technological assistance which will enable Greece
   to establish maintenance and repair facilities for
   civil and military aircraft.

4. Acceptable indirect offsets include nonmilitary
   technology transfer and investment, transportation, tourism (maximum 10% of obligation) and
   new energy sources. The French may select projects and Greek partners from an eligibility list
   prepared by the Greek Ministry of National
   Economy.

5. The total value of Greek imports will be covered
   by French government loans.

Partner country: United States (General Dynamics with Greek Air
                   Force and Hellenic Aerospace Industry Co.)

Import: Coproduction of aircraft and technology transfer; pur-
                         chase of 40 F-16 jet fighters

Export: Indirect offset is 40% of total offset and includes ex-
                         port of unspecified products

Value: $900 million

Year: 1985

Duration: 15 years

Type: Military offset, mixture of direct coproduction and in-
                         direct offset. Offset obligation is 100%: 60% to be ful-
                         filled through direct coproduction arrangements with
                         Greek defense industry (primarily aerospace), and 40%
                         to be indirect offset including export of products, in-
                         vestment, and tourism. Indirect offset may include ship
                         repair. Fulfillment is divided into three five-year pe-
                         riods, with 40% fulfillment during the first period and
                         30% during each of the remaining two periods.

Comment: There are unconfirmed reports that the U.S. govern-
                         ment offered Greece concessionary FMS financing on
                         the sale of the F-16s in return for reduction in the di-
                         rect offset obligation to 40% of the transaction value;
                         this would have saved Greece $50 million. The alleged
                         reason behind the offer was that the Pentagon wanted
                         to control the flow of technology to Greece. However,
                         Greece decided that it wanted the technology and re-
                         jected the FMS financing.

Partner country: Federal Republic of Germany (Daimler-Benz with
                         Greek firm Steyr-Hellas S.A.)

Import: 10,000 jeep-type military vehicles

Export: Coproduction of vehicles

Value: Unspecified

Year: 1985

Duration: Unspecified

Type: Coproduction offset; 80% offset on parts and compo-
                         nents imported into Greece

Partner country: Bulgaria (with Greek Ministry of National Economy
                         and state-owned Eleusis Shipyards)

Import: Machinery, fertilizers, metal products; see ''Com-
                         ment'' below

Export: Ship repair; alumina, 200,000 tons per year

Value:	$40 million per year ($400 million total)
Year:	1985
Duration:	Ten years
Type:	Bilateral clearing agreement
Comment:	Bulgaria will settle $9 million worth of social insurance claims of Greek nationals with products consisting of capital goods, consumer items, and semifinished goods.

Partner country:	China (China National Chemicals Import–Export Corp. with the Greek firms Chemical Industries of Northern Greece, S.A., and Hellenic Chemical Products and Fertilizers Co. S.A.)
Import:	Chemicals
Export:	Compound fertilizers, 130,000 tons
Value:	$22 million (value of fertilizer)
Year:	1985
Duration:	Unspecified
Type:	Bilateral clearing agreement

Partner country:	China
Import:	Textiles, watches, decorative household items
Export:	Fertilizers, steel products, cables, construction materials, turnkey plants
Value:	$50 million each side
Year:	1985
Duration:	Unspecified
Type:	Bilateral clearing agreement

Partner country:	Albania
Import:	Electric power, asphalt, petroleum products, agricultural products
Export:	Metal products, machinery, semifinished industrial products; construction of a chromite processing plant in Albania
Value:	$80 million (value of chromite plant, $7 million)
Year:	1985
Duration:	Unspecified
Type:	Bilateral clearing agreement

Partner country: United Kingdom (ML Engineering)
Import: Upgrading of Athens-Thessaloniki railway system; automatic signalling system
Export: Unspecified
Value: £ 3.17 million
Year: 1985
Duration: Unspecified
Type: Civilian offset; 100% offset

Partner country: United States (Cravat Coal Co. and United Energy Resources, both of Cadiz, Ohio, with Greece's Public Power Corp.)
Import: Coal
Export: Clinker (cement pellets), other products
Value: $28 million
Year: 1985
Duration: Unspecified
Type: Civilian offset; value of counterpurchase obligation is $7.2 million, which is 25% offset
Comment: Up to 50% of the counterpurchase obligation can be satisfied by shipping the coal on Greek carriers

Partner country: Iran
Import: Oil
Export: Flour, chicken, eggs, tobacco, cigarettes, paper, chemicals, cables, footwear, other products
Value: $400 million
Year: 1984
Duration: 18 months
Type: Bilateral trade agreement

Partner country: Algeria
Import: Oil
Export: Construction of 3000 houses in the towns of Biskra and Zizel; export of unspecified products
Value: $200 million
Year: 1985
Duration: 12 months
Type: Bilateral trade agreement

21 Malaysia

COUNTERTRADE

Countertrade Policy

Malaysia issued formal countertrade guidelines in 1982. Countertrade is not mandatory, though in practice it appears to be required for most civil and military procurements; additionally, the government urges private sector companies to ask for countertrade from their foreign suppliers. Most observers agree that Malaysia began its offset program as a reaction to Indonesia's aggressive export promotion activities and resultant countertrade program. The two countries are direct competitors in many products, and Indonesia had begun to displace Malaysia in several important markets. As Malaysia has gained experience in countertrade, the government has become less reactive and more proactive in its policy and practices.

Malaysia's countertrade policy was originally considered to be one of the most flexible among developing countries. However, offset is now frequently demanded instead of "invited," and the terms of offsets have become quite restrictive, especially in regard to offset percentages, types of products available for counterpurchase, and liquidation of goods in third countries. A major problem, from the foreign vendor's point of view, is the government's practice of arranging offsets on a case-by-case basis; one vendor may get relatively easy terms, while another will encounter various restrictions. The government is expected to issue a revised policy in the near future. This policy should formalize the current unofficial practices and make offset requirements more equitable among vendors.

The objectives of the original policy, as stated by the government, were additionality of exports; development of new export markets; increased access to markets where protectionism or competition had hindered the growth of Malaysian exports, primarily industrial country markets; diversification of exports; promotion of nontraditional, high-value-added exports, primarily manufactures and semimanufactures; maintenance of market share for traditional exports; facilitation of exports to countries with foreign exchange shortages, particularly the CMEA countries; and balancing trade with specific countries. To date, the emphasis has been almost exclusively on counter-purchase as the means to achieving these ends, though the government is beginning to regard technology transfer as an important export development tool.

Major features of the original policy, new developments, and unofficial practices are listed below.

Original Policy and Related Changes in Practice

1. The government agency which evaluates, approves, and makes the final decision on countertrade proposals is the Unit Khas Countertrade (Special Countertrade Unit) of the Ministry of Trade and Industry. Unit Khas approves proposals on a case-by-case basis. New development: Unit Khas now sets the terms of the offsets and closely monitors the administration of offset transactions.

2. Foreign vendors are "invited" rather than required to include countertrade proposals in their bids, though the government has stated that a good countertrade proposal might win the contract, all other things being equal. This has not changed, since countertrade is still not officially mandatory. New development: Unit Khas, rather than the foreign vendor, has the responsibility of organizing the offset, selecting counterpurchase products, and so on.

3. The offset obligation can be assigned to a third-party trading company for liquidation. (No change.) Most countertrade obligations are handled by three major Malaysian trading companies: Malaysian International Trading Corporation, (MITCO; government); Malaysian Overseas Investment Corporation, (MOIC; quasi-government); and Bumiputra International Corporation, (Bumi, private). The fees charged by these companies usually range from 5% to 7% of the value of the transaction.

4. Goods produced in Malaysian free trade zones are not eligible for counterpurchase. (No change.)

5. Offsets are not supposed to be required for public works projects involving financing by international lending agencies such as the World Bank or the Asian Development Bank. (No change.)

6. Malaysian exporters selling products through countertrade can arrange alternate methods of repatriation of export proceeds with Bank Negara Malaysia (the Central Bank). For conventional export transactions, proceeds must be repatriated in full in specified foreign currencies or Malaysian ringgit within six months from the date of shipment. (No change.)

7. Products targeted for import through countertrade are military equipment and vehicles, industrial machinery and equipment, sugar, rice, animal feed, iron ore, coal, chemicals, fertilizers, cotton, and wheat. (No major change.) In practice, most Malaysian offset to date has been in state railway

improvement, highway construction, electrification programs, large water treatment programs, rural water supply projects, and defense procurements.

8. Types of products eligible for counterpurchase: The Malaysian government prefers that primary commodities and semiprocessed raw materials be reserved for developing and socialist countries, while takebacks destined for industrial countries are supposed to be semimanufactures and manufactures. (No change.) This policy has never been strictly enforced, though Unit Khas has recently stepped up its efforts to get industrial country vendors to take nontraditional products. To date, most of the counterpurchases have been traditional exports, regardless of destination: crude petroleum, petroleum products, processed palm oil, rubber, timber, sawn logs, and wood products.

New Developments

1. Destination of counterpurchased exports: As of 1986, Unit Khas prohibits liquidation of takebacks in third country markets when the Malaysian procurement contract is valued at less than M $10 million (about U.S. $4.3 million). Above that figure, a percentage of offsets (often as little as 30%) may go to third countries. Originally, the liquidation of counterpurchases was by product rather than by value of contract. Goods were divided into two groups: Schedule A products, which had to be sold in the home market of the vendor, and Schedule B products, which could be liquidated anywhere.

2. The penalty for nonfulfillment of offset obligations is 15%, as of 1986. The foreign vendor must post a security deposit equal to 5% of the value of the offset obligation, in the form of a bank guarantee against nonfulfillment; the other 10% is left open as good faith on the vendor's part.

3. Offset percentages vary, ranging from 50% to 100%. The Ministry of Industry and Trade estimates that the average offset is 92%; however, a check of past Malaysian deals indicates that most offsets are around 80%.

Unofficial Practices

1. Unit Khas has sometimes required that 100% of the takebacks be liquidated in the foreign vendor's country, regardless of the value of the contract. (See Item 9.) Furthermore, this requirement has often been imposed in midtransaction, long after the foreign vendor had arranged to sell the counterpurchases in a third country. Vendors affected by these practices have included Tradeks (on behalf of Sapura of Japan) and C. Itoh of Japan.

2. There have been instances of *forward offset*, in which Malaysia will not take delivery of imported products until after the offset obligation has been fulfilled. The first known forward offset was imposed on British Rail Engineering by Malayan Railways.

3. Unit Khas has an unofficial policy of allowing only 100% Bumiputra (ethnic Malaysian) trading houses to assume offset obligations on a nonrecourse basis.

Malaysia is a strong supporter of the NIEO and is interested in the promotion of South–South trade, particularly with other Islamic countries. The government views countertrade as a permanent fixture of its trading relationships with both developed and developing countries. Indeed, some Malaysian officials are very outspoken concerning countertrade as a mechanism to penetrate industrial country markets. The Minister of Trade and Industry, Tengku Razaleigh Hamzar, said at a 1986 conference that countertrade would help private Malaysian companies "circumvent Western protectionism." An official of MOIC, Tan Sri Ghazali Shafie, stated at a 1985 seminar that countertrade was "the only way to circumvent Western protectionism." Mr. Shafie is also generally credited as the first person to make the now famous prediction that countertrade would account for 40% of world trade by 1990.

The value of Malaysian public sector countertrade is estimated by the authors at U.S. $321.8 million for the years 1982 through 1985, based on the values of known countertrade deals, with over half of the value accumulated in 1985. The estimated total value, including 1986 countertrade, is U.S. $500 million. The Ministry of Industry and Trade estimates that private sector countertrade from 1983 through 1985 generated M $336 million in exports and M $28 million in imports (about U.S. $143.4 million and $11.9 million, respectively). When one tries to translate the private sector figures into offset percentages, they do not make much sense, as the result is 1100% offset. Possibly the term "generated" refers to incremental exports that occurred after the countertrade transactions were completed.

Malaysia has bilateral clearing agreements with Brazil, China, Czechoslovakia, Nigeria, the Philippines, and Romania.

Products Available for Countertrade

The products Malaysia wants to export to industrial countries through countertrade are manufactures and semimanufactures such as food products, articles of rubber and wood, textiles, electrical components, electrical goods, and footwear. A locally produced automobile, the Proton Saga, may also be promoted in countertrade if test marketing through conventional channels does not show acceptable results. Products Malaysia has given in countertrade include cocoa and cocoa products, coffee, pepper and other spices, crude and processed palm oil, crude petroleum, petroleum products, refined pump oil, pump oleins, pump stearin oil, tin, methanol, urea, blended fertilizers, dental alloys, sawn logs, timber, wood products (plywood, veneers), rubber and rubber products (tires, hoses, gloves, etc.), cotton textiles, cotton yarn, rubber processing machinery, furniture, and footwear.

Key Government Agencies and Private Companies

Unit Khas Countertrade
International Trade Division
Ministry of Trade and Industry
9th Floor, Block 10, Government
  Offices Complex
Jalan Duta, Kuala Lumpur, Ma-
  laysia
Telephone: 940033/946022/948044
Telex: DANANG MA 30634

Malaysian International Trading
  Corporation (MITCO)
11th Floor, Block E, Plaza Peke-
  liling, No. 2
Jalan Pekeliling, Kuala Lumpur,
  Malaysia
Telephone: 917122
Telex: MA 31731 MITCO

MITCO is a government agency, established in 1982. Ownership is equally divided among four of Malaysia's largest state enterprises, which together control the production of Malaysia's most important primary commodities (palm oil, rubber, cocoa, petroleum, tin, etc.): Federal Land Development Authority of Malaysia (FELDA), Kuok Brothers, Malaysian Mining Corporation (MMC), and Petronas (National Oil Corporation of Malaysia). MITCO has handled countertrade deals with Brazil, the Philippines, Romania, Japan, the United States, and Germany.

Malaysian Overseas Investment
  Corporation (MOIC)
91, SS 21/1A, Damansara Utama,
Petaling Jaya, Selangor, Malaysia
Telephone: 787656/89/787377/
  787022
Telex: TACKOH MA 37395

MOIC, established in 1984, is an independent consortium of seven companies; three of the best known are the Malaysian Mining Corp., Sunblest, and Multipurpose Holdings–Guthrie. Since some of the companies are state enterprises, MOIC is considered to be a quasi-government rather than a private organization. One of MOIC's major functions is to promote countertrade on a government-to-government basis (South–South), and its primary areas of operation are the Indian subcontinent, the ASEAN countries, the South Pacific and East Asian regions, and Eastern Europe. MOIC has handled countertrade deals with Brazil, Sweden, Austria and Romania among other countries. MOIC has incurred heavy financial losses, however, and the government may disband it.

Bumi, a private corporation founded in 1985, is a French–Malaysian joint venture between Safic Alcan and Co. (45% of equity) and Manan Othma, the former Malaysian minister of agriculture (55%). It is Malaysia's first private company specially incorporated to liquidate offset obligations. Bumi is particularly interested in handling military offset, and has conducted several small deals with suppliers from the United States and Western Europe. The company has also handled offsets incurred by Germany and France for public works projects.

Other Malaysian companies that will take over offset obligations include Sine Darby Pernas Trading Corp; Perdama Corp; Malaysian Transnational Trading Corp., Guthrie Malaysia Trading Corp., and Mulpha International Trading Corp.

TRADE CONTROLS

Some imports require licensing, and some others, such as motor vehicles, are subject to quantitative restrictions designed to protect local industries. Imports of raw materials and machinery for the manufacturing sector are eligible for preferential duties. Licenses are required for many exports, including cement, scrap iron, formic acid, wheat flour, rice, bran, sugar, textiles, tiles, and bricks. All trade with Israel and South Africa is prohibited.

INTERNATIONAL TRADE

Imports

Malaysia usually has a small trade surplus; recently it has been about $2 billion per year. Import growth, which averaged 9.0% per year for the seven-year period 1979–1985, has slowed considerably. The last year in which imports showed strong growth was 1980, when value increased by 37.1%. From 1981 through 1983, growth was around 7% annually. Efforts of the Malaysian government to cut imports resulted in growth of only 1.5% in 1984, and a drop in imports of 5.8% in 1985.

About 40% of annual Malaysian imports are machinery and transport equipment. Of the remainder, about 17% are basic manufactures, 15% mineral fuels and 10% food, with the other product groups accounting for less than 7% of imports. The top import products are transistors and valves, which account for about 11% of annual imports; refined petroleum products, 9.5%, miscellaneous electrical machinery, 8.7%, and crude petroleum, 5.0%. Other important products are civil engineering equipment; passenger motor vehicles; iron and steel universals, plates and sheets; special industry machinery; aircraft; iron and steel shapes; ships and boats; telecommunications equipment; paper and paperboard; tin ores; and iron and steel structures and parts, which each account for 1% to 3% of imports. These 15 products account for 54% of total Malaysian imports.

Most Malaysian imports, 56% come from Asia. About 18% come from the Americas (primarily North America), 17% from Europe (14% from the

Import Total, Malaysia (thousands)

	Value	Growth (%)
1979	7,848,509	——
1980	10,763,526	37.1
1981	11,549,484	7.3
1982	12,400,205	7.3
1983	13,251,000	6.8
1984	13,457,000	1.5
1985	12,663,900 (est.)	−5.8

EEC, 2% from EFTA, and 0.4% from the CMEA countries), and 5% from Oceania. Japan is Malaysia's major import trading partner, with a 25.4% share of the Malaysian market, followed by the United States with a 16.1% share, and Singapore with a 13.9% share. Other important suppliers are Australia, Germany, the United Kingdom, Saudi Arabia, Thailand, China, and France.

Exports

Export performance has been a little erratic. Exports went up by 16.8% in 1980, down by 9.3% in 1981, and back up by 2.5% in 1982. Performance was very good during the next two years: sales increased by 17.3% in 1983 and by a further 16.8% in 1984. In 1985, however, the value of exports dropped by 6.1%. The average annual growth of exports for the period, 6.3%, is somewhat lower than the growth of imports. Malaysia will need further stimulation of exports in order to maintain its trade surplus.

Malaysia's major export groups are mineral fuels and crude materials, which account for 29% and 27% of annual exports, respectively. Machinery and transport equipment accounts for 15% of exports, animal and vegetable oils and fats for 11% and basic manufactures for 9%. Food products, mis-

Export Total, Malaysia (thousands)

	Value	Growth (%)
1979	11,078,566	——
1980	12,944,692	16.8
1981	11,737,742	−9.3
1982	12,031,418	2.5
1983	14,117,520	17.3
1984	16,490,442	16.8
1985	15,469,867 (est.)	−6.1

cellaneous manufactures and chemicals make up the remainder of exports and are relatively unimportant.

The top export product is crude petroleum; exports are valued at about $3.6 billion per year and account for 23% of the Malaysian export total. Transistors and valves are the second most valuable export product category, accounting for 14% of 1985 exports at $2.1 billion, followed by palm oil, 11.2% of the total at $1.7 billion, rough wood (mostly hardwood logs), 10% of the total at $1.5 billion; and natural rubber, 7.7% of the total at $1.1 billion. These five products account for 66% of Malaysian exports. Other important export products are tin, shaped wood, plywood, petroleum products, telecommunications equipment, and copper ore, each accounting for 1% to 5% of exports.

Malaysia is the major world supplier of palm oil, with a 65% market share; hardwood logs, 60% share; and tin, 27% share. It is the second ranked supplier of natural rubber (after Thailand), with a 26% world market share.

Asia is Malaysia's most important export market area; 62% of exports go there. Europe is second in importance, taking 16% of all Malaysian exports (EEC, 14.6%; CMEA countries, 2.4%), followed by North America, 14.5% of exports. A small percentage of exports, 1.6%, go to Oceania. Singapore and Japan are the top export country markets, taking 22.5% and 19.7% of Malaysian exports, respectively. About 14% of exports go to the United States. Other important export trading partners are the Netherlands, Germany, the Republic of Korea, the United Kingdom, Thailand, India, and the Soviet Union.

RECENT COUNTERTRADE TRANSACTIONS, MALAYSIA

Partner country:	Poland (Stalexport with Malaysian Railway Administration)
Import:	Rail tracks
Export:	Rubber, refined pump oil, coffee, cocoa products, pepper, sawn timber, spices, cotton fabrics, tin, textile yarn
Value:	M $9.6 million (about U.S. $4.0 million; value of rail tracks)
Year:	1985
Duration:	18 months
Type:	Public procurement offset, counterpurchase
Partner country:	Yugoslavia (Energo)
Import:	Construction of federal highway across Malaysia from Malacca to Johore

Export:	Rubber, tin, pepper, refined petroleum, sawn timber, rubber hoses, tires, plywood, cotton fabrics, furniture, footwear
Value:	M $86 million (about U.S. $36.6 million)
Year:	1985
Duration:	Unspecified
Type:	Public procurement offset, counterpurchase
Comment:	Offset is 45%; Energo will receive M $47 million in cash and M $39 million in products

Partner country:	Republic of Korea (Samsong)
Import:	Naval patrol boats
Export:	Crude petroleum, refined pump oils, sawn timber, rubber gloves, cocoa powder
Value:	M $20 million (about U.S. $8.5 million; value of boats)
Year:	1984
Duration:	Unspecified
Type:	Defense offset, counterpurchase

Partner country:	Romania
Import:	Pharmaceuticals, cotton, ferromanganese
Export:	Crude petroleum, rubber, tin, palm oil, cocoa, pepper
Value:	U.S. $50 million
Year:	1985
Duration:	Eighteen months
Type:	Reciprocal trade

Partner country:	Federal Republic of Germany (Standard Elektrik Lorenz)
Import:	Microwave transmission system
Export:	Refined pump oil, cocoa products, rubber manufactures, cocoa products, various semimanufactured goods
Value:	M $130 million (about U.S. $55.4 million)
Year:	1985
Duration:	Unspecified
Type:	Offset, counterpurchase
Comment:	Offset is 80%

Partner country:	Japan (C. Itoh and Co., with Kelang Port Authority
Import:	Dockside crane

Export: Timber products, plywood, veneer
Value: M $3.6 million (about U.S. $1.5 million)
Year: 1985
Duration: Unspecified
Type: Public procurement offset, counterpurchase

Partner country: United Kingdom (Guthrie Corp., with the Malaysian
                           Fire Brigade)
Import: Water tenders
Export: Palm oil, rubber products
Value: M $3 million (about U.S. $1.2 million)
Year: 1985
Duration: Unspecified
Type: Public procurement offset, counterpurchase

Partner country: Sweden (SIAB and MOIC)
Import: Two hospitals with ancillary services, to be construct-
                           ed in Kuala Lumpur and Penang
Export: Unspecified counterpurchase items
Value: M $300 million (estimated) (about U.S. $120 million)
Year: 1985
Duration: Unspecified
Type: Public procurement offset, counterpurchase

Partner country: United States, Japan, Federal Republic of Germany
                           (unspecified private companies, with MITCO)
Import: Ammonium sulfate, muriate of potash
Export: To U.S. company: pepper, cocoa, plywood, sawn tim-
                           ber, dental alloys, rubber goods, tin alloy
                               To Japanese company: pepper, cocoa, plywood, ve-
                           neers, refined pump oil, blended fertilizers, rubber ma-
                           terials, furniture
                               To German company: pepper, cocoa, plywood,
                           sawn timber, refined pump oil, furniture, footwear
Value: M $4.75 million (about U.S. $1.92 million)
Year: 1985
Duration: Unspecified
Type: Offset, counterpurchase

22 Soviet Union

COUNTERTRADE

Countertrade Policy

Although the Soviet Union does not formally require countertrade, the government promotes compensation trade, and usually favors vendors offering reciprocity over those who do not. The goals in countertrade have historically been technology transfer and equipment procurement; however, export development has recently become an important feature. Most Soviet countertrade with the West has been associated with large-scale industrial cooperation projects in which the Western vendor buys back part of the plant's production. In its extensive countertrade with developing countries, the Soviet Union takes the Western position: the Soviets build facilities or sell capital equipment, taking back resultant products or unrelated counterpurchases. The government downplays "countertrade" per se, stating that it only accounts for about 15% of Soviet trade. This low figure apparently does not include the value of trade conducted through clearing arrangements with the CMEA and developing countries.

Major changes are under way in Soviet trade with the West. In 1986, the entire Soviet foreign trade sector was reorganized, resulting in a decentralization strategy with emphasis on increasing exports through incentives for FTOs. The reorganization was not directed specifically towards increasing compensation trade, but for reasons to be explained it will probably have that effect. Compensation trade was already on the rise before the reorganization: during the 1981–1985 economic plan period, 40 large industrial projects valued at a total of 6 billion rubles were financed through compensation trade, and there was a 270% increase in the value of Soviet takebacks in compensation deals compared to the 1976–1980 period. The increase in countertrade was due in part to declining Soviet oil income, which depleted foreign exchange reserves.

The Soviet reorganization is designed to transfer complete authority for foreign trade from the Ministry of Foreign Trade to individual ministries and production associations, and to the enterprises that report to them; these entities will be responsible for policy implementation. Policy supervision of foreign trade is the responsibility of the recently created State Commission for the External Economy, a part of the Council of Ministers.

The following are the major points of the Soviet foreign trade reorganization:

1. Selected Soviet enterprises have been granted foreign trade rights. They have the right of direct access to foreign markets for import and export, and may make independent decisions concerning technical and industrial co-operation with foreign partners. As further incentives, they may retain 90% of their foreign exchange receipts for their own purposes, and will receive foreign exchange "bonuses" when they exceed export quotas. These incentives are expected to encourage the enterprises to pressure their Western partners and vendors for countertrade percentages higher than the traditional 5% to 20%. Over 60 Soviet enterprises received foreign trade rights in 1986; the authorization will be extended to virtually all enterprises in 1987.

2. Soviet enterprises with foreign trade rights may now form equity joint ventures with Western firms. The Western company is allowed to own up to 49% of the equity, and may repatriate dividends and capital. Profits may be reinvested. The joint ventures will not be subject to production targets or investment constraints. This development represents a considerable relaxation of Soviet regulations on joint ventures, and should provide many opportunities for business expansion in both conventional trade and countertrade.

3. The aforementioned Soviet enterprises must finance all of their hard currency imports with exports, as well as all foreign exchange costs incurred in forming joint ventures. They may obtain four-year loans from the Soviet Bank for Foreign Trade, to be repaid from their export earnings. However, the responsibility of earning the foreign exchange will probably cause these enterprises to increase their countertrade demands.

4. Many FTOs have been transferred from the Ministry of Foreign Trade to individual ministries, production associations, and state committees, though the FTOs that deal exclusively in raw materials and commodities (petroleum, grain and other agricultural products, timber, etc.) will remain under the Ministry of Foreign Trade. The effect on countertrade will be initial confusion in locating the appropriate FTO for a particular deal.

5. FTOs not attached to a ministry may be able to offer only their own products as counterpurchases. Under the old arrangement, the Western vendor could select products from other FTOs, and thus had a wide choice of takebacks. The new regulations may force Western companies to accept surplus inventory or uncompetitive products.

Existing regulations on nonfulfillment penalties and third country markets for counterpurchase products remain unchanged. The penalty is very high, ranging from 15% to 50%. There are restrictions on reselling counterpurchases in third country markets where the Soviet Union is already selling the product; however, the product may be sold in countries where market access has been difficult for Soviet exporters.

Compensation contracts are rigid, but the Soviets are reliable in meeting their obligations. There are usually three contracts in a compensation deal: (1) the contract between the Western exporter and the Soviet FTO; (2) the financing agreement between a Western bank and/or government agency and Vneshtorgbank (Soviet Foreign Trade Bank); and (3) the contract between the Soviet FTO exporting the return product and the Western importer. The contract fulfillment period generally ranges from 6 months to 24 months.

According to the Soviet government, the new goals of compensation trade with the West should be greater diversification of exports (about 40 different products were exported through countertrade during 1981–1985) and the use of compensation financing to modernize existing facilities as well as to procure capital equipment. Ideally, takeback products should be competitive, value-added items.

The Soviet Union has bilateral clearing agreements with the CMEA countries and with 26 other countries: Afghanistan, Argentina, Bangladesh, Brazil, Colombia, China, Cuba, Egypt, Finland, Greece, Guyana, India, Iran, Laos, Mali, Malta, Nepal, Pakistan, Peru, Somalia, Syria, Thailand, Turkey, Vietnam, Yugoslavia, and Zambia.

Products Available for Countertrade

Products the Soviet Union has offered in countertrade include food products (such as honey, jam, and fish), vodka, brandy, tobacco, crude petroleum, natural gas, coal, gasoline, diesel fuel, chemicals (including polyethylene, phthalic anhydride, fumaric acid, urea, paraxylene, methanol, monoethylene glycol, aromatics, polyvinyl chloride, ammonia, orthoxylene naphtha, polystyrene, caprolactum, and acrylonitrile), fertilizer, lumber, wood chips, wood pulp, iron ore, iron ore pellets, nickel, asbestos, chromium ore, raw cotton, textiles, aluminum, paper, scrap metal, steel, tools, bearings, large engines, electric motors, construction and mining machinery, hydroelectric turbines, capital goods and various heavy manufactures, tractors, motor vehicles, aircraft, motorcycles, bicycles, floating docks, typewriters, and toys. Services offered include civil engineering services. The range of products offered to developing countries in compensation trade is usually wider than that offered to industrial countries; this is probably due to the unacceptability of some Soviet manufactured products (product quality and level of technology) in industrial country markets.

INTERNATIONAL TRADE

Detailed data on Soviet trade is not available because the Soviet commodity nomenclature is not very compatible with the SITC. The following statistics are accurate, but do not represent a complete trade picture on a disaggregate product basis.

Imports

Soviet imports have shown moderate, slightly erratic growth in recent years. Valued at $68.5 billion f.o.b. in 1980, they rose by 6.4% to $72.9 billion in 1981 and by 6.6% to $77.7 billion in 1982. Growth slowed in 1983, with imports rising by 3.1% to $80.2 billion, and in 1984 there was hardly any growth: imports went up by only 0.4% to $80.6 billion. In 1985, growth was a little better at 2.4%, with imports increasing to $82.5 billion. The average annual import growth rate for the 1980–1985 period was 3.7%.

The Soviet Union maintains a trade surplus each year, though it is not very large relative to total imports. The surplus was $7.9 billion in 1980 and $6.0 billion in 1981. It increased for the following three years, at $9.1 billion in 1982, $11.0 billion in 1983, and $11.3 billion in 1984, but fell sharply to $4.6 billion in 1985.

According to the U.N. data available, the top Soviet import product is iron and steel products, accounting for 6.1% of annual imports at $5 billion. Imports accounting for 3% to 5% of the total ($2.7 billion to $3.8 billion) are wheat, sugar, and ships and boats. Products accounting for 1% to 2.9% ($870 million to $2 billion) are metalworking machine tools, special industry machinery, mechanical handling equipment, and data processing equipment. Accounting for 0.6% to 1.9% of imports are knit outerwear, agricultural machinery, railway vehicles, medicinal products, civil engineering equipment, centrifugal pumps, motor vehicle parts, fresh and frozen meat, power generating equipment, parts for nonelectric machinery, wine, furniture, cigarettes, raw wool, buses, and industrial food processing machinery. Since these 24 products account for only 35% of Soviet imports, there is obviously a good deal of data on disaggregate products that are either not being reported or are not convertible to the SITC.

Most Soviet imports, 47.5%, come from the CMEA. About 12% of imports come from the EEC, 8.5% from developing America, 6.6% from EFTA, and 4.7% from developed America. Developing Asia supplies 3.4% of imports; developed Asia, 3.3%; Africa, 2.7%; and centrally planned economies in Asia, 2.7%. The USSR's major import trading partner is the German Democratic Republic, which supplies 10.9% of imports, followed by Czechoslovakia, 9.5%; and Bulgaria, 8.7%. Other important suppliers are Poland, which has a 7.9% share of the Soviet market; Hungary, 7.0%; Cuba, 5.9%; the Federal Republic of Germany, 4.6%; Yugoslavia, 4.1%; Finland, 3.8%; the United States, 3.4%; Japan, 3.3%; and Romania, 3.2%. (Shares for 1985.)

Imports from other centrally planned economies account for 50.2% of total Soviet imports. Suppliers from developed countries account for 27.8% of imports, and developing country suppliers account for 21.8%. The remaining small percentage of imports comes from OPEC countries.

Imports, USSR (thousands, f.o.b.)

	Value	Growth (%)
1980	68,522,000	——
1981	72,960,000	6.4
1982	77,792,000	6.6
1983	80,267,000	3.1
1984	80,624,000	0.4
1985	82,578,000	2.4

Exports

Although the Soviet Union has a trade surplus each year, it seems to be having some difficulty with exports; their growth rates are quite erratic compared to imports. Exports were valued at $76.4 billion in 1980, and increased by 3.3% to $79.0 billion in 1981. In 1982, exports jumped by 10% to $86.9 billion, but this growth was not sustained; value grew by only 5% in 1983, reaching $91.3 billion. There was virtually no growth in 1984, with exports increasing by 0.3% to $91.6 billion. (This was also a slow year for imports.) Exports fell in 1985, dropping by 4.8% to $87.2 billion.

Soviet exports are less well documented than imports, though about 70% of exports can be identified by using aggregate product codes. Exports are poorly diversified: crude petroleum accounts for about 42% of annual exports (roughly $40 billion). The Soviet Union is the world's second ranked supplier of petroleum, following Saudi Arabia, and has an estimated market share of 20%.

The other major Soviet export is natural gas, which accounts for about 10% of total exports; it is valued at roughly $9 billion annually. Products accounting for 1% to 3.4% of the export total ($920 million to $3 billion) are iron and steel, power generating equipment, coal, raw cotton, iron ore, metalworking machinery, sawn conifer lumber, crude minerals, manufactured fertilizers, motor vehicle parts, electric current, construction and mining machinery, aircraft, miscellaneous manufactured products, and trucks.

Soviet export market areas follow the same general pattern as import areas. Almost half of total exports (47%) goes to the CMEA. The EEC is the Soviet Union's next most important market area, accounting for 17.7% of exports followed by developing America, 5.8%; centrally planned economies in Asia, 5.1%; developing Asia, 3.4%; and Africa, 1.7%. The import and export patterns diverge here. Developed Asia, which supplies 3.3% of Soviet imports, takes only 1.2% of exports; and developed America supplies 4.7% of imports but takes almost no Soviet exports, 0.4%. This is due mostly to problems in exporting to Japan and the United States. The GDR is the Soviet Union's major export trading partner, accounting for 10.5% of Soviet exports. The next most important markets are Czechoslovakia, which takes 9.4% of exports, and Poland, which buys 8.9% of exports. Other top markets are Bul-

Exports, USSR (thousands f.o.b.)

	Value	Growth (%)
1980	76,450,000	——
1981	79,004,000	3.3
1982	86,912,000	10.0
1983	91,330,000	5.0
1984	91,649,000	0.3
1985	87,201,000	−4.8

garia, the destination of 8.8% of Soviet exports; Hungary, 6.2%; the Federal Republic of Germany, 5.8%; Cuba, 5.3%; Yugoslavia, 4.3%; Italy, 3.4%; Finland, 3.1%; France, 3.0%; and Romania, 2.6%. (1985 shares.)

About 52% of Soviet exports go to other centrally planned economies; 25.6% to developed countries; and 22.4% to developing countries. The remaining exports go to OPEC countries.

RECENT COUNTERTRADE TRANSACTIONS, USSR

Partner country:	Greece
Import:	(During 1986) wheat, 100,000 tons; corn, 100,000 tons; steel tubes, 10,000 tons; olive oil, 4000 tons; alumina from Hellenic Alumina
Export:	Ship repair contracts (for ships to be repaired in Greece); compensation financing of alumina plant; other items
Value:	Unspecified
Year:	1986
Duration:	Unspecified
Type:	Bilateral trade agreement
Comment:	The alumina plant is financed by the Soviet Union's Tsvetmetpromexport and is valued at $450 million. Originally, Bulgaria agreed to buy 33% of the plant's output; however, they pulled out of the deal, and the Soviet Union agreed to buy the entire output of the plant.

Partner country:	Brazil (State of Párana)
Import:	Microcomputers, automation equipment
Export:	Food products, alcoholic beverages, food processing equipment, construction/engineering services for a hydroelectric plant; also joint ventures in deep-sea fishing and a tractor factory

Value:	$35 million
Year:	1986
Duration:	Unspecified (several years)
Type:	Bilateral clearing agreement

Partner country:	China
Import:	Soybeans, corn, fruit, metals, light manufactures
Export:	Lumber, steel, fertilizer, aircraft, motor vehicles, heavy manufactures
Value:	$14 billion
Year:	1986
Duration:	Five years
Type:	Bilateral clearing agreement

Partner country:	United States (Occidental Petroleum)
Import:	Facility for the storage and handling of fertilizers and fertilizer materials
Export:	Fertilizers; annual export value, $441 million
Value:	$10 billion over life of contract
Year:	1974
Duration:	Twenty-four years (1974–1997)
Type:	Buyback; export of the buyback products began in 1978

Partner country:	United States (Union Carbide) and United Kingdom (CJB)
Import:	Polyethylene plant
Export:	Polyethylene
Value:	$70 million; annual export value, $7 million
Year:	1974
Duration:	Fifteen years (1974–1989)
Type:	Buyback; export of the buyback products began in 1980.

Partner country:	United States (Union Carbide) and United Kingdom (CJB)
Import:	Polyethylene plant (second deal with Union Carbide and CJB for a polyethylene plant)
Export:	Polyethylene
Value:	$162 million; annual export value, $16 million
Year:	1977

Duration: Sixteen years (1977–1993)
Type: Buyback; export of the buyback products began in
                    1983

Partner country: France (Creusot Loire)
Import: Ammonia plant
Export: Ammonia; annual export value, $27 million
Value: $270 million
Year: 1974
Duration: Fifteen years (1974–1989)
Type: Buyback; export of the buyback products began in
                    1980

Partner country: Federal Republic of Germany (Krupp/Koppers)
Import: Dimethylterephthalate plant
Export: Dimethylterephthalate
Value: $100 million; annual export value, $10 million
Year: 1976
Duration: Fourteen years (1976–1990)
Type: Buyback; export of the buyback products began in
                    1981

Partner country: Japan (Mitsui/Toyo)
Import: Four ammonia plants
Export: Ammonia; annual export value, $11 million
Value: $240 million
Year: 1976
Duration: Twenty years (1977–1997)
Type: Buyback

Partner country: France (Technip)
Import: Two aromatics complexes
Export: Aromatics; annual export value, $95 million
Value: $950 million
Year: 1976
Duration: Thirteen years (1976–1989)
Type: Buyback; export of the buyback products began in
                    1980

Partner country: Japan (KS Industries)
Import: Forestry handling equipment

Export:	Timber products
Value:	$1.1 billion
Year:	1974
Duration:	Unspecified
Type:	Buyback

Partner country:	Italy (ENI)
Import:	Large diameter pipe
Export:	Natural gas
Value:	$3.2 billion
Year:	1971
Duration:	Unspecified
Type:	Buyback

APPENDIX
Directory of Selected Countertrade Service Organizations

Note that this directory of selected countertrade service organizations does not include the names of major oil companies, CPAs, and law firms involved in countertrade since they are known to the reader.

Aceco—Association Pour La Compensation
Des Exchange Commerciaux
28 Avenue Hoche
75008 Paris, France
Tel: 33-1-4225 3640
Telex: 640912

Alfa-Laval Intertrade
P.O. Box 7
Lamezanstrabe 17
A-1232 Vienna, Austria
Tel: 43-222-67 76 419
Telex: 111825 ait a

Andre & Cie S.A.
7, Chemin Messidor
CH-1002 Lausanne, Switzerland
Tel: 41-21-21 11 11 - 021/20 11 11,
    Fax. 41-21-21 1429
Telex: 24470

ASEA Trade and Barter
P.O. Box 3284
S-103 65 Stockholm, Sweden
Tel: 08-143180
Telex: 10760 ELVESTS

Astro
International Association of State Trading Organizations
of Developing Countries
P.O. Box 92
Titova 104, 611109 Ljubljana, Yugoslavia
Tel: 38-3441777 - Telex: 31709 YU
    STRO

Atlantic Petroleum Corp. N.V.
Hammond House
117 Piccadily
London W1V9FJ, United Kingdom
Tel: 01-629-2484
Telex: 291015 PortagG

Atwood Richards Inc.
Interchange S.A.R.L.
11 Rue La Boetie
75008 Paris, France
Tel: 33-1-42 65 62 60
Telex: 649-660

99 Park Avenue
New York, NY 10016

USA
Telex: 125234
Tel: 1-212-490 1414

AWT International Handels
Schottenring 12
A-1013 Vienna, Austria
Tel: 63-36-06-0
Telex: 11-4787

Bank of Boston
767 Fifth Avenue
New York, NY 10153 USA
Tel: 212-350-0785
Telex: ITT 420 676
Cable: CORPBOS NYK

Bank of Helsinki, Ltd.
Aleksanterinkatu 17
sf-00100 Helsinki 10, Finland
Tel: 358-0-162 0262
Telex: 124536 hbank sf

Bankamerica World Trade Corp.
915 Front Street
San Francisco, CA 94111 USA
Tel: 415-622-2298
Telex: 279-026 BAWT

Banque de L'union Europeene
4, Rue Gaillon
BP 89, 75060 Paris Cedex 02,
   France
Tel: 33-1-42 66 20 30
Telex: 210 942 bue. Cable: NO-
   REBANK

**Banque De Paris Et Des Pays-Bas
(Paribas)**
12 Boulevard de Paris de la Made-
leine
75009 Paris, France
Tel: 33-1-298 1234

**Banque Francaise Du Commerce
Exterieur**
645 Fifth Avenue
New York, NY 10022 USA

Tel: 212-872-5000
Telex: 620463

Barex World Trade Corporation
777 W. Putnam Avenue
Greenwich, CT 06830, USA
Tel: 203-531-1059
Telex: 240007 BAREX UR

**Bartrade International Trade &
   Finance Co., Ltd.**
9 Had Ha'am Street, 23rd Floor
Tel Aviv 65251, Israel
Tel: 972-3-660121/660643
Telex: 342 226 LCNC IL

Berger & Borum
Michael Drewsens Vej 17
DK 8270 Hejbgerg, Denmark
Tel: 45-6-292233
Telex: 65244 BERBO DK

Business International Corp.
One Dag Hammarskjold Plaza
New York, NY 10017 USA
Tel: 212-750-6300
Telex: 234 767

Schwarzenbergplatz 8/7
A-1030 Vienna, Austria
Tel: 43-222-7261

**Canadian Department of External
   Affairs**
Trading House & Countertrade
   Division
125 Sussex Drive
Ottawa, Ontario K1A 0GZ, Cana-
   da
Tel: 613-992-7722
Telex: 053-3745

Canadian Export Association
99 Bank Street, Suite 250
Ottawa, Ontario K1P 6B9,
   Canada
Tel: 613-238-8888

Carney & Associates
6, Girod de L'Ain

1290 Versoix
Geneva, Switzerland
Tel: 41-022-47 11 33 or 55 50 68
Telex: 422 500 or 427 452

**Caterpillar World Trading
  Corporation**
100 NE Adams Street
Peoria, IL 61629-1485 USA
Tel: 309-675-5551
Telex: 404 435 CAT PEORIA
Cable: CATERPILAR

G.P.O. Box 3069
Hong Kong
Tel: 852-5-832-6333
Telex: 73305
CFEL HK
Cable: CATFAREAST

P.O. Box 456 1208
Geneva 6, Switzerland
Tel: 41-22 374444
Telex: 22 706 CATCH
Cable: CATOVER SEAS GENE-
VA

Centro Bank
Centro International Handelsbank
  Aktiengesellschaft
Tegetthoffstrasse 1
A-1015 Vienna, Austria
Tel: 0222-51520-0
Telex: 136 990

Ceteco Countertrade BV
P.O. Box 520
1110 AM Diemen, The Nether-
  lands
Tel: 31-20-900-741
Telex: 14699 ctec nl

Chase Manhattan Bank
Countertrade Unit
1 World Trade Center, 78th Floor
New York, NY 10048 USA
Tel: 212-432-8076
Telex: 667-266 CWIC (WUI)

CGL' Handelsgesellschafl MBH
Boerseqasse 11
A-1010 Vienna, Austria
Tel: 0222-6624
Telex: 134665 CGLA

China/Tech Ltd.
430 Tenth Street, S-206
Atlanta, GA 30318 USA
Tel: 404-873-3485
MCI 65 251 5885

**Citicorp International Trading
  Co., Inc (CITC)**
399 Park Avenue
New York, NY 10043 USA
Tel: 212-559-8100
Telex: 662503

Coca-Cola Trading Co.
P.O. Box 104
Atlanta, GA 30301 USA
Tel: 404-676-2121
Telex: 542373 COCA COLA Atl

Combaro S.A.
Route d'Oron 2
Ch-1010 Lausanne, Switzerland
Tel: 41-21-33 51 51
Telex: 26 672 CARO

**Combustion Engineering Trading
  Company**
P.O. Box 9308
Stamford, CT 06904 USA
Tel: 203-328-2341
Telex: 2372

Commerce Union Bank
One Commerce Place
Nashville, TN 37219 USA
Tel: 615-749-3342
Telex: 749317

Connaught Trading Corp.
1–4 Connaught Place
London, W2 2EX, United Kingdom
Tel: 012621212

Contitrade Services Corp
ContiTrade Services
1 State Street Plaza
New York, NY 10004 USA
Tel: 212-248-7800
Telex: WU 129 241
Cable: MERBANINT

Merban Limited
49/51 Bow Lane
London EC4H 9HA, United
  Kingdom
Tel: 44-1-236-7684
Telex: 884 604 MERBAN

Merban Pacific Ltd.
1503 Bank of America Tower
12 Harcourt Road
Hong Kong
Tel: 852-5-237 071
Telex: 64858 MERBAN HX

CSI International Corp.
800 Second Avenue
New York, NY 10017 USA
Tel: 1-212-687-5600
FAX 212-867-6115

Countercorp Trading Ltd
583 Orchard Rd #05-03
Forum, Galleria
Singapore 0923
Tel: 732-8077
Telex: RS 50235 CT CORP

Countertrade, Barter & Finance
2627 NE 203 Street, Suite 212
North Miami Beach, FL 33132
  USA
Tel: 305-937-4550
Telex: 514210 CB&F MIA

Cyrus Eaton World Trade Ltd.
1111 Superior Avenue, NE
Cleveland, OH 44114 USA
Tel: 216-523-5000
Telex: 98-5312

Davis Group
301 West 53rd Street
Suite 1611
New York, NY 10019 USA
Tel: 212-977-8482

Deerfield Communications Corp.
210 East 39th Street
New York, NY 10016 USA
Tel: 212-685-0066
Telex: 710581236 TWX

Douglas Trading Company
P.O. Box 200 77-100
Long Beach, CA 90846 USA
Tel: 714-952-6217
Telex: 674357

Enerfin S.A.
Energy & Finance, ENERFIN.
  S.A.
10 Rue Albert Gas
1206 Geneva, Switzerland
Tel: 41-22-46 76 87 and 46 78 19
Telex: 421 754 CMW CH

European Interamerican Finance
  Corp.
The Eurinam Group
400 Madison Avenue, Suite 401
New York, NY 10017 USA
Tel: 212-751-2200
Telex: 225 180 EURIN UR

Federal Mogul Trading Company
26555 North Western Hwy.
P.O. Box 1976
Southfield, MI 48076 USA
Tel: 313-354-7700
Telex: 170357

FFV Trading AB
P.O. Box 10103
S-100 55 Stockholm, Sweden
Tel: 46-8-65 34 00
Telex: 16325 ffvtra

First Interstate Trading Co.
707 Wilshire Boulevard
Los Angeles, CA 90017 USA
Tel: 213-614-3000
Telex: 674421 FICAL LSA

First National Bank of Chicago
Trade Finance Division
One First National Plaza, Suite
  0042
Chicago, IL 60670 USA
Tel: 312-732-8874 or 732-8261, or
  44-1-240-7240 (London)
Telex: 887 716 FNBCLNG; 190
  201 FNBC UT

**First Union National Bank Export
  Trading Co.**
301 S. Tryon Street-CORP-14
Charlotte, NC 28288 USA
Tel: 704-374-4458
Telex: 825515

Fischli Ag
Seefeldstrasse 9
8008 Zurich, Switzerland
Tel: 41-1-251 2801
Telex: 813 073 safz ch

Focus International Inc.
8260 College Parkway
Suite 204
Fort Myers, FL 33907 USA
Tel: 813-433-3443
Telex: 522719 Focus Int UD

Ford Direct Markets, Inc.
P.O. Box 600
Wixom, MI 48096 USA
Tel: 313-344-5560
Telex: 669777 FORD DMO WIX

Gebr. Volkart AG
Postfach 8401
Winterthur, Switzerland
Tel: 052/ 84 31 31
Telex: 76243

**General Electric Trading
  Company**
570 Lexington Avenue
New York, NY 10022 USA
Tel: 212-750-3751
Telex: ITT 420214

General Foods Trading Company
250 North Street
White Plains, NY 10625 USA
Tel: 914-335-1595
Telex: 646742 GF INTL

Gisbert Brinkschulte
Gmbtt & Co. KG
Kolkstrabe 4
D-2800 Bremen 1, Federal Repub-
  lic of Germany
Tel: 0421-170521
Telex: 17-421-2017 GIBRI BR

Graficomex S.A.
20 rue de la Ville l' Eveque
75008 Paris, France
Tel: 33-1-47 42 07 06
Telex: 211 280 F

Grindlays Bank Plc
Minerva House, Montague Close
London SE 1 9DH, United King-
  dom
Tel: 44-1-626 0545
Telex: 885-043

Hab Mercator
Biblioteksgtan 12
111 46 Stockholm, Sweden
Tel: 46-8-10 50 92

Hibogan (Belgium) S.A.
Boniverlei 29
B-2520 Edegem, Belgium
Tel: 32-3-455-74-95
Telex: 71162

Icon International, Inc.
501 Fifth Avenue

New York, NY 10017 USA
Phone: 212-741-3518
Telex: 429.01 SOBRIEN

**InterBarter Systems/Priority
   Marketing**
155 N. Michigan Ave, Suite 764
Chicago, IL 60601 USA
Tel: 312-938-1919
Telex: 955329

**International Business and
   Consulting**
Missiehuislei 8
2180 Kalmthout, Belgium
Tel: 32-3-666 5314
Telefax: 32-3-666 5314
Telefax: 32-3-666 6618
Telex: 335 60 Ibco b

International Countertrade
P.O. Box 634
Dayton, OH 45409 USA
Tel: 513-293-4348
Telex: 955-2125

International Countertrade
Chaussée de la Hulpe 187
1170 Brussels, Belgium
Tel: 02-673-99-20

**International Market Information
   System**
3433 Paces Forest Road, NW
Atlanta, GA 30327 USA
Tel: 404-237-6248
Telex: 804 294 SPEDEX

ITCO
International Trade Company
   ITCO, SA
B. Konstantinou Av. 44
GR-11635 Athens, Greece
Tel: 30-1-723 02 14 or 721 90 50
Telex: 225 020 ITCO Gr

C. Itoh & Company, Ltd.
335 Madison Avenue

New York, NY 10017 USA
Tel: 212-818-8000
Telex: 12297 CITOCH-NYK

A. Johnson & Co. Eastern AB
S-103 75 Stockholm, Sweden
Tel: 08-788-5000
Telex: 12134 AXEAST S

K-Mart Trading Service
3100 West Big Beaver
Troy, MI 48084 USA
Tel: 313-643-1000

Kemira Oy Trading
Malminkatu 30
SF-00100 Helsinki 10, Finland
Tel: 358-0-694 2911
Telex: 124 633 kehki sf

Kodak CT Division
343 State Street
Rochester, NY 14650 USA
Tel: 716-724-4000
Telex: 97-8481

Krusoe & Company Ltd.
24 St. Mary Ave
London EC3A8DE, United King-
   dom
Tel: 01-626-5766
Telex: 885649

Lister-Petter, Ltd.
Dursley
Gloucestershire GL 114HS,
   United Kingdom
Tel: 44-453-4141
Telex: 43261

Lockheed-California Company
P.O. Box 551, Dept. 51-80
Unit 35, Plant A-1
Burbank, CA 91520 USA
Tel: 818-847-4927
Telex: 67208

Mack Trucks International, Inc.
International Operations Division
2100 Mack Blvd.
Allentown, PA 18105 USA
Tel: 215-439-3011
Telex: 847429

Management Associates, Inc.
USA Headquarters
18200 Von Karman Ave.
Suite 760
Irvine, CA 92715 USA
Tel: 714-553-8040
Telex: 140 476 TAB
TELEX 19

**Manufacturers Hanover World
Trade Corp.**
140 East 45th Street
New York, NY 10017 USA
Phone: 212-808-0830
Telex: 968020 CITIC

The Mapro Group
Marshall House
5 Kingston Road
Tolworth, Surbiton
Surrey KT59PE, United Kingdom
Tel: 01-330-4343
Telex: 261316 MAPRO G

Marcotrade S.A.
10 Cours de Rive
1204 Geneva, Switzerland
Tel: 41-22-36 1920
Telex: 421 333 Ara Ch

Marine Midland Bank
140 Broadway
New York, NY 10015 USA
Tel: 212-440-1000
Telex: 421800 MMBYI

Marubeni America Corporation
200 Park Avenue
New York, NY 10166 USA
Tel: 212-599-3700
Telex: 12424

**McDermott International Trading
Company**
1010 Common Street
New Orleans, LA 70112 USA
Tel: 504-587-4411
Telex: 587412

MG Services Co.
520 Madison Avenue
New York, NY 10022 USA
Tel: 212-715-5210
Telex: 423540 MGSUI

Mitsubishi International Corp.
520 Madison Avenue
New York, NY 10022 USA
Tel: 212-605-2318
Telex: WU 12482

Mitsui & Co. (USA), Inc.
200 Park Avenue
New York, NY 10166-0130 USA
Tel: 212-878-4000
Telex: 232 613 (RCA); 420
153(ITT); 620 251 (SUI)

Monsanto International
800 N. Lindbergh Blvd.
St. Louis, MI 63167 USA
Tel: 314-694-1000
Telex: 44-7282

Montore Metals Ltd.
Thorne House
152 Brent Street
London NW4DR, United King-
dom
Tel: 01-202-2656
Telex: 27312

Motors Trading Corporation
3044 West Grand Boulevard
Detroit, MI 48202 USA
Tel: 313-556-2591
Telex: 425543

Nissho Iwai Corporation
4-5 Akasaka 2-chome, Minato-ku

Tokyo 107, Japan
Tel: 81-3-588-3654
Telex: 222 33

Noble Trading Company
1150 South SE. Asaph St.
Alexandria, VA 22314 USA
Tel: 703-549-5966
Telex: 4974294

Noranda Sales
P.O. Box 45
Commerce Court West
Toronto, Ontario M5L 1B6, Canada
Tel: 416-982-7000
Telex: 065-24231

O'Neill Global Trading, Inc.
5575-B Chamblee Dunwoody
 Road
Atlanta, GA 30338 USA
Tel: 404-392-9244
Telex: 543368

Pepsico International
Anderson Hill Road
Purchase, NY 10577 USA
Tel: 914-253-2000
Telex: 62848

Philipp Brothers, Inc.
1221 Avenue of the Americas
New York, NY 10020 USA
Tel: 212-575-5900
Telex: 233 031 or 420 808
Cable: PHIBRO NEW YORK

**Philippine International Trading
 Corporation**
Philippines International Centre,
 Tordesillas St.
Salcedo Village, Makati, Metro
 Manila 3116 (P.O. Box 1056
 MCC), Phillippines
Tel: 63-2-818 9801 to 30
Telex: 63745 PITCPN; 45286
 PITCPM; 14860 PITC PS
Cable: PITC MANILA

Postipankki
International Trading Unit
Unioninkatu 20
Helsinki 7 00007, Finland
Tel: 358-0-1641
Fax: 358-0-164 3634
Telex: General 121698PGIRO SF

Produce Studies Ltd.
Northcroft House, West Street
Newbury, Berkshire RG13 1HD,
 United Kingdom
Tel: 44-635-46 112
Telex: 849 228 PROMAR G

**Prudential-Bache Trade
 Corporation**
100 Gold Street
New York, NY 10292 USA
Tel: 212-406-6613 or 406-6607
Telex: 6720090 PBTC UW

Rabobank Nederland
Boerenleenbank BA, Netherlands
245 Park Avenue, 36th Floor
New York, NY 10167 USA
Tel: 212-916-7816
Telex: 640452

Ranier International Trading Co.
Rainier Tower, P.O. Box 3966,
 T22-1
Seattle, WA 98164 USA
Tel: 206-621-6188
Telex: 62930229 EASY LINK

**Rockwell International Trading
 Company**
600 Grant Street
Pittsburgh, PA 15219 USA
Tel: 412-565-7118
Telex: 866213

Royal Bank of Canada
200 Bay Street, 5th floor, South
 Tower
Royal Bank Plaza, Toronto, Ontario M5J 2J5, Canada

Tel: 416-974-4310
Telex: 062 2231

**Security Pacific Trade Finance,
Inc.**
595 Madison Avenue, 18th floor
New York, NY 10022 USA
Tel: 212-644-0020
Telex: 421 748 SPTF

**Shearson Lehman Trading Co.,
Inc.**
American Express Tower
World Financial Center
New York, NY 10285 USA
Tel: 212-298-6660
Telex: 177 837 (SLTCO UT)

**Shell Chemical International
Trading Company**
One Shell Plaza
Houston, TX 77001 USA
Tel: 713-241-6161

Sib Hegner AG
Wiesenstrasse 8
8022 Zurich, Switzerland
Tel: 01/256 7272

Sic, Inc.
(Societe International de Compen-
sation)
PO Box 659, Station A
Montreal, Que H3C 2T8, Canada
Tel: 514-937 9577
Fax: 514-937 1697
Telex: CNP 5-267 585 BARENG
MTL
Cable: BARENG MTL

**Sumitomo Corporation of
America**
345 Park Avenue
New York, NY 10154 USA
Tel: 212-207-0520

Sun Oil Trading
200 W. Lancaster Avenue

Wayne, PA 19087 USA
Tel: 215-964-3676
Telex: 845 230 SUNINTL

**Scandinavian Trading
International, Ltd.**
3 Queen Street, Mayfair
London WIX7PH, United King-
dom
Tel: 44-1-409-2840
Telex: 8953133 TRADEAG

**Skandinaviska Enskilda Banken
International**
Kungstradgar dsgatan 8
106 40 Stockholm, Sweden
Tel: 46-8-763 8712
Telex: 11 00 essbh s

Sodechanges S.A.
Societe de Development des
Echanges S.A.
Rue Pedtor-Meylan 5
P.O. Box 203
1211 Geneva 17, Switzerland
Tel: 41-22-36 71 11
Telex: 270 72 sosa ch

Sorimex S.A.
Route de la Reine 17
92100 Boulogne-Billancourt,
France
Tel: 33-14-604 91 74
Telex: 203 758 F

Straits Petroleum & Partners
Park House
165/177 The Broadway
London SW191AQ, United King-
dom
Tel: 01543-2133
Telex: 9177910 STRAIT G.

Sukab
Box 7458
S-103 92 Stockholm, Sweden
Tel: 46-8-23 47 95
Telex: 19146 SUKAB S

3M International
P.O. Box 33800
St. Paul, MN 55133 USA
Tel: 612-733-4032
Telex: 277434 TRIMINCO

Trading Mercantil
Av. Andres Bello No. 1
Apartado 789
Caracas 1010-A, Venezuela
Tel: 507-1226
Telex: 28387 BMER-VC

Transnational Trade Development Corp.
866 Second Avenue
New York, NY 10017 USA
Tel: 212-759-6201
Telex: 429292 TNTDC

UHAG
Ueberseehandel AG
Utoquai 55
8022 Zurich, Switzerland
Tel: 01 47 74 00

Unico Trading Handelsgesellschaft M.B.H.
Sterngasse 6A
A-1010 Vienna, Austria
Tel: 43-222-63 32 41
Telefax: 43-222-630 723 74
Telex: 136385 UNICO A

Voest Alpine Intertrading
Vait
PO Box 22
A-4010 Linz, Austria
Tel: 43-732-280 4281
Telex: 225 11 VAI A

Westinghouse Trading Corporation
500 Center Boulevard
Pittsburgh, PA 15222 USA
Tel: 412-925-7079
Telex: 866307

XPORT Trading Company
One World Trade Center
63 East
New York, NY 10048 USA
Tel: 212-466-3248
Telex: 427346 NYANDNJ

Select Bibliography

BOOKS AND MONOGRAPHS

Association for Compensatory Trade. 1985. *Practical Guide to Countertrade.* New York: Metal Bulletin, Inc.

Batis, Ltd. 1986. *Countertrade with the Middle East.* London: Need House.

Business International. 1984. *Exploring Countertrade Opportunities in Africa.* Geneva: Business International.

Business International. 1985. *101 Checklists for Coping with Countertrade Problems.* New York: Business International.

Business International. 1984. *Threats and Opportunities of Global Countertrade; Marketing, Financing and Organizational Implications.* New York: Business International.

Countertrade Outlook, *"Directory of Organizations Providing Countertrade Services 1986,"* Alexandria, VA: Countertrade Outlook. 1986.

Ehrenhaft, P. 1983. *Countertrade: International Trade Without Cash,* New York: Law & Business.

Jones, S. 1984. *North–South Countertrade: Barter and Reciprocal Trade with Developing Countries.* London: Economist Intelligence Unit.

Organization for Economic Co-operation and Development. 1985. *Countertrade: Developing Country Practices.* Paris: OECD.

Organization for Economic Co-operation and Development. 1979. *Countertrade Practices in East–West Economic Relations.* Paris: OECD.

Organization for Economic Co-operation and Development. 1981. *East–West Trade: Recent Developments in Countertrade.* Paris: OECD.

Outter-Jaeger, I. 1979. *The Development Impact of Barter in Developing Countries.* Paris: OECD.

United Kingdom, Department of Trade and Industry. 1984. *Countertrade: Some Guidance for Exporters.* London.

U.S. Congress, House Committee on Banking, Finance and Urban Affairs, Subcommittee on Economic Stabilization. 1984. *The Impact of Countertrade and Offset Agreements on the U.S. Economy.* Washington, DC: U.S. Government Printing Office.

U.S. International Trade Commission. 1982. *Analysis of Recent Trends in U.S. Countertrade: Report of Investigation Number 332-125, Under Section 332 of the Tariff Act of 1930.* Washington, DC: U.S. Government Printing Office.

U.S. International Trade Commission. 1985. *Assessments of the Effects of Barter and Countertrade Transactions on U.S. Industries,* Washington, DC: U.S. Government Printing Office.

U.S. Office of Management and Budget. 1985. *Impacts of Offsets in Defense-Related Exports.* Washington, DC: U.S. Government Printing Office.

U.S. Department of the Treasury. 1983. *Offset Coproduction Requirements in Aerospace and Electronics Trade: Report of a Survey of Industry.* Washington, DC: U.S. Government Printing Office.

Verzariu, P. 1985. *Countertrade, Barter, and Offsets: New Strategies for Profit in International Trade.* New York: McGraw-Hill.

Verzariu, P. 1980. *Countertrade Practices in East Europe, The Soviet Union and China: An Introductory Guide to Business.* Washington, DC: (U.S. Department of Commerce, International Trade Administration) U.S. Government Printing Office.

Verzariu, P. 1984. *International Countertrade: A Guide for Managers and Executives.* Washington, DC: U.S. Department of Commerce, International Trade Administration, U.S. Government Printing Office.

Verzariu, P., S. Bozek, & J. Matheson. 1978. *East–West Countertrade Practices: An Introductory Guide for Business.* Washington, DC: U.S. Department of Commerce, Industry and Trade Administration, U.S. Government Printing Office.

Welt, L. 1982. *Countertrade: Business Practices for Today's World Market.* New York: American Management Association.

Welt, L. 1984. *Trade Without Money: Barter and Countertrade.* New York: Law & Business.

ARTICLES

Alexandrides, C.G., & Barbara L. Bowers, "International Countertrade Strategies," *Business Administration Bulletin,* September 1986.

Alexandrides, C.G., & Barbara L. Bowers, "Finding Markets for Countertrade Products," *Countertrade and Barter Quarterly* (series of three articles), Winter, Summer, Fall, 1985.

Banks, Gary, "The Economics and Politics of Countertrade," *World Economy,* June 1983.

Barovick, R. L., "New Trading Company Law Heightens Interests in Exporting," *Business America,* March 7, 1983.

Cohen, Stephen S., & John Zysman, "Countertrade, Offsets, Barter and Buybacks," *California Management Review,* Winter, 1986.

Dennis, Robert D., "The Countertrade Factor in China's Modernization Plan," *Columbia Journal of World Business,* Spring 1982.

Dizard, John W., "Is Countertrade Worth the Effort?" *Institutional Investor,* January 1982.

Dizard, John W., "The Explosion of International Barter," *Fortune*, February 7, 1983.

Finley, E.S., "The ABC's of Countertrade," *American Import-Export Management*, March, 1985.

Griffin, Joseph P., "Antitrust Law Issues in Countertrade," *Journal of World Trade Law*, May/June 1983.

Kaikati, J.G., "Marketing Without Exchange of Money," *Harvard Business Review*, November/December 1982.

Khoury, Sarkis J., "Countertrade: Forms, Motives, Pitfalls, and Negotiation Requisites," *Journal of Business Research*, June 1984.

Korth, Christopher M., "Barter—An Old Practice Yields New Profits," *Business*, September/October 1981.

Kyung, Matton, "Countertrade: Trade Without Cash?" *Finance & Development*, December, 1983.

Lochner, "Guide to Countertrade and International Barter," *International Law*, 725, 1985.

Matthews, Gordon, "U.S. Banks Take Different Serious Approaches to the Spreading Practices of Countertrade," *American Banker*, September 21, 1984.

McVey, Thomas B., "Countertrade: Commercial Practices, Legal Issues and Policies Dilemma," *Law & Policy International Business*, September 1984.

Nelson, Carl A., "Guidelines for Using Countertrade," *American Legal Export Management*, September 1984.

Potter, Philip H., "East–West Countertrade: Economic Injury and Dependence Under U.S. Trade Law," *Law and Policy in International Business*, No. 2, 1981.

Roessler, F., "Countertrade and the GATT Legal Systems," *Journal of World Trade Law*," November–December 1985.

Sender, Henriette, "The Booming World of Countertrade," *Dun's Business Month*, January 1984.

Verzariu, Pompiliu, "Communist Countries Are Strengthening Commercial Ties With the Third World," *Business America*, February 25, 1980.

Walsh, James I., "Countertrade: Not Just For East–West Anymore," *Journal of World Trade Law*, January/February 1983.

Walsh, James I., "The Effect on Third Countries of Mandated Countertrade," *Journal of World Trade*, November–December 1985.

Welt, Leo G. B., "Forms of Countertrade," *American Import-Export Management*, December 1984.

Wiegand, Robert E., "Barters and Buybacks: Let Western Firms Beware!" *Business Horizons*, June 1980.

Yafie, Roberta, C., "Countertrade Can Open Markets," *American Metal Market*, July 31, 1985.

Yoffie, David B., "Profiting From Countertrade," *Harvard Business Review*, May–June, 1984.

Index